About the Author

Eric B. Ross is an anthropologist who was educated at the University of Pennsylvania and subsequently Columbia University. For many years he taught at various North American universities, including Mount Holyoke College, the University of Michigan at Ann Arbor and the University of Florida. In 1986 he was appointed a Senior Lecturer at the University of Huddersfield in the UK, before moving to the Institute of Social Studies in the Hague in 1992.

He is the author and editor of a number of works, including *Beyond the Myths of Culture: Essays in Cultural Materialism* (New York: Academic Press, 1980) and *Death, Sex and Fertility: Population Regulation in Pre-industrial and Developing Societies* (New York: Columbia University Press, 1987).

Other Zed Titles on Population and Development

A. Adepoju (ed.), *Family, Population and Development in Africa*

Asoka Bandarage, *Women, Population and Global Crisis: A Political-Economic Analysis*

Braidotti, Charkiewicz, Hausler and Wieringa, *Women, the Environment and Sustainable Development: Towards a Theoretical Synthesis*

S. Correa, DAWN, *Population and Reproductive Rights: Feminist Perspectives from the South*

Peter Custers, *Capital Accumulation and Women's Labour in Asian Economies*

A. Hardon and L. Hayes (eds), *Reproductive Rights in Practice: A Feminist Report on the Quality of Care*

Hardon, Mutua, Kabir and Engelkes, *Monitoring Family Planning and Reproductive Rights: A Manual for Empowerment*

Petchesky and Judd (eds), *Negotiating Reproductive Rights: Women's Perspectives across Countries and Cultures*

Visvanathan, Duggan, Nisonoff and Wiegersma (eds), *The Women, Gender and Development Reader*

The Malthus Factor

Population, Poverty and Politics
in Capitalist Development

ERIC B. ROSS

ZED BOOKS
London & New York

For Reuben and Mimi

The Malthus Factor was first published by
Zed Books Ltd, 7 Cynthia Street, London N1 9JF, UK,
and Room 400, 175 Fifth Avenue, New York, NY 10010, USA in 1998

Distributed in the USA exclusively by St Martin's Press, Inc.,
175 Fifth Avenue, New York, NY 10010, USA

Typeset by Lucy Morton & Robin Gable, Grosmont
Cover designed by Andrew Corbett

A catalogue record for this book is available from the British Library

Library of Congress Cataloging-in-Publication Data
Ross, Eric B.
The Malthus factor : poverty, politics and population in capitalist
development / Eric B. Ross
  p.   cm.
Includes bibliographical references (p.   ) and index.
ISBN 1–85649–563–9 (hb). — ISBN 1–85649–564–7 (pb)
  1. Malthus, T. R. (Thomas Robert), 1766–1834. 2. Overpopulation—
Economic aspects. 3. Poverty. 4. Capitalism. 5. Economic
development. I. Title.
HB863.R67 1998   98–29913
338.9—dc21   CIP

Transferred to digital printing 2005

ISBN 1 85649 563 9 (Hb)
ISBN 1 85649 564 7 (Pb)

Contents

Acknowledgements

Like most books, this one has changed immeasurably since its original conception, and, like most such projects, it remains unfinished, at least in its author's mind. It arrived in its present form through a long process of intellectual encounters, with the materials and ideas out of which the book is composed; with my students at the Institute of Social Studies (ISS), with whom, more than with anyone else, I have shared many of those ideas; with a few special ISS colleagues, who gave me hope that academics can sometimes be truly meaningful in a highly political world; and with the exigencies of life in general.

Among the students I want to thank for their encouragement and friendship are: Ranjit Drivedi, Philomen Harrison, Alex Izurieta, Kara Johnston Molina, Daniel Koster, N.C. Narayanan, Nina Orlova, Babette Resurreción, Edsel Sanjor, Imani Tafari-Ama and Maria Piedad Villaveces.

Academic life is not generally a place where genuine intellectual comradeship thrives. Ashwani Saith has been the exception that proves the rule. This in no way diminishes my gratitude, however, to special people within the ISS community who, in one way or another, often against the odds and sometimes unwittingly, helped to create the intellectual environment in which this work developed. Among them are Loes Keysers, Wicky Meynen, Rene Pittin, Ken Post, Graham Pyatt, Peter Waterman and Ben White. Some people simply were good friends at the right time; they include Avril Digby, George Groenewald, Jolanda Kaloh and Emiliano Ruiz.

It is also incumbent on me to note that this book originated within the framework of the Population and Development programme at the ISS, which was then a part of a global training programme of the UNFPA. Despite this, the ideas expressed here were never intended to reflect the thinking of that organisation. The freedom to develop my own ideas owes much to the intellectual integrity of the director of the global programme, Dr Mohammed Masouz. I will always be grateful to him for his support and confidence.

I want to thank Barbara MacDermott, for her political commitment, which would never allow me to take any comfort just in being an academic. I hope she will always understand how important this has been.

My parents, Julian and Sylvia Ross, died too soon to see this book, but I hope it honours their ideals and the struggles which shaped them. In small measure, it also pays belated homage, on my father's behalf, to the memory of his youthful friend Aaron Lopoff, who died in Spain in the struggle against fascism.

Above all, because my parents never expected me to repay anything I owe them, but only to reinvest it in my children, I dedicate this book to Mimi and Reuben. Their strong passion for justice has been my chief inspiration and strength and is my greatest source of hope for the future.

Eric B. Ross
The Hague, 1998

Introduction

Since the publication of Thomas Malthus's first *Essay on the Principle of Population* in 1798, Malthusianism has become a way of explaining poverty, death and environmental degradation as products of human population pressure on resources. This book examines the nature of such explanations and how they have served to rationalise or obscure the aims and contradictions of capitalist development.

Although Malthus is widely considered one of the "patron saints" of modern demography (James and Pullen 1988: 320; Wrigley 1989; Coleman and Schofield 1986; Caldwell and Caldwell 1986: 5), he was primarily an economist. He wrote his essay not, as is often averred, as a precocious youth engaged in dispute with his father, but at the age of 32, when he was already established as a cleric in the Church of England and wrote with a clear sense of purpose. Among his principal aims was to explain the nature and origins of poverty in a way which not only would suggest that there was no viable alternative to capitalist economy, but which would also contribute to the evolution of that economy in the form of certain policy prescriptions – most notably the abolition of the old poor laws, the closest thing that existed in his time to social welfare – which he justified in terms of his "law" of population (cf. Chamberlain 1970: 3–4). Whatever Malthus's contribution to population theory has been, and that is not my principal concern here, his most enduring influence has been to shape academic and popular thinking about the origins of poverty, and to defend the interests of capital in the face of the enormous human misery which capitalism causes. The merits of his work in this regard were quickly realised, and he was rewarded with the first Professorship in Political Economy, at the East India College at Haileybury.[1]

Most theories about the roots of poverty or underdevelopment fall into two general camps. One regards poverty as sociogenic in nature and susceptible to practical amelioration through the structural transformation of society. The other assumes that it is largely the product of circumstances beyond human control, because those circumstances refer to innate physical/genetic features of the population in question (May 1981), to relatively intractable cultural or psychological characteristics of that population (Harrison 1985), to aspects of their environment which seem to impede economic and social development (Kamarck 1972, 1976), or to the inevitable consequences of population increase, as in the case of Malthusian theory. Between these two general perspectives – one seeking systemic change, the other denying its likelihood or necessity – lies a world of irreconcilable political aims over which people have contested strenuously for centuries (see, for example, Kegel 1958; Harvey 1974). These differences are not simply theoretical, however. For too many people, their implications have been a matter of life and death.

Explanations which tend to naturalise poverty and underdevelopment and to neutralise the influence of alterable economic and social conditions are not separate and discrete; in practice, they commingle in many ways, mutually reinforcing each other. But there is one identifiable line of argument which has remained remarkably persistent and which has predominated over the others for two centuries, despite formidable and compelling criticism (cf. Coontz 1961): that associated with the writings of Malthus and his followers.

The view that poverty is "natural" has a long history. But what Malthus did for the first time was to purport to have discovered a "law of nature" which explained poverty as natural and inevitable. As Beales notes:

> The Malthusian theory rests, at bottom, on the view that poverty and indigence are the inescapable lot of man, his natural inheritance. (1953: 10)

This is not strictly true. As Rothschild (1996) has suggested, Malthus and those who thought like him acted as if they believed that wholly different laws of nature applied to the rich and the poor. Poverty may have been the inevitable fate of most people, but it was certainly not theirs.

---

1. It is difficult to underestimate the meaningfulness of this appointment. In the beginning of the nineteenth century, at a time when ruling-class power was intensely concentrated in the English Parliament, there were more than 100 members of the East India Company sitting in the House of Commons (Philips 1961: 151). Malthus's access to the makers of public policy, even if indirectly, was ensured.

In Malthusian thinking, the pressure of population on resources is regarded as the paramount cause of human misery, while the effects of such misery – disease, starvation, etc., his so-called "positive checks" – are regarded as the chief routes through which that pressure can (and even should) be alleviated. When Malthus considered that there might also be preventive checks, he meant delayed marriage or what he called (after 1803) "moral restraint", which depended on the poor acquiring the middle-class habits of prudence and self-discipline. But, of course, since it was the apparent absence of such habits that had made them poor in the first place, it was never likely that such traits could ever really be developed except through draconian measures.

Obviously, there were other possibilities for curbing fertility, and, if Malthus was really the uncompromising anti-natalist he is often regarded as and if population growth was truly the great source of all human misery, as he implied, "One might think," as Langer writes, "that Malthus, with his conviction that the root cause of pauperism was the excessive procreation of the lower classes, would have welcomed any reasonable plan for the limitation of population through measures of birth control" (1975: 269). Yet, he generally regarded most of the means available to the poor as morally unacceptable. At a time when they clearly were seeking to control their fertility (Langer 1975; McLaren 1984), either directly or indirectly – as in the case of infanticide by neglect (Sauer 1978) – Malthus recognised that a desire for children could be moderated by "human reason and ingenuity", but failed to advocate any particular methods, including non-coital sex, *coitus interruptus*, abortion and contraception, and actually branded them as "vice" or "improper arts" (Malthus 1930). Nevertheless, one of these so-called vices – *coitus interruptus* or "withdrawal" – which McLaren (1984: 75) describes as "the main brake on fertility" in nineteenth-century Europe (cf. Seccombe 1986; Schneider and Schneider 1992), continued to be one of the most popular and effective forms of contraception well into the second half of the twentieth century (Santow 1993; Glass 1966: 228), largely because it was safe, free and remarkably effective.

Malthus's opposition to such widespread and practical strategies, even on moral grounds, necessarily calls into question the assumption that he truly comprehended the varied ways in which people would attempt to alter their reproductive output in accord with their means and quality of subsistence. Indeed, there is little in his work to suggest that he appreciated the relationship between working-class fertility and the effective demands on the household economy.

By the late eighteenth century, these demands were generally forcing the poor to depend increasingly on their children's labour (Harris and

Ross 1987: 109–122). During Malthus's lifetime, the process of industrial-isation advanced at such a pace that "Machinery was soon developed to the point at which few men were needed and widespread unemployment among them was often accompanied by the over-working and intense exploitation of women and especially of children" (Morton 1979: 344). As new industries came to regard young children as a significant reserve of labour, the poor responded by marrying earlier and doing what they could to increase the survivorship of their offspring. It was not their fault that ultimately they were defeated by the overcrowded, insanitary urban living conditions in which tuberculosis, typhoid and other infec-tions took their chronic toll (Harris and Ross 1987: 110–113; Ross 1991: 28–30), so that, while industrial capitalism stimulated a higher birth-rate, it also eventually produced a dramatic rise in early childhood mortality. In the midst of such contradictions, the poor tried to exercise some control over their reproduction.

But what Malthus commended was a choice between the entirely impractical path of moral restraint and the crueller alternative repre-sented by the operation of what he termed "the laws of nature" (1830: 41). The seeming paradox of his position is fairly easily resolved by appreciating that Malthusian theory never aimed to be the basis of a policy of fertility regulation. On the contrary, it not only suggested that the fertility of the poor was the main source of their poverty, but implied that it was actually best if that fertility was not significantly controlled by human intervention, because that would reduce poverty and with it the chief stimulus for the poor to seek work.

Up until the middle of the eighteenth century in Western Europe, population growth was regarded as a major source of political and economic strength and innovation (cf. Tomaselli 1989 passim; see also Strangeland 1966). The English philosopher Thomas Hobbes exemplified this view when he wrote:

> Concerning multitude it is the duty of them that are in sovereign authority to increase the people, in as much as they are governors of mankind under God Almighty, who having created but one man, and one woman, declared that it was his will they should be multiplied and increased afterwards. And seeing this to be done by ordinances concerning copulation, they are by the law of nature bound to make such ordinances concerning the same, as may tend to the increase of mankind. (quoted in McLaren 1984: 60)

While this view is still advocated in modified form by some writers today (e.g., Boserup 1965; Simon 1981), during the eighteenth century a major shift began to occur toward the perspective which is largely associated with Malthus. Yet, Malthus himself was not unambiguously anti-natalist. While he is famous for arguing that poverty was the result of "the natural tendency of the labouring classes of society to increase beyond the demand for their labour, or the means of adequate support" (Malthus 1830: 74), he also viewed population growth and competition among workers as "a necessary stimulus to industry" (in Glass 1953: 29). As I have suggested, he had no intention of removing such pressures, but only of reducing the material obligation of the rich to mitigate the human misery caused by chronic or periodic unemployment. Such an obligation was, in his view, fundamentally incompatible with the ultimate rights of private property (Malthus 1830: 73). So it was that his so-called law of population acquitted the property-owning class of any such accountability, by arguing that poverty was the "natural" product of the fertility of the poor, rather than of the social or economic system. The solution therefore was a matter of individual, not systemic, responsibility.

Many of the contradictions and inconsistencies in Malthus's own writings can be resolved by reference to this political agenda – the defence of the system of private property (cf. Waterman 1991) as a means of organising resources and the removal of accountability by that system. These aims became increasingly important in the last decades of the eighteenth century, as English society underwent profound structural changes which simultaneously put new pressures on the poor and created new opportunities for wealth accumulation.

As Marx often observed, the essence of Malthusian theory was not new (Marx 1867). Robert Wallace, another cleric, had published a book called *Various Prospects of Mankind, Nature and Providence* in 1761, which also had described a disproportionate relationship between population and the means of subsistence (Beer 1984: 70–71; Boner 1955: 10–11). Such work had prompted Marx to observe: "with this very 'principle of population', struck the hour of the Protestant parson" (in Meek 1971: 89). But there was a crucial difference between Wallace and Malthus. While the former regarded the dismal effects of population pressure as an eventual problem, Malthus viewed it as imminent, even immediate. It was therefore responsible for current poverty. The main explanation for this difference is that Malthus intended his work to bear on contemporary debates in a time when the whole landscape of the English economy was being transformed. There was mounting pressure by employers for the creation of a cheap labour market, which required a working population which was not too costly to maintain and neither immoderate nor too modest in its reproductive habits.

His principle of population was meant to hold the struggle for a better world for the majority in check. Even if the poor wanted, at least, to address the question of how to exert some control over their fertility – not because this would resolve every economic or social problem, but because it might contribute to their aspirations to participate more fully in the determination of their own fate – Malthus again counselled against any expectation that human effort could be effective. "It is to the laws of nature, therefore," he wrote in 1830, "and not to the conduct and institutions of man, that we are to attribute the necessity of a strong check on the natural increase of population" (Malthus 1830: 41).

It is hardly surprising that Malthus had no wish to advocate effective human means of limiting population. If the reproduction of the poor was necessary for the production of wealth and if poverty was necessary to make the poor work cheaply, the pressure of population on the means of subsistence was, as Marx and Engels argued, part of the fundamental and necessary dynamic of capitalist economy. That remains true today, and it has made Malthusianism an equally necessary element of mystification in the dynamic of capitalist ideology. It has ensured that, while Malthus is remembered chiefly as the originator of a theoretical perspective which has left us with an unremitting anxiety about "over-population", his greatest achievement, in fact, was to devise such an enduring argument for the prevention of social and economic change.

While such an argument has impressed intellectuals and proven useful for policy-makers, it has never managed to constrain the aspirations and the dreams of the poor. That would not have escaped Malthus's attention, especially when the Swing uprisings of 1830 reached the county of Hertford where Haileybury is situated. As such events, locally or magnified on a larger scale, from the French Revolution to the peasant revolutions of the twentieth century, from the Russian Revolution through the decades of the Cold War, have frightened the rich and privileged, for whom "over-population" has always simply been a shorthand for "the majority", they have ensured that Malthusianism would be continually revived and revised in the defence of the changing strategic interests of capital.

As an ideological framework which naturalised poverty, which sought to reconcile the contradiction between hunger and abundance by attributing poverty and starvation to personal inadequacy and excess fertility, contested the philosophical premises of socialism and defended the private property system for over a century, the Malthusian vision acquired a firm place in the ideology of capitalism. With the inclusion of "birth control" in its practical armoury, it has proven to be a perspective which, in its compelling simplicity and practical application, could give the cover of legitimacy to Western interests, as expressed in their development theories and strategies (such as the Green Revolution), in a world defined by those interests as engaged in a fundamental struggle between systems based on private or collective ownership, capital or labour. Among the many explanations of poverty – genetic, cultural, environmental, etc. – which depend for their credibility on a superficial and opportunistic reading of history, none ever has managed to achieve the effect of the Malthusian argument because, in presenting over-population as the root cause of most human ills, it could always threaten us with such apocalyptic scenarios that reasoned debate about alternative explanations has been consistently overwhelmed. The fear of pending famine has systematically distracted attention from the fact that it is not the reproductive habits of the poor, but the contradictions and motives of capitalist development – of the morbid inequalities upon which the productive potential of such a system is based – that are the principal source of most of the misuse or waste of the world's human and material resources.

As we shall see, Malthusianism has been employed, not only to justify policies designed to resist criticism of such development, but also to contain the potential for the revolutionary transformation of capitalist economy throughout (but not only within) the developing world. From Ireland in the early nineteenth century to India, Guatemala and the Philippines in the mid-twentieth, it has rationalised development policies – above all, the advance of commercial agriculture – which have led to the gradual displacement of peasant cultivators. The aim of the present work is to explore how and why this has happened; to question the validity of the Malthusian vision of the necessity of inequality, of a world deemed incapable of progressive change; and to challenge the economic and political agenda of those who have gainfully employed that vision. In so doing, it seeks to reaffirm the priority of the hopes of the many over the privileges of the few.

1

Politics and Paradigms: The Origins of Malthusian Theory

It is clearly the duty of each individual not to marry till he has a prospect of supporting his children; but it is at the same time to be wished that he should retain undiminished his desire of marriage in order that he may exert himself to realize this prospect, and be stimulated to make provisions for the support of greater numbers.

Thomas Malthus

When Malthus's first Essay was published, England was in the midst of an agricultural revolution which was transforming long-standing agrarian relations between landlords and tenants; it was on the verge of an industrial revolution which would soon make it the paramount manufacturing nation in Europe; and it was five years into a counter-revolutionary war with its growing commercial rival, Napoleonic France.

It is hardly surprising that landlords, mercantilists and industrialists were all preoccupied with the question of property relations. Not only were new social and economic pressures pushing old institutional frameworks to their limits, but the French Revolution, which "destroyed the landmarks of the old established order in politics, economics, social life and thought" (Thomson 1966: 49), had unleashed many threatening ideas about the fundamental legitimacy of private property. Malthus's work emerged as a response to the anxieties which these produced in England.

Historian Carl Becker once called attention to the fact that the Jacobin spirit produced much the same response politically among the English that Bolshevism did in America over a century later (Becker 1932). As he wrote, long before the advent of Senator McCarthy and the rise of Henry Kissinger:

To the Castlereaghs and Metternichs of our day the word "Bolshevism" is the symbol of all that is horrendously antisocial, just as the word "Jacobinism" was to the Castlereaghs and Metternichs of 1815; and the words "soviet" and "communism" have for the beneficiaries of modern democracy the same ominous import that the word "republicanism" formerly had for the beneficiaries of the age of kings and nobles. (1932: 166)

One of the earliest important English expressions of this attitude, appearing in 1790, was Edmund Burke's *Reflections on the Revolution in France*. This book was especially notable for provoking two immediate and important rejoinders. One was Mary Wollstonecraft's *A Vindication of the Rights of Men* (in 1790);[1] the other was Thomas Paine's *Rights of Man* (in 1791) (Wollstonecraft 1994; Paine 1969).

The former explicitly accused Burke of championing property and of narrowly equating the defence of liberty with the maintenance of a system of unequal property ownership. But it was Paine's work which achieved the greatest distribution and notoriety (Claeys 1989: 67–82, 112). The pamphlet became a catalyst for the organisation of local branches of what was known as the London Corresponding Society (LCS). But this development was itself a symptom of the state of the country and it justified the government's fears of the turmoil that lay on the horizon, not only at home but in Ireland as well, where The United Irishmen had formed in 1790 and took as their main objective "to form a Republic, independent from England or France; to form a constitution upon the French model" (quoted in Claeys 1989: 118).

The seeming threat of widespread insurrection (Wells 1983) led the government to take repressive measures. Noted radicals were put on trial, the Habeas Corpus Act was suspended, the Treason Act was widened (Claeys 1989: 141). One of the government's targets was Mary Wollstonecraft's husband, William Godwin, whose *Enquiry Concerning Political Justice* was published in 1793 and who barely escaped standing trial for treason. All this was obviously made easier by the onset of war with France, which provided an admirable rationale for a crack-down on radicals. It also helped to blame the state of unrest on an imported ideology, at a time when the English working class had ample reasons of its own for protest.

By the time Malthus published his Essay in 1798, the very year that the United Irishmen actually attempted an uprising, the dangers represented by the French Revolution seemed quite real. Malthus, who had no intention of letting his readers misunderstand his aims and allegiances, grandly entitled his pamphlet *An Essay on the Principle of Population as It Affects the Future Improvement of Society, with Remarks on the*

---

1. Followed two years later by *A Vindication of the Rights of Woman* (Wollstonecraft 1975).

Speculations of Mr. Godwin, M. Condorcet, and Other Writers. Godwin, of course, was an easy and logical target. Condorcet was a more esoteric reference. But it is easy to see why Malthus singled him out: a mathematician and biographer of Voltaire, Condorcet represented revolutionary Paris in the new Legislative Assembly, in which he was one of the first members to call for a republic. Unlike Malthus, who regarded material want as essential to goad the poor into serious effort, Condorcet believed that government should actually ensure that people were not "exposed to misery, to humiliation, to oppression"; for him, it was a duty of government to guarantee "That all members of society should have an assured subsistence each season, each year, and wherever they live; that those who live on their wages, above all, should be able to buy the subsistence they need" (quoted in Rothschild 1996: 341).

Over the following decades, as the character of the European social landscape changed dramatically, Malthus was encouraged to expand and embellish his essay, to adapt it to emerging conditions. As the radical impulses of the French Revolution began to wane and the Napoleonic state emerged, the ensuing struggle between France and England, which lasted over twenty years, did much to unleash the productive forces of industrial capitalism, especially in England. As antagonisms between capital and the working class intensified, the threat from French republicanism began to seem far less important than that from the advocates of socialism. Malthus's theory of population became less and less a critique of Godwin's ideas of progress and was adapted to the debates that arose out of the process of English capitalist development.

But what never changed was the role of Malthusian theory in the legitimisation of private property arrangements. It remained committed to the view that Godwin's idea of progress, which was associated with the abolition of private property, was wholly negated by the dismal consequences of population increase pressing on the available means of subsistence. It thereby absolved such a system of responsibility for human misery by describing the latter as a natural effect of irrepressible biological urges on the part of a class that, innately or otherwise, was viewed as having little capacity for rational control. And, finally, it argued that any public obligation to mitigate that misery was fundamentally incompatible with the ultimate rights of property, since any form of social welfare was bound to be little more than a way of subsidising the fertility of the poor at the expense of the well-to-do and therefore of creating further misery. (This studiously ignored the question of how the well-to-do managed to maintain themselves, if not at the expense of the poor.) In this way, Malthus not only offered the authority of natural law in defence of established property relations, but created a general explanatory framework which was to prove one of the most enduring bulwarks against any argument for the mitigation of economic or social injustice. That it has retained this role over two centuries underscores how little fundamentally has changed between his time and our own.

Toward an End of the Old Poor Laws

...the Poor Law discussion formed the minds of Bentham and Burke, Godwin and Malthus, Ricardo and Marx, Robert Owen and John Stuart Mill, Darwin and Spencer.

Karl Polanyi

The debates which Malthus joined reflected the concerns of English capitalists, industrial and gentry alike (since the distinction was not always a clear one; cf. Ward and Wilson 1971), who felt constrained by many of the institutional arrangements, inherited from preceding centuries, which now seemed to them to restrict opportunities for investment and profit. A major focus of their opposition was the old Elizabethan poor laws which provided for parish relief, paid for by local taxation. It is important to underscore that these laws had not originated as a form of charity. Far from it. Both in England and on the continent, such legislation had been promulgated in the sixteenth century as a form of social control, directed especially against the great numbers of poor who had been displaced by enclosures and driven to seek a living wherever and however they could (Jordan 1959). After decades of ineffectual measures, in 1597 the English Parliament passed what was called "An act for the relief of the poor", which created the system of parish relief which Malthus and others would seek to abolish two hundred years later. This law

> remained, with numerous reaffirmations and quite minor amendments, the central law of the land relating to poor relief for very nearly two and one-half centuries. It fixed the parish as the unit of ultimate responsibility not only because the facts regarding poverty were best known there, but probably more importantly, because the whole scheme of poor relief rested on the assumption that a stable society, a non-migratory society, offered fewer social perils to the state. (Jordan 1959: 97)

By the late eighteenth century, however, the Tudor poor laws were regarded by employers as an unnecessary drain on private income and the principal impediment to the creation of the free and mobile labour reserve which emergent industrial capitalism required. It was not to be until 1834, the year of Malthus's death, that the Poor Law Reform Act, passed by a new Whig government dominated by merchants and industrialists, finally "set the seal on unfettered free trade in the labour market" (Dobb 1963: 275). Until then, less brutal mechanisms were devised. Polanyi (1944) regarded 1795 as a watershed because, in that year, the magistrates who administered the poor law in the county of Berkshire met in the village of Speenhamland to revise the system of local relief. The result, which was soon emulated in many other parts of England, was imperfect and contradictory; but it highlighted the widespread discontent among the landed gentry with the nature of relief, even while it reflected their interest in maintaining a system which guaranteed the local reserves of cheap, casual labour that English agriculture, not yet mechanised, still required.

Speenhamland reflected arguments against the poor laws that had been mounting for some time. Twelve years before Malthus's Essay, another English cleric, Joseph Townsend, had published a pamphlet (1786), entitled *Dissertation on the Poor Laws*, which had not only argued for their abolition but had suggested, as Malthus would, that such corrective efforts were in vain, since "wretchedness has increased in proportion to the efforts made to relieve it" (quoted in Chase 1982: 55). Townsend's writings contain many of the essential features, as well as the spirit, of Malthusianism. Neither man really believed, for example, that a disparity between population growth and food production – the essence of the latter's law of population – was entirely natural or pre-ordained. After all, both wrote in a period of unprecedented agricultural productivity. Between 1750 and 1840, when the population of England and Wales almost doubled, cereal production did as well (Hobsbawm and Rudé 1969: 27–9). This partly reflected the fact that, after 1801, Irish grain harvests counted as British; and it owed a great deal as well to the stimulus to grain production provided by the Napoleonic Wars and the Corn Laws. Under any circumstances, it meant, as Townsend observed, that it was "indeed possible to banish hunger". The problem, he emphasised, was that this would only have undesirable effects. More food would encourage the poor to breed more recklessly, whereas hunger and disease would curb the numbers of those he described as the "unworthy" (thus demonstrating why Malthusianism would ultimately find an intellectual ally in eugenics a century later).

Equally important, Townsend also regarded hunger as a necessary incentive for people to pursue employment. Anticipating Malthus, he wrote of how

> Hope and fear are the springs of industry.... The poor know nothing of the motives which stimulate the higher ranks to action – pride, honour, and ambition. In general it is only hunger which can spur and goad them on to labour; yet our laws [i.e., the Poor Laws] have said that they shall never hunger. (in Snell 1985: 123)

Like Townsend, Malthus also did not wish to see the poor guaranteed such entitlements. In his first Essay he had called for the "abolition of all the present parish laws" (Digby 1983: 97). For a man who described a world in which the means of subsistence were said to be continuously under threat from rising population, he was, as we have seen, remarkably judgemental and restrictive in his view of how that threat might be reduced by practical efforts. Yet perhaps to some extent this was because the spectre of over-population was too important and necessary as a rationale for the policies he wanted to prescribe. If it was the chief cause of human misery, he could plausibly argue against the poor laws on the grounds that they artificially subsidised the fertility of the poor. He could therefore say that it was as much in the interests of the poor as of the rich that they should be abolished, as did Malthus's friend, the economist David Ricardo. Ricardo observed that the rising costs of relief "make the rich poor" (there was little evidence for this, but this is how the rich always feel), while "every friend to the poor must ardently wish for their abolition" (Ricardo 1988: 345). (Again, it is common to hear how such entitlements degrade the poor, even more than poverty itself.)

In private, however, Malthus acknowledged that this was a theoretical assumption for which there was no real evidence, a view which has been sustained by recent research (Huzel 1969). But for the landed and commercial interests, whose arguments against the poor laws were fuelled by their disdain for the rising costs of parish relief, the Malthusian frame of reference offered the compelling line of argument that the fertility of the poor was being stimulated by the security which poor relief seemingly offered. It made the reproductive habits of the poor accountable for their poverty, for the process of proletarianisation which was a predominant feature of this period, especially in the rural areas, and for the burdens which the poor laws increasingly placed on people of property. But, in fact, neither the rise of a proletariat nor the rising cost of poor relief was really due to increasing population *per se*. It owed far more to the intense commercialisation of agriculture, especially during the Napoleonic Wars, which forced the enclosure of common lands across England during this period (Hammond and Hammond 1987; Hobsbawm and Rudé 1969: 27) and of which Malthus took remarkably little account.

Enclosures, Corn Laws and the Defence of Property

The enclosure process was not only the hallmark of the increasing pressure of commercial agriculture in these years. It represented the privatisation of the last vestiges of communal rights and property. As Blum writes:

> Enclosure and consolidation transformed land in which an entire community had rights of use into land in which only the individual occupant had the right of use. (1978: 263)

Between 1750 and 1850, about a quarter of England's cultivated acreage was transformed from open field, common land or waste into private property. Most of this occurred between 1760 and 1815 (Hobsbawm and Rudé 1968: 27). Many of the dispossessed could find no secure alternative employment either in the countryside or in the towns and, in the face of rising food prices, they were driven to depend on poor relief. As a result of the increasing number of claimants and the Speenhamland formula, the cost of relief nationally rose steadily during this period.

We are now told that the commons leads to tragedy (cf. Hardin 1968). But in reality it was the loss of the commons which was the tragedy, as it destroyed the economic viability of households. Even Arthur Young, the prominent agricultural writer and secretary of the Board of Agriculture, who initially regarded enclosure as part of a necessary process of modernisation, came to view it as destroying the basis of rural self-sufficiency. From first-hand experience, he had come to see how "before the enclosures, the despised commons had enabled the cottager to keep a cow, and this, so far from bringing ruin, had meant in very many cases all the difference between independence and pauperism" (in Hammond and Hammond 1987: 83).

And while enclosure proceeded, alternative rural opportunities were also shrinking, as landlords pushed their advantage, reflecting the un-democratic temper of the period. One of the few means by which the rural poor could enhance their depleted diet (Hobsbawm 1964) was by poaching, but the penalties for poaching were becoming increasingly harsh. According to Morton,

> In 1800 poachers became liable to hard labour and to two years' imprison-ment for a second offence. In 1803, it was enacted that any poacher who pointed a gun or attempted to cut or stab while resisting arrest should be hanged as a felon. In 1817 any person not belonging to the class entitled to pursue game who might be found in any park or wood with a gun or any other weapon became liable to transportation. (1979: 371)

All that remained of the idea that the poor had any right to subsistence was the old poor laws, and these were plainly in the sights of the proponents of Malthusian theory.

Under such circumstances, it was natural that part of the defence against enclosure rested on an almost Arcadian ideal of rural England. If anyone ever represented this ideal and used it as effective polemic against the tide of commercialisation sweeping over rural England in the early nineteenth century, it was William Cobbett. Cobbett was a man of robust contradictions. He had first made his reputation as a Tory pamphleteer, but sometime early in the nineteenth century, after living in the United States, probably due to the influence of Paine, he emerged as the greatest radical writer of his era (Williams 1983: 23ff.). For Cobbett, the enclosures were just part of a wholesale transformation of rural England which had created a new system that had

> drawn the real property of the nation into fewer ... hands ... made land and agriculture objects of speculation ... in every part of the kingdom, moulded farms into one ... almost entirely extinguished the race of small farmers. (in Williams 1983: 12)

But even without the potato, the rural populace was being squeezed by the strategy of enclosure, initiated for landlords by a legislature run by landlords.

It has been argued that, despite this, enclosure was as necessary as the abolition of the poor laws, to modernise the economy. In the late eighteenth century, Young had been one of the most notable champions of this view. But reexamination of the data he collected suggests that he greatly overdramatised the positive impact of enclosure, that they

> do not support the conclusion that enclosures or capitalist farming caused the growth in English grain yields. This was just landlord ideology in the eighteenth century. (Allen and Ó Gráda 1988: 116)

And if productivity increased during the Napoleonic Wars, it was as much in response to the boom market for grain as anything else.

Moreover, as with the Green Revolution in our own time (Lindenbaum 1987; Franke 1987), increased food production did not necessarily correspond to greater purchasing capacity for the poor. It was actually the opposite after the war, when the Corn Laws kept an artificial floor under grain prices and pushed up the price of bread. The cost of a 4 lb loaf in London doubled between 1790–94 and 1810–14 (Mathias 1969: 474), making the issue of the price of bread one of the central focal points of working-class protest after 1815 (Thompson 1963).

Meanwhile, the enclosures, by forcing new cohorts of landless rural families to seek wage labour, were also intended to bring more workers within the orbit of English employers and to accustom them to the new realities of the market economy (Snell 1985: 120) – to the discipline and other supposed moral virtues that it required – and to moderate the level of wages. But new opportunities for wage employment did not often materialise (Snell 1985: 183). As a result, poor relief expenditures tended to rise in the wake of enclosures (Snell 1985: 195ff.). Because the process of enclosure was irreversible, landowners and employers then sought to dismantle the whole edifice of poor relief. Speenhamland was a relatively modest step in that direction, although by pegging relief to the price of bread, it had created a new set of problems. (Under the system which they devised, the working poor were to obtain a wage pegged to the price of bread; when and if their wages were insufficient, relief would raise their income to the appropriate threshold [Watson 1969: 9–10].)

But it was Malthus three years later who provided the most persuasive argument, which in the end finally won the day in the unremitting attack on the poor laws. It gained strength through the years from the evidence that there were, indeed, increasing numbers of dependent poor. But it obscured the fact that, to a very large degree, they had been made, not born.

In its particular focus on population, then, Malthusianism provided a way of looking at the origins of poverty – and, by extension to more recent times, to underdevelopment – which effectively mystified the central role of capitalist relations of production. Nowhere is this better illustrated than by Malthus's defence of the English Corn Laws. As a result of these laws – which were not repealed until 1846 (Morton 1979: 404) – the poor suffered nutritional stress, not because of an absolute scarcity of food, as classical Malthusian thinking would argue, but because of state policy, dictated by and operating in the interest of the landowners and large farmers who controlled Parliament up to the early 1840s.

There is no doubt that, at various times during the Napoleonic Wars, there were real food shortages in Britain and even famine – in 1794–96 and 1799–1801, for example (Wells 1988). While Malthus was undoubtedly influenced by these events, which would have lent his views a certain credibility, he must have recognised that they were the result, not of population growth, but of the dynamics of a war economy. Yet, again, the effects of the Napoleonic Wars on British economy and society seem to have been easily overlooked. Even as the war created an enormous national debt which forced up prices and reduced real wages, he published a pamphlet in 1800, called *An Investigation of the Cause of the Present High Price of Provisions*, which attributed rising prices solely to "the attempt in most parts of the kingdom to increase parish allowances in proportion to the price of corn" (Keynes 1956 : 24–5). That is, he blamed the poor laws.

During much of the period during which Malthus wrote, British grain production was on the increase. Aside from the introduction of new farming methods and technologies – and access to Irish grain – this owed much to the fact that large amounts of land were being enclosed, in response to the high war-time grain prices. These enclosures were a major cause of the rural poverty that Malthus no longer wished to have assisted by parish relief. In the long run, however, many of the rural poor either left for the towns and cities or remained as a local under-class. If the latter were not highly regarded as workers (Kerr 1943: 366), with the growth of factory production, "town workers ... were no longer making annual excursions into the country for harvest work" (Kerr 1943: 373). At crucial periods, English farmers actually faced a labour scarcity which had to be met by importing Irish workers (Collins 1969), whose availability was the direct result of the chronic underemployment with which British rule had inflicted Ireland.

The movement of rural population into new urban centres began in earnest in the last quarter of the eighteenth century. New wealth from the conquest of India (Baran 1957: 146) and lucrative profits derived from the Atlantic slave trade and the development of plantation economies in the Caribbean provided capital for investment in manufacturing (Mathias 1969: 105). The rapid technical expansion of English industry owed everything to the emergence of a new global colonialist system whose complex texture Deane describes so well:

> Weapons, hardware, spirits from Britain, and calicoes from India were shipped to West Africa and exchanged for slaves, ivory, and gold. The slaves were sold in the West Indies for sugar, dyestuffs, mahogany, logwood, tobacco, and raw cotton. The gold and ivory were shipped to the East and Near East for teas, silks, calicoes, coffee, and spices. The tropical goods were sold in Europe for Baltic timber, hemp, pitch, and tar (all essential naval stores), Swedish and Russian iron; and, in the fourth quarter of the century, they paid for the foreign grain which was vital when the harvest failed and which was regularly required in most years even when the harvest did not fail. (1979: 55)

But, above all, it was the English cotton textile industry that was transformed. It is here that we confront the obverse of the European picture of the developing world as one retarded by traditionalism in the idea that Europe developed economically because of the intrinsic genius of its people. This is belied above all by the nature of the transformations that are referred to as the "Industrial Revolution", the catalyst for which seems rather to have been the English gift for conquest, pillage and duplicity. The turning point in particular was Robert Clive's victory at Plassey in Bengal, a victory that was ensured less by Clive's tactical brilliance than by the fact he had bribed many of his opponent's soldiers not to fight. As Brooks Adams wrote:

> very soon after Plassey, the Bengal plunder began to arrive in London, and the effect seems to have been instantaneous; for all the authorities agree that the "industrial revolution" ... began with the year 1760. (quoted in Baran 1957: 146)

Clive himself, officially an employee of the East India Company, returned to England a year later with over £300,000 in personal treasure (Bence-Jones 1974).

Of course, the riches from India were not the only new wealth which England capitalised upon. There was also the slave trade and the Atlantic "triangular trade", of which it was an integral part (Williams 1944). Liverpool especially grew rich on sugar and slaves (Aikin 1968); and, as its merchants enriched themselves, they invested their profits in textiles and other industries in the surrounding towns of Lancashire (Mathias 1969: 105).

Despite this, Wilkinson, in his book *Poverty and Progress*, which was hailed as a sophisticated reworking of Malthus (Boulding 1973), portrayed the rise of industrial Europe and England in particular as a matter of local responses to ecological depletion. He makes little reference to colonies – neither Ireland nor the Caribbean (or West Indies) is mentioned in the index – and in a brief account of the displacement of the woollen industry by cotton textile production – a process so complex that books have been written about it – he makes a reference to India that is perfunctory at best. According to Wilkinson,

> Although cotton was – like wool – a landbased resource, the fact that it depended on the exploitation of land in India and America rather than in England meant that it could provide a way out of the domestic impasse. The manufacture of clothing could be expanded without threatening the production of food. (1973: 128)

Of course, it did threaten food production, just not in England. Moreover, it was not from India that raw cotton came initially. On the contrary, India produced excellent-quality cotton textiles which dominated the English market up to the early eighteenth century (Mantoux 1961: 199–200) until Parliament decided to restrict their import and, through a long succession of acts, eventually managed to decimate Indian cotton manufacture (Morton 1979: 337; Dutt 1940: 124ff.). It was partly to compete with superior Indian cottons that English textile manufacturing had been impelled to contemplate new techniques of production.

Contrary to Wilkinson, "raw cotton came largely from the Levant, the southern States of America and the West Indies" (Deane 1979: 88); India was not a major supplier until after 1815. But what Wilkinson wholly overlooks in his compulsion to reduce such history to a ruthlessly simple Malthusian calculus is that cotton did not supplant wool in England from the late eighteenth century onward simply because of its extra-territorial provenance, but because it was grown by slaves on Caribbean plantations. Those slaves, in turn, were fed on provisions imported from another English colony – Ireland – with catastrophic results for the diet of the Irish peasantry, as we will see in the next chapter.

The Caribbean plantations and, later, India were able to provide England with cotton in such prodigious quantities that cotton manufacturing not only displaced woollen production throughout Lancashire, but triggered the rise of new factory towns almost overnight (Chadwick 1862: 14). As the price of cotton dropped from 2 s. per lb in the 1780s to 1 s. in the 1820s (and halved again over the next twenty years) (Barrett Brown 1974: 87), imports soared from just over 4 million pounds of raw fibre in the period 1755–64, to 24.45 million pounds in 1775–84, to almost 43 million pounds in 1785–95 (Wilson and Lenman 1977: 121). The expansion of cotton textile manufacturing brought a commensurate rise in the demand for labour, which had a marked effect on fertility among workers.

While the enclosures were forcing rural labourers to seek new sources of income, the technical transformation of cotton production in the second half of the eighteenth century (Pinchbeck 1969: 115–17) created new opportunities. Initially, improvements were limited to the spinning of yarn and had the chief effect of providing greater supplies for domestic weaving. It led to what Pinchbeck called "the golden age" of the weaver (Pinchbeck 1969: 117). This was an inducement for earlier marriage and an interest in the positive nurturing of offspring in a new economic climate where their labour value was of increasing importance. Infant and early childhood mortality declined (Wrigley and Schofield 1981: 249). The result was that the annual population growth rate rose from 0.48 in 1745 to 1.35 in 1800 (Wrigley and Schofield 1981: 213).

With the shift in the early nineteenth century from domestic to factory production, the demand for the labour of children would become at times greater than that for their parents. In such circumstances, parents were not only eager to see their children employed, but often could not even obtain poor relief unless they sent their children to work (Morton

1979: 344). Moreover, as a result of demographic trends since the late eighteenth century, the English population had become extremely young. By 1826, some 40 percent was represented by children under the age of 16 (Wrigley and Schofield 1981). Under such circumstances, increased employment of children in an age of industrial expansion was inevitable.

Malthus, meanwhile, could only describe the increase in fertility among the English working class as a symptom of their irrationality. He was never able to see it as a strategic accommodation to the new relations of production that characterised the emergent factory system. And, if he showed so little sensitivity to the impact of the factory system on the reproductive strategies of the working class, he was equally oblivious of the conditions which increasingly affected childhood morbidity and mortality.

During the years when he was Professor of Political Economy at Haileybury, improvements in mechanisation steadily reduced the need for adult male labour and "widespread unemployment among them was often accompanied by the over-working and intense exploitation of women and especially of children" (Morton 1979: 344). By the 1830s, male unemployment was chronic in urban areas and all of a family's productive resources had to be mobilised to ensure survival. A survey in 1833 of 48,645 workers in various industrial firms in Lancashire and Cheshire found that 41 percent were under 18 years of age, while 22 percent were under 14 (Collier 1964: 68). Of 565 children working in calico print works in Lancashire, Cheshire and Derbyshire, who were sampled by the Children's Employment Commission in 1843, nearly two-thirds had begun work before the age of 9 (Hutchins and Harrison 1966: 124; cf. Chadwick 1862: 47).

Women – single or married – were also a major source of industrial labour (Anderson 1971: 73), and while this was imperative from the viewpoint of household economy, it had adverse consequences for child mortality. Maternal employment required early weaning. Wet nursing was not an option for the working class, cows' milk was expensive and often unhealthy anyway, and new manufactured infant foods were an impractical, unaffordable alternative. It was not until around 1870 that cheaper tinned condensed milk appeared, but it was deficient in vitamins A and D – and therefore was conducive to rickets – and was also likely, if used, to be diluted (like much infant formula in the Third World today) with unclean water (Hewitt 1958: 147–8). Thus, the factory system, which came to depend so much on child labour, also created material conditions which were fiercely prejudicial to the survival of the young. This can be seen clearly enough in mortality trends in the northern industrial towns. In Preston, Lancashire, for example, the proportion of all deaths climbed from 29.3 percent among the under-fives in 1783 to 53.4 percent in 1841 (Harris and Ross 1987: 115). For the working class, there was an irreconcilable tension between the need for their children to work and the detrimental impact on children of their fathers' insecure employment and their mothers' low-waged labour.

Poor nutrition, crowded and sunless housing, new infectious diseases such as cholera and typhoid which thrived on the insanitary conditions of urban industrial life (Rosen 1958: 201ff.), all combined to produce a high level of infant mortality that remained a feature of English working-class communities up to the eve of the Second World War. In the end, the most common working-class strategy was simply not to invest too much in children until they were past the period of highest risk and then to fatten them up as they approached an age when they could go out to work.

Malthus in the Age of Industrialisation

With the end of the Napoleonic Wars, boom times for large farmers and speculators ceased. But grain prices never fell to pre-war levels because of the Corn Laws, which attempted to maintain prices, in large part by restricting grain imports (so that wheat imports were forbidden whenever the price fell below a certain level) (Morton 1979: 401). Dutifully, Malthus, who had argued that poverty was a matter of personal responsibility, published a pamphlet in 1815 which was entitled *The Grounds of an Opinion on the Policy of Restricting the Importation of Foreign Corn*. Growing rich was clearly a matter of government responsibility. So, for thirty years, while the Corn Laws stood as a prime example of market intervention, their effect on the price of bread was a significant factor in the declining living standards of the working class. Throughout the same period, the argument was made with great self-assurance, by Malthus, Ricardo and others, that poverty was the result of over-breeding on the part of the poor themselves.

During that same time, the commercialisation of English society – a society which subsidised large farmers on the one hand and took away common lands on the other – created enormous wealth, but also growing inequality. As the Hammonds wrote,

> The lives of the judges, the landlords, the parson, and the rest of the governing class were not becoming more meagre but more spacious in the last fifty years [to 1830]. During that period many of the great palaces of the English nobility had been built, noble libraries had been collected, and famous galleries had grown up, wing upon wing. [Meanwhile] the agricultural labourers whose fathers had eaten meat, bacon, cheese and vegetables were living on bread and potatoes. (1987: 241)

Potatoes, which had become an increasingly important part of the rural diet as the Corn Laws pushed up the price of bread, were, as the radical journalist William Cobbett continually noted, another means of impoverishing farm workers and enriching landlords. As early as 1770, Arthur Young had written in *A Six Months Tour Through the North of England* that

> these roots are everywhere considered as an excellent fallow crop, greatly ameliorating the soil, and preparing in every respect for wheat in particular, or for any other grain in a very superior manner. It is extremely evident ... that their culture is uncommonly profitable. (1967: 12–13)

It was attractive advice for any landlord poised to enclose the local commons. Just six years later, in *The Wealth of Nations*, Adam Smith also advocated the wider use of the potato, again with the profits of large farmers in mind. Because the tuber was so productive,

> the same quantity of land would maintain a much greater number of people, and the labourers being generally fed with potatoes, greater surplus would remain after replacing all the stock and maintaining all the labour employed in cultivation. A greater share of this surplus too would belong to the landlord. Population would increase, and rents would rise much beyond what they are at present. (1947, Vol. 1: 145)

But Cobbett was aware – and we shall see this in the next chapter – that the same strategy had subverted the food security of rural Ireland. He understood how the potato would be another factor in the process of cheapening the value of workers' labour. Thus, in 1834, while he was travelling in Ireland, Cobbett wrote in his *Political Register* on the subject of the debate in the British Parliament about the New Poor Law. He suggested that, in the name of morally improving the poor, the abolition of out-door relief and the choice between poverty wages and entering the poor-house would force many people to accept the lower wages that employers would now offer. As a result, he argued, English workers would be forced to eat, not bread, but potatoes, as they were squeezed between the Corn Laws and low wages. All this, he maintained, was sanctioned by the economic philosophy of Malthusianism, which argued that the poor had no claim on society, even in the face of starvation. After all it was Malthus, in the second edition of his Essay, supposedly a more compassionate update of the first, who had written:

> A man who is born into a world already possessed, if he cannot get subsistence from his parents on who he has a just demand, and if the society do not want his labour, has no claim of right to the smallest portion of food, and, in fact, has no business to be where he is. At nature's mighty feast there is no vacant cover for him. She tells him to be gone. (in Meek 1971: 8)

Of course, it was not Nature which said "be gone", but Malthus, land-lords and Parliament. But it was on the basis of this view, of class interest disguising itself as disinterested nature, that poor law reform was proposed.

Considerations of Malthus's work and influence have often over-looked just how much his theory of population was subservient in this way to a defence of private property relations (Harvey 1974). But it was this service that made Malthus's ideas congenial not only to the eco-nomic and political elite who encouraged the development of his ideas, but also to a whole generation of intellectuals and thinkers who laid the basis of classic Western economics. Foremost among them was David Ricardo, who, like Malthus, was firmly convinced of the immutability of the established order. His major work, *On the Principles of Political Economy and Taxation* (1817), rested securely on Malthusian foundations in its conception of the origins of poverty. In it, he observed:

> It is a truth which admits not a doubt, that the comfort and well-being of the poor cannot be permanently secured without some regard on their part, or some effort on the part of the legislature, to regulate the increase of their numbers, and to render less frequent among them early and improvident marriages. The operation of the system of poor laws has been directly con-trary to this. They have rendered restraint superfluous, and have invited imprudence, by offering it a portion of the wages of prudence and industry. (1988: 345)

Thus, one of the great figures of classical economics talks about the "prudence and industry" that made individuals like himself wealthy and not wanting any of his wealth spent on the poor, who had died in battle during the war with France or gone hungry because of war-time prices or in the wake of the enclosure of common land, or who were trans-ported to Australia for the crime of poaching, in order to feed their children. What prudent and industrious things did Ricardo do during the war? Ricardo was a stockbroker and a good friend of Malthus, with whom he maintained a continuous correspondence between 1811 and his own death in 1823. According to Keynes,

> During the Napoleonic Wars, Ricardo was ... a principal member of a Syndicate which took part in operations in Government stocks correspond-ing to what is now effected by "underwriting". His Syndicate would take up by tender from the Treasury a mixed bag of stocks of varying terms known as the *Omnium*, which they would gradually dispose of to the public as favour-able opportunities offered. On these occasions Ricardo was in the habit of doing Malthus a friendly turn by putting him down for a small participation without requiring him to put up any money, which meant the certainty of a modest profit if Malthus did not hold on too long, since initially the Syndicate

terms would always be comfortably below the current market price (Keynes 1956 : 30–31)

Not long after the end of the war, in 1817, Ricardo published his *Principles of Political Economy and Taxation*. War-time speculation had undoubtedly been quite profitable, because he was soon able to retire. He became a landed proprietor and entered Parliament in 1819, at a time when it was dominated by large landowners with a keen interest in passing bills of enclosure.

Another economist whose Malthusian sentiments have had lasting effect is the less well-known figure, William Forster Lloyd. Like Malthus an ordained minister in the Church of England, Lloyd held the Drummond Chair of Political Economy at Oxford. The author of a collection of essays entitled *Lectures on Population, Value, Poor-Laws and Rent* (1837), he is chiefly remembered, indirectly, as the inspiration for the biologist Garrett Hardin's famous essay "The Tragedy of the Commons" (1968) (see Chapter 3), and thus represents an important conceptual bridge between Malthusianism and one its most influential contemporary incarnations.

In 1833, Lloyd published his *Two Lectures on the Checks to Population*, which, in addition to expounding Malthus's central arguments, described what he regarded as the theoretical arguments against common property. There are several notable features of his argument, which would be harnessed later by Garrett Hardin to his Cold War vision of population and economy. First, it assumed that the threat to communal property came from individualism, as if this were an immutable feature of human nature, rather than a cultural and historical trait. Secondly, the whole point of Lloyd's argument was to advance Malthus's own use of the theory of population against the development of the common property regimes that he disparagingly referred to as "systems of equality". Like Hardin later, Lloyd maintained that democratic and open access to a "commons" – whether this were a pasture or the employment market – would offer little reason for people not to expand their numbers to fill it, because there would seem to be "no adequate individual benefit to be derived from abstinence" (Lloyd 1980: 484). This, he presumed, would probably occur only where a system of private property granted a limited number of people certain and guaranteed shares in a resource. Thus, for Lloyd, the "principle of population ... furnishes a reason for the institution of private property" (1980: 496).

In addition – and here one catches intimations of the eugenicists still to come – any system of equality seemed, to Lloyd, to lead inevitably to a general lowering of standards, whereas social differentiation would ensure that people had drive and ambition. "A state of perfect equality," he wrote, "by its effect in lowering the standard of desire, and almost reducing it to the satisfaction of the natural necessities, would bring back society to ignorance and barbarism" (1980: 496). It is an old elitist argument – here, based on Malthusian precepts which were so congenial to such an argument – that democracy creates mediocrity. But it is certainly not unique to Lloyd. This anti-democratic temper (with its reference point, either explicitly or implicitly, in assumptions about biological differences) remains a central feature of Malthusian and Neo-Malthusian thinking to the present day.

Lloyd and Malthus both had clearly perceived the central issues of their time. As a result, long before Malthus's death, his theories had become the cornerstone not only of the campaign against the old poor laws, but of the increasingly bitter struggle against socialism. The means by which they fulfilled this role were varied, however. Arguments such as Lloyd's were one, which ultimately was revived by Garrett Hardin. Another was beginning to emerge as early as 1822, when what came to be called Neo-Malthusianism first began to develop. In that year, Francis Place, a disciple of Jeremy Bentham, wrote that working people, in their own interest, should curb their fertility in order to drive up wages and resolve all the problems that affected working people. As he said to them:

> Many indeed among you are compelled for a bare subsistence to labour incessantly from the moment you rise in the morning to the moment you lie down again at night, without even the hope of ever being better off.
> The sickness of yourselves and your children, the privation and pain and premature death of those you love but cannot cherish as you wish, need only be alluded to ... what, you will ask is the remedy? Howe are we to avoid these miseries?
> The answer is short and plain: the means are easy. Do as other people do, to avoid having more children than they wish to have, and can easily maintain. (in Hardin 1969: 192–3)

The important departure here from conventional Malthusian thinking was that Place believed that this should be done not simply through moral restraint but by birth control (Thompson 1963: 777). But, of even greater strategic significance, he regarded this as more desirable than the structural transformation of society or any form of working-class militancy, even trade unionism. As Gordon has observed, he "offered contraception encapsulated in an ideology that promoted acceptance of the capitalist mode of production and distribution ... as part of a theory that denied the concept of exploitation" (1976: 81). Place's efforts set the stage for the evolution of a birth control movement which was so divorced from sensitivity to the fate of working people that it would eventually find common cause with many of their enemies.

Toward a New Poor Law

For the time being, however, Place's advocacy of birth control fell far short of the concrete demands of an increasingly active working class. According to Hobsbawm (1964: 30), the first "labour dispute" took place in 1831. But a year earlier, rural labourers across the south and east of England, under growing pressure from new commercial production, mechanisation, enclosures, the Corn Laws, had launched a violent, but short-lived campaign for agricultural reform, under the name of "Captain Swing" (Hobsbawm and Rudé 1968). In its aftermath, hundreds were "transported" to Australia for real or alleged participation in the riots (Hughes 1987: 197–200) and the government put Cobbett on trial for supporting the agricultural workers (Morton 1979: 374).

The Swing riots, which were also called "The Last Labourers' Revolt", reflected the fact that the old agrarian order was generally on the wane (Blum 1978). Across Europe, the power of old landed interests was being challenged, especially by the ambitious middle class, frustrated in its efforts to forge a modern, competitive market. So, in the same year as the Swing riots, a wave of liberal revolutions also swept the continent. In France, a Bourbon king, restored after the defeat of Napoleon, was dethroned. Belgium was liberated from Holland. In England, where change was almost always more temperate, the Whigs took control of Parliament from the Tories. One of their first major legislative achievements was the passage of the 1832 Reform Bill, which widened the franchise, not radically, but enough to begin to consolidate Whig power by diminishing the influence of the old landed interests that controlled small borough constituencies (Morton 1979: 390–94). The Tories still remained a significant force, but the bill meant that "the bourgeoisie had shown its teeth" (Moore 1966: 32), and the manufacturing and commercial interests, especially in the large northern towns, at last acquired some political influence. It is also necessary, however, to see the bill as a defence against the more radical impulses of the time. It defined a voter as the owner or tenant of a property worth at least £10 a year, which was sufficient to disenfranchise virtually the entire working class.

While this may have had the general (if not enduring) effect of disillusioning the working class with the potential of parliamentary politics (Morton 1979: 393), it is perhaps ironic that even such a mild reform made it possible for a few individuals such as Cobbett to enter Parliament. Radical interests in the Lancashire cotton-manufacturing town of Oldham, who had previously learned how to put pressure on traders and merchants in the form of boycotts, repeated those tactics with great success in the parliamentary elections of 1832. As a result, Cobbett and another radical, John Fielden, "enjoyed tremendous majorities over their employer-backed Whig and Tory opponents" (Foster 1974: 54).

Although Cobbett was a singular minority within that Parliament, it was forced by outside events to pass the first really effective factory legislation to curb child labour in the textile industry. This largely resulted from the "pressure of a most violent working class agitation throughout the whole of the North of England" (Morton 1979: 378), which itself must be related to the cholera pandemic of 1831–82, which had profound political repercussions throughout much of Europe (cf. Blum 1978: 343). In general, however, the new Parliament consolidated the interests of the industrial class. While Cobbett continued to write and speak for the working class against the emergence of what he called an "unnatural system", while he attacked the spirit of Malthus and his supporters, the Whig Parliament prepared to reform the poor laws once and for all, to create the free labour market that industry demanded. The New Poor Law was passed in 1834, a final tribute to Thomas Malthus, whose "views were of central intellectual significance in shaping the debate over poor-law policy for nearly 40 years before the decisive reform" (Digby 1983: 104).

Whatever else this legislation pretended to be, this Act "and its subsequent administration ... was perhaps the most sustained attempt to impose an ideological dogma, in defiance of the evidence of human need, in English history" (Thompson 1963: 267). At a time when the condition of the English working class was perceptibly worsening, the New Poor Law instituted a system of workhouses in which circumstances were deliberately made so bad that people would choose to take the poorest paid work rather than enter them. That was the whole idea. "Our intention", one Assistant Poor Law Commissioner said, "is to make the workhouses as like prisons as possible", while another declaimed: "our object ... is to establish therein a discipline so severe and repulsive as to make them a terror to the poor and prevent them from entering" (in Thompson 1963: 267). It is little wonder that, within a short time, the Poor Law Commissioners and their Secretary, Edwin Chadwick, who had been one of the principal authors of the new law, had become "the most detested men in England" (Morton 1979: 397).

The irony, of course, is that, in order to create a so-called free labour market, employers had to *force* workers to compete. But, while classical economic theory said that a competitive market was optimal, workers defied both the prevailing theory and the interests of their employers by struggling to organise themselves against the brutality of a system in which unemployment and low wages were endemic. The combination of the New Poor Law, the Reform Bill and, as William Morris observed, "the simplest and most powerful of all causes – hunger" (Morris 1984: 172) politicised the English working class (Desmond and Moore 1991: 264). In 1837, while founding the London Workingmen's Association, William Lovett wrote "The Charter", whose simple demands soon became the rallying call of the working poor. Seemingly mild by today's standards, Marx and Engels, who allied themselves with the Chartist cause, acknowledged that their enactment would have been tantamount to a revolution (Morton 1979: 430ff.). The Whigs, however, had not reformed the poor laws just to concede political rights to workers, and the Chartists' demands were strenuously resisted (Moore 1966: 34).

By 1846, moreover, the repeal of the Corn Laws did much to disempower Chartism and to strengthen the position of the industrial elite. In Marx's words, it "reduced production costs, expansion of foreign trade, increase in profits, a reduction in the main source of revenue, and hence of the power, of the landed aristocracy, and the enhancement of their own political power". To be sure, the landed gentry survived, and still retain considerable political influence in Britain today. But the repeal of the Corn Laws was certainly one of the signs of the dawning of a new world order, the beginning of the thrust by the English – for that matter, the European – bourgeoisie to create a world market based on industrial production (which would eventually industrialise agriculture as well). That was finally possible in just a few years' time, after another wave of European revolutions in 1848 "had been precipitated by the last, and perhaps greatest, economic crisis of the ancient kind, belonging to a world which depended on the fortunes of harvests and seasons" (Hobsbawm 1979: 28).

There is no doubt that this "great European upheaval" (Thompson 1966: 204) was in large part a response to widespread political oppression. That this was a pivotal moment in the evolution of European political life is evidenced by the fact that 1848 – exactly a half century after Malthus's first Essay – was also the year of the publication of *The Communist Manifesto*. But, at a deeper level, it reflected a final crisis in the nature of the agrarian systems of Europe, pushed to their limits in a time of rapid urban industrial development. When a potato blight arrived in Western Europe from the United States in 1844–45 and spread rapidly wherever the potato had become a staple crop (Blum 1978: 273–6), it revealed how insecure food production was.

Another symptom of the increasing vulnerability of the European system at mid-century was the recurrence of epidemic disease. And it is probably no coincidence that the year of revolution, 1848, saw the first great cholera pandemic since the early 1830s (R.J. Morris 1976: 13). In Ireland, where, as we shall see in the next chapter, the failure of the potato crop had its most disastrous consequences, and where cholera was just one of the diseases that accompanied it (Woodham-Smith 1962: 380–81), Malthusian theory was quickly brought into play, to attribute the ensuing famine and death, not to colonial underdevelopment, but to over-population.

Just as the potato blight was about to hit, Engels published his *Outlines of a Critique of Political Economy*. In it, although he made no specific reference to events in Ireland, he commented on the contradiction which Malthus, now dead, had sought to obscure through his principle of population. "I will not accept", wrote Engels,

> any defense of the Malthusian theory as competent which does not begin by explaining to me, on the basis of the theory itself, how a people can die of hunger from sheer abundance, and which does not bring this explanation into harmony with reason and the facts. (in Meek 1971: 61–2)

The irony is that Malthus had already conceded that the disparity between population and resources was not entirely natural, that it was not separable from the system of production. He had written in an especially revealing passage:

> it is unquestionably true that the laws of private property, which are the grand stimulus to production, do themselves so limit it, as always to make the actual produce of the earth fall very considerably short of the power of production. (Malthus 1830: 36)[2]

This was so because, if capitalists must earn a profit, they would inevitably tend to exclude from use any land that could only be cultivated at an unacceptable cost. For Engels, this revealed the theoretical inconsistency at the heart of Malthusian thinking, and he maintained that it was actually "From [Malthus's] theory we derive the most powerful economic arguments in favor of a social reorganization" toward a system not predicated upon competition (quoted in Meek 1971: 62).

---

2. A good example is provided in William Hinton's report on China in the late 1980s after capitalist reforms had been introduced in the countryside. He writes of how

> Dams, terraces, and other collective engineering works were falling apart. We saw abandoned irrigation systems and washed-out earthworks. It was quite clear that many of them never would have been built under a private economy and that they would not now be restored short of recollectivization. (Hinton 1990: 144)

But if Malthus admitted that an alternative system of common owner-ship might make it possible to exploit such land without regard for profits in the strict sense and so allow a far greater population to sub-sist, he immediately countered that greater productivity would simply engender more people. But more importantly, he regarded capitalism as the only admissible system, because private property embodied the "laws of nature" (Malthus 1830: 71–3).

By 1830, Malthus had taken his theory of population well beyond its humble beginnings, when he had first responded to the writings of Godwin and Condorcet over three decades earlier. But, in slowly adapt-ing his work to the demands of the new market economy (Desmond and Moore 1991: 264–8), he had revealed not only the essential flaw in his own argument – that population increase was only a problem relative to the means of production – but his central and unrelenting aim: to justify and affirm the established order of inequality. In the process, he sought to prove that anything that humans might do through their own social or political efforts to redress inequalities or to mitigate suffering was counterproductive because it would only increase population and place more pressure on the means of subsistence. If anyone argued that it was possible to avoid this by changing the social nature of production, Malthusians would reply that this was an affront to the "natural" order of things. The poor would prove to have their own ideas.

2

Ireland:
The "Promised Land"
of Malthusian Theory?

Begin with pauperizing the inhabitants of a country and when there is no
more profit to be ground out of them, when they have grown a burden
... drive them away.

Karl Marx

Momentous changes in British capitalism and in the nature of Ireland's
role in the British economic system at the end of the eighteenth and
beginning of the nineteenth century ensured that Irish poverty and
famine would come to be regarded as classic manifestations of Malthusian logic. In Ireland, it was an exceptionally profitable time for landlords and, as Engels would have predicted, a time of growing misery
among the rural Irish. And in England, the government was increasingly
repressive toward growing popular opposition at home and anxious to
prevent the egalitarian ideals of the French Revolution from exacerbating revolutionary aspirations in Ireland, where many Tories owned great
estates (Morton 1979: 354; Wells 1983).

But it was too late. The United Irishmen, vanguard of the insurrectionary movement in Ireland, had "declared for the abolition of church
establishments, and of tithes; for resistance to rack-rents; and, ultimately,
for sweeping measures of agrarian reform" (Jackson 1970: 119). They
were made illegal, but by early 1798 "the whole of Ireland was declared
in a state of insurrection and placed under military law" (Morton 1979:
355). Overt rebellion was not suppressed until 1805, but discontent and
local resistance percolated through the following decades, and it is no
coincidence that it was precisely during these years, when nothing
England did could pacify the country, that a Malthusian consensus began
to emerge which defined colonial Ireland as a resource-poor country
whose poverty, agricultural crises and general unruliness were principally
the result of surplus population. Over the next half-century, this view

coalesced into one of the great myths of Malthusian theory and, as such, came to figure centrally in Western ideas about the very nature of underdevelopment, the innocence of colonial rule, and the causes of peasant unrest.

Malthus himself published an anonymous essay in 1808 in *The Edinburgh Review*, a journal extremely sympathetic to his ideas, in which he highlighted the significance of Thomas Newenham's recent work on Ireland's population increase (Anon 1808). What he overlooked was how Newenham had connected this to the nature of Ireland's export economy, observing that

> An increased exportation of the native produce and manufactures of a country denotes an increased demand for labour. And an increased demand for labour must necessarily be followed by an increase of people. (Newenham 1805: 176)

There was bound to be opposition to Malthus's oversimplifications about Ireland, as there was to Malthusian thinking generally, and the lines of debate reflected the general polarisation of English political life during this period (Wells 1983: 2ff.). But it was the Welsh-born industrialist Robert Owen, one of Malthus's most eminent opponents and certainly the most influential socialist of the first half of the nineteenth century (Beer 1984: 131), who, in the early 1820s, would emphasise the central anomaly of Ireland's situation, that the Irish were impoverished despite the fact that Ireland was "competent to maintain, not only its own inhabitants, but more than double the whole population of Great Britain and Ireland, in comfort heretofore unattained by any nation or people, at any period of the world" (Owen 1823: 22). This was the very paradox of capitalist development that Engels and Marx had described.

It was to be the so-called Great Famine of 1846–49, however, which provided what seemed like the definitive confirmation of Malthus's judgement and helped to consolidate the argument that Irish underdevelopment was largely due to endogenous factors. It so marked Ireland, in Marx's words, "as the promised land of the principle of population" that, a century after Owen's remarks, it was commonly accepted that the famine had occurred chiefly because "population had increased up to the limit of subsistence" (Griffin 1926: 61–2). As we shall see, that limit was largely imposed by the imperatives of colonial interests.

It was hardly in England's interest, however, to admit that rural distress and periodic famine were actually the results of its colonial rule which had created a role for Ireland within the wider British economy that made agricultural crises endemic. That role was special indeed. As the earliest English colony, Ireland had set the stage for future colonial enterprise. It was the "colonial prototype" which served as the strategic and intellectual model that defined subsequent encounters, from North American Indians to peasants in India (Cook 1993; Jones 1964: 167–79). It materially subsidised other ventures, in particular the plantations of the English Caribbean, which Irish agricultural output sustained to a singular degree. And, eventually, England's ascendancy as the first and paramount industrial nation in Europe also depended upon Ireland providing a strategic reserve of cheap labour and agricultural products. It was inevitable, then, that Ireland came to play a crucial role in assumptions about the causes and consequences of underdevelopment in general. And if the Malthusian paradigm predominates today among models of underdevelopment, it is partly because the great Irish famine of 1846–49 was taken as the definitive embodiment of its essential principles. It is still widely regarded as *the* classic Malthusian crisis, the culmination of a half-century during which the population of rural Ireland seemed to press steadily on the country's means of subsistence.

Yet Malthusian theory could never rely solely on the presumption that the poor, Irish or otherwise, simply allowed their fertility to go unchecked, because this never actually seemed to be the case (Harris and Ross 1987). It depended, as we saw in the previous chapter, on some variant of the premise that the poor were not rational enough to practise sufficient self-restraint. In the particular case of Ireland, demographic growth was largely attributed to a seemingly irrational dependence on the potato, which was believed to have transformed that lack of restraint into Malthusian tragedy. As one anonymous writer put it,

> The fatal luxuriance with which this vegetable flourished in the soil of Ireland, caused population to run fearfully ahead of the requirements and capabilities of the country. (Anon. 1847: 37)

This was the view expressed by Malthus himself as early as 1808 (Semmel 1963: 36). As a result, according to the conventional scenario, when the fungus *Phytophthora infestans* destroyed most of the potato crop in the 1840s, the Irish population, having nothing else to sustain it, inevitably crashed. The ensuing famine was therefore regarded as an exemplary case of what occurred when Malthus's preventative checks seemed to have failed.

This popular account of the wellsprings of the Irish potato famine assures us that increasing dependence on the potato, an American cultigen introduced into Ireland probably in the seventeenth century (Salaman 1985), encouraged early marriage and land-subdivision because "Irish men and women were prepared to live almost exclusively on potatoes" (Drake 1969: 66). The implication was that the Irish were easily satisfied with the minimal standard of living that the potato could readily supply because it summoned forth certain intrinsic traits in the Irish themselves. In his eccentric work *The Evolution of Man and Society*, the prominent English plant geneticist C.D. Darlington would write of how

> The growth of the potato had in a hundred years doubled the population of Ireland. The Irish cultivator had at last found a crop whose dangerously easy cultivation suited his temperament. (1969: 454)

As a result, the potato was seen as the catalyst for what a leading Neo-Malthusian today describes as a "gradually accelerating increase in population growth relative to available resources, so that crop failure in the 19th century brought mass starvation" (Abernethy 1979: 97).[1] According to such reasoning, it was only the profound trauma of the famine that finally induced a fundamental change in the formerly profligate reproductive habits of the Irish, triggering a pattern of delayed marriage, high rates of celibacy and emigration (cf. Bodley 1976: 89; Friedl and Ellis 1976: 23–4).

More recently, the eminent Italian demographer Massimo Livi-Bacci, in his book *A Concise History of World Population*, has recapitulated many of the arguments advanced over forty years ago by K.H. Connell (1950). Although he glancingly acknowledges that England played a role in Ireland (referring briefly to English demand for Irish food during the Napoleonic Wars), he endorses Connell's thesis that the Irish had "a natural tendency" to marry early. Connell related this to "their improvident temperament", suggesting, like Darlington, the operation of innate character traits. According to Livi-Bacci (1992: 62–3), these formerly had been inhibited by land scarcity, but, conveniently for the English, were unleashed by the advent of the potato, which was so productive per acre that people could subsist easily on smaller holdings and indulge their natural inclinations. There is no mention that, in 1700, the Irish diet still was not confined to the potato (Lucas 1960; Cullen 1981); that it only grew in importance among the rural Irish as Ireland became increasingly productive as an export economy; nor any reference to how the potato made landlords wealthy as it made the poor so vulnerable. England is completely exonerated when Livi-Bacci confidently asserts that "*one may accuse the potato of having impoverished Irish peasantry* [my italics]" (Livi-Bacci 1992: 63).

---

1. Over time, this general scenario has been pared down to almost epigrammatic form. In a popular anthropology textbook, Harris refers to how "The potato was taken to Ireland where it produced a population explosion followed by crop failures, a famine, and a mass exodus to America" (1971: 190).

English Colonial Rule and the "Limits of Subsistence"

Long before the Industrial Revolution, according to the English historian James Froude, Ireland "was regarded as a colony to be administered,
not for her own benefit, but for the convenience of the mother country"
(in MacNeil 1886: 15). Over the centuries, military incursions, land
confiscations and paralegal interventions all contributed to the establishment of a relatively manageable colonial regime which left Ireland with
only fictive autonomy. As early as 1495, all the laws passed by its Parliament had to be approved by the English Privy Council. But this did
not mean that Ireland was wholly pacified, and for the next two centuries
the English had to assert their dominance with periodic military campaigns. In 1649, Cromwell – still regarded in England as the champion
of parliamentary democracy – himself led an invasion to take Ireland in
the name of the Puritan Commonwealth and to carve it up among the
merchants and speculators who had bankrolled Parliament's army.
Ireland's population was decimated within the next few years; thousands
of Irish prisoners were shipped to the West Indies (Williams 1944: 13),
while English and Scottish settlers were brought in to fill the vacuum
(Morton 1979: 264).

Catholic landownership was reduced from about 59 percent in 1641
to 22 percent over the next four decades. By 1703, after a major military
intervention by William of Orange in his war with James II, another
wave of land confiscation further reduced Irish Catholic landownership
to a mere 14 percent (Hechter 1975: 103–4). At the same time, England
pressured the Protestant-controlled Irish Parliament into passing a series
of what were loosely called "penal laws", which collectively consolidated
Anglo-Irish power and privilege by depriving Catholics of their basic
political, social and economic rights. Between 1695 and 1727, they were
forbidden to buy land, bear arms, own a horse worth more than £5,
become lawyers, etc.

In 1801, Ireland and England were officially joined into one kingdom. Mokyr has tried to minimise the adverse impact of this development, suggesting that Ireland only stood to benefit by becoming "part
of a large economic unit which also happened to contain the most
advanced industrial nation in the world" (1985: 288), but the fact is that
it sealed the fate of Ireland's poor, while effectively obscuring Ireland's
colonial status. Of course, as far as most of the Irish were concerned,
the Act of Union merely formalised a loss of sovereignty which had
begun centuries earlier. But the timing was crucial. The war with
Napoleonic France was costly and the union enabled England to tap
the rich reserves of Ireland's treasury. Within the first sixteen years of

the union, Ireland's national debt rose 250 percent, compared with only 50 percent for England (Kennedy 1973: 33); and when the exchequers of the two countries were actually combined in 1817, Ireland, which had been one of the most prosperous countries in Western Europe at the turn of the century, was virtually bankrupt (Smart 1964: 488).

The effect on Irish industrial development was profound, as the union exposed Ireland to competition from English manufactures, while it drained the island of vital investment capital (Probert 1978: 30). The consequence was that unemployment became a chronic feature of Irish life – one which had been present in the eighteenth century, but which certainly worsened in the nineteenth – and there was a steady migration, both seasonal and permanent, to England, where Irish workers provided a cheap, flexible labour force, or into the English Army, for which Ireland provided "an inexhaustible nursery of the finest soldiers", according to the historian Thomas Babington Macaulay (in Woodham-Smith 1962: 28), who otherwise despised the Irish as lazy and troublesome.

These developments also had a profound effect on the Irish diet. In the eleventh century, the Irish economy was largely pastoral, with milch cows providing the dietary staples of milk and cheese. As late as 1600, extensive forests (McCracken 1971: 15–22) had also provided mast for foraging swine, so that there was a steady supply of pork as well. Cereal cultivation rounded out the diet (Lucas 1960). This picture changed dramatically in the course of the next two centuries. Wars that destroyed fields of grain encouraged the use of the newly introduced tuber, which survived rampaging armies (Salaman 1943: 15–16; Longfield 1929: 116, 204). But, above all, landlords came to recognise in the potato a remarkable opportunity to create an economy geared to export trade with the emerging Caribbean plantations. Because it markedly increased output per acre and could be grown over a wider range of micro-habitats – including poorer, wetter soils – than grains, landlords encouraged tenants to cultivate the potato, while they took over more prime land for wheat or pasture.

By the middle of the seventeenth century, the colonial economy of Ireland was given over to grazing cattle to such an extent that, according to Crotty, it had "what was certainly the largest livestock export trade in the world at that time" (1983: 107). Some animals were shipped to England to be fattened for the London market. But it was the development of a provisions trade with England's Caribbean colonies that distinguished this period. After 1660, under pressure from English cattle farmers, protectionist legislation prohibited the import of Irish animals, leaving Irish graziers little choice except to engage in a trade which in the end proved to be extremely lucrative for them and essential for the growth of the West Indies plantation economy. As the book *The Interest of England in the Preservation of Ireland*, published in 1689, observed,

The islands and plantations of America are in a manner wholly sustained by the vast quantities of beef, pork, butter, and other provisions of the product of Ireland. (in O'Donovan 1940: 73)

This remained the case until the 1760s, when Ireland exported a total of 213,000 barrels of beef per annum, 50 percent of which went to the plantations, 48 percent to the continent and only 1 percent to Britain. But significant changes in this pattern began to occur toward the middle of the eighteenth century when the demand in England for Irish foodstuffs increased and gradually took priority over exports to the West Indies. This shift reflected various factors. The combined effects of English industrial expansion and urbanisation created considerable pressure on food supplies in the manufacturing districts. The onset of the Napoleonic Wars, which cut off England from its continental food supplies, added to the problem, and there were periods of real nutritional distress after 1795 (Wells 1988; Boner 1955).

The passage of Foster's Corn Law in 1784, which lifted restrictions on the importation of Irish cereals (Hechter 1975: 85), had guaranteed that meat and dairy products were not Ireland's sole exports. But it took the Napoleonic Wars to shift the emphasis of Irish production decisively toward grain. By 1800, the total export of beef had fallen to 147,382 barrels – most of which (79 percent) now went to Britain. And as land use became more intensive and potatoes became an even more important part of the rural Irish household economy, the rearing of pigs (to the outsider, another hallmark of Irish peasant poverty) grew in importance, as potatoes provided an important source of fodder (cf. Ross 1983: 103–4). This was reflected in the increase in pork exports between 1764 and 1800, from 30,328 barrels to 107,530. The proportion which was exported to Britain rose from virtually zero to 87 percent (O'Donovan 1940: 114–16).

While grain took over significantly from cattle rearing, the latter was never wholly displaced, however, largely because it was a crucial resource for the provisioning of the English Army during this period. In 1813, toward the end of the Napoleonic Wars, the British War Office's Commissariat contracted for 14.3 million lb of Irish salted beef, in addition to 12.6 million lb of salted pork (House of Commons 1836: 514). Between 1813 and 1835, it acquired almost 70 million lb of salted beef and 78 million lb of salted pork from Ireland (House of Commons 1838: 514). It was only as a soldier in the English Army that many Irish youth finally had a chance to eat the family pig.

Nevertheless, cattle grazing generally diminished as the wartime economy stimulated a more intensive agricultural regime, both in England and in Ireland (Jones 1983). This was reflected in an explosive rise in Irish grain exports from 31,423 barrels in 1771–73 to over 863,000 by 1791 (Newenham 1805: 48–50). This more intensive land use depended on allocating more land for commercial production and on an increased workforce.

The Ascendancy of the Potato

Landlords sought to achieve these ends not only by encouraging tenants to grow more potatoes on marginal land, but also by using it as an inducement for them to marry earlier and raise children on smaller holdings. Among the various incentives for the poor was the fact that the potato was one of the few major food crops that was not tithed (Gill 1925: 35–6). But the chief virtue of the potato, for landlord and tenant alike, was its productivity. In *The Wealth of Nations*, Adam Smith had already advocated its use a means of improving landlords' profits. And, indeed, it not only enabled them to increase cereal production, but compelled the rural Irish to compete for tenancies, which drove up rents, which, in some districts, rose as much as 85 percent between 1746 and 1783 (Johnson 1970: 229). As a result, the pro-natalist policies of landowners, which would not have been feasible in the absence of the potato, proved especially rewarding. There is certainly little evidence that rising population during the late eighteenth century had a damaging effect on the Irish economy in general. On the contrary, it was a major factor underlying an unprecedented increase in the prosperity of the ruling class. By 1805, Thomas Newenham would observe:

> We know that within these last five-and-twenty years the rent of land has doubled in most places and trebled in many. We know that a vast number of superb country mansions, besides splendid townhouses, have been built within these last twenty years: a circumstance which clearly evinces a very great increase of wealth among the landlords of Ireland. (1805: 143)

This would not have been possible if the potato had not been productive and versatile enough to guarantee peasants a basic livelihood, while they were forced to live on a steadily contracting subsistence base. Despite this, however, by the beginning of the nineteenth century, Malthusian biases were beginning to portray the potato as the source of virtually all of Ireland's problems. This is despite the fact that in other parts of Europe, where the potato had become a popular crop, there was no obvious or consistent association with demographic trends (Morineau 1979: 22–3).

The way in which the English assigned responsibility to the potato for triggering a great upturn in Irish population which ultimately was held accountable for the 1840s' famine depended, not on any concrete evidence, but on the essentially racist view that the Irish were intrinsically content to live solely on the potato, because they were lazy and unambitious and because the potato could satisfy all their apparent wants. Few, if any, other peoples in Europe had to endure such opprobrium for having embraced the potato as a staple crop which was widely respected for its ability to grow in areas where grain was marginal. Ireland was not the only country where it had proven capable of opening up new zones for food and fodder production (cf. Ross 1983). But only in Ireland, where a colonial power sought endless justifications for its policies, was reliance on the potato closely associated with the negative characterisations that the Irish suffered. Even as the blight was spreading in 1846, one writer would exclaim how it was "that rational and intelligent men, with heads upon their shoulders, and hands capable of working, should, by their indolence and want of common energy, have so long cheated themselves of even the common comforts of life" (Niven 1846: 23) because of their over-dependence on their "favourite root" (Niven 1846: 21). Only in Ireland, among the potato-eating regions of Europe, was the vicious circle posited that the potato made people lazy, while their laziness led them to depend solely on the potato. In the English mind, the potato seemed to summon forth the worst traits of the Irish, traits which the English, as colonial rulers, already believed – or needed to believe – were there.

Scarcity in the Irish Export Economy

Opponents of Malthus who had any familiarity with Ireland knew better. Michael Sadler, the radical Tory MP, who gained renown for his advocacy of children's rights, published a book in 1829 entitled *Ireland; Its Evils and Their Remedies*, in which he cogently observed that the destitution which characterised rural Ireland could hardly be blamed on the potato or on surplus population, since Irish poverty and famine had existed long before the potato became a major food crop and before Irish population had begun appreciably to rise (1829: 2). The view that Ireland's population was dramatically increasing had, in fact, only developed in the late eighteenth century. In the first half of the 1700s, Ireland's population was scarcely excessive and it was even argued that its prosperity depended upon more, rather than fewer, people. Yet the crop failure and famine of 1740 was, in relative demographic terms, as catastrophic as – perhaps more than – that of the 1840s (Kennedy

1973; Dickson 1995: 55). The principal problem, then as later, was not that Ireland produced too many people or too few (or only) potatoes, but that, when the potato crop failed, the unrelenting demands of landlords prevented tenants from being able to retain enough food for themselves. Ireland, as Sadler observed, "instead of not producing sufficient for the sustenance of its inhabitants, produces far more than they ever consume, exporting a greater quantity of its edible products than probably any other country of equal extent in the whole world" (1829: 9). But it was the increasing insecurity of subsistence cultivation which was the issue. Hugh Boulter, the Lord Primate of Ireland, wrote to the Archbishop of Canterbury in 1727 of how

> Our present tillage falls very short of answering the demands of this nation … the occasion of this evil is, that many persons have hired large tracts of land, on to 3 or 4000 acres, and have stocked them with cattle, and have no other inhabitants on their land than so many cottiers as are necessary to look after their sheep and black cattle; so that in some of the finest counties, in many places there is neither house nor corn field to be seen in 10 or 15 miles travelling. (Boulter 1769–70: 221–2)

A century later, the situation had deteriorated dramatically. By then, Irish population had indeed risen, but not because the rural Irish were impelled by an irrational desire to immiserate themselves by an excessive love for children or potatoes. Far more mundane material factors were at work. Chief among them was the increasing commercialisation of agriculture, and this, in turn, was related to the course of industrial development in England. The need in England for cheap grain for a burgeoning urban, industrial population had already led, in 1784, to the passage of Foster's Corn Law, which lifted previous restrictions on the import of Irish cereals (Hechter 1975: 85). Land use shifted from pasture to tillage (Hechter 1975: 85), and it is estimated that in the dozen years after this bill, "more corn [i.e., grain], meal, and flour were sent out of Ireland than had been exported in the entire period from 1700 to 1784" (Green 1956: 98). Demand continued to grow after the Napoleonic Wars cut off England's continental sources. And as cattle gave way to grain, the need for rural labour grew.

There was another important aspect of the industrialisation process that has long been overlooked, which also led rural families in Ireland, facing increased economic stress, to increase fertility in order to improve their precarious subsistence opportunities. Industrialisation of the cotton textile industry in England was the pivotal development in late-eighteenth-century British capitalism. It displaced wool, which had been severely limited in terms of the domestic supply of raw fibre, with a material which could be provided in virtually unlimited quantity by newly colonised tropical and semi-tropical regions. But production was crucially limited by a major technical constraint: that cotton textiles could not initially be machine-produced with a warp strong enough to manufacture an all-cotton cloth. English machine-woven cotton depended on supplies of Irish linen yarn to produce a material known as "fustian". In many parts of Ireland, flax raising and linen yarn production became a major cottage industry in response to the English market, and it is estimated that Ireland exported almost 47 million yards of linen by 1796, most of it wheel-spun (Horner 1920: 312).

This was especially the case in the poor western province of Connacht, where flax growing and the spinning of linen yarn were both attractive to land-hungry peasants whose subsistence base was contracting while dependence on the potato was increasing. Flax, moreover, combined readily with potato production on small holdings, and seemed even to grow especially well on land previously used to raise potatoes (Gill 1925: 36n). Surveying the state of linen manufacture, Robert Stephenson noted in his *Journal of a Tour of Inspection* in 1755 that "Every potato garden in the kingdom is fitter to produce flax than any ground whatever" (in Gill 1925: 36n). Thus, the English market for yarn was another major stimulus to potato cultivation during this period.

From the peasant's viewpoint the advantages of flax were varied. According to Gill,

> A flax crop yielded on the whole a larger return from a given area than any other crop which a peasant could grow, and, secondly ... the careful hand-labour needed in its harvesting made it particularly valuable for very small holdings. Further, the preparation of yarn, although it was ill-paid labour, brought at any rate some increase to the trifling income of the cottier's household. In certain parts of the country flax crops were the more attractive because they were exempted by custom from tithe. Moreover, it was found that flax could be grown satisfactorily after potatoes – which were also exempted from tithe – and thus a small farmer ... could use a flax crop in establishing a simple rotation. (1925: 35–6)

Flax and linen yarn production also markedly enhanced the labour value of children, and the increased value of spinning among young women probably reduced the age of marriage during this period. Thus, it is unlikely to have been a coincidence that the period when Irish population rose most dramatically was precisely when the country's linen exports more than trebled (Gill 1925: 163), or that the centre of flax production, Connacht, was where "women married earliest" and 'parcellation of the land was most acute" (Connell 1965: 429).

Clearances and "Over-population"

In such regions, to consolidate their possession of good arable land, landlords were also pushing peasants onto poorer lands, where only the potato could at first be cultivated and where it was used to bring otherwise useless land into cultivation, to increase the resource base available for rentable tenancies on which potatoes would eventually give way to commercial crops. Under these circumstances, concern among landlords in Ireland about rising population only emerged *after* the Napoleonic Wars, when the boom market in grain collapsed – although grain exports to England continued to rise (Green 1956) – and landowners sought to reestablish the earlier pattern of extensive cattle raising. Only then did landlords begin "to utter bitter complaints of surplus population ... [and] to ventilate their grievances through the English and Irish press, saying that their land was overrun by cottiers and squatters – the main cause of all this being kept in the background" (O'Rourke 1902: 46), that is, the clearance of the Irish countryside.

In testimony to a parliamentary committee in 1881, Andrew Kettle, a farmer in County Dublin, who had grown up during the famine, described how the appearance of "over-population" had resulted from what was actually a process of depopulation.

> To begin at the beginning, I would say that because it became profitable for the landlords to get rid of the people, and to let their land in large tracts to graziers, owing to the great price paid for the article of fresh meat in England; and in that way, owing to the nature of their tenures, the people looked upon themselves as insecure. I might push that point further, and say, that it had the effect of with-drawing so much land from the Irish people as to leave undue competition for the remainder of the lands, near the Cities and towns and centres of population, into which the people had to go.... I remember to have seen whole groups of homeless people coming into Dublin from the districts around; and in County Meath I saw the remains of many houses in districts that were depopulated. (Royal Commissioners on Agriculture 1881: 422)

Thus, the "excess population" swarming around Dublin consisted largely of people whom landlords no longer wanted on land which would otherwise have been capable of supporting them. As the Halls wrote of the clearing of the fertile lands of Meath:

> The county ... is the great grazing ground of Ireland, and consists almost entirely of pastureland, vying in its external aspect with the richest of the English counties, and, perhaps, surpassing any of them in fertility.... Much of the apparently prosperous character is, however, hollow and insubstantial; the large farmers are indeed wealthy, but of small farmers there are few or none: the policy of the "graziers" has been, for a long time, to devote the produce of their soil to the raising of cattle; and the "clearing of estates" in Meath has,

therefore, been proceeding at a very disastrous rate.... The small plots of ground are "wanted for cattle"; and as the cabins cannot exist without them, they are in rapid course of removal. (Hall and Hall 1984, Vol. 2: 301)

Such clearances had already created great insecurity in the decades before the Great Famine. When, as happened even without blight, the potato failed, the rural poor could not afford to buy or to eat anything else, even when they produced it themselves. Other produce had to be used to pay the rent, taxes and tithes, and was then exported to Britain. As Archbishop John MacHale wrote at the time of a potato crop failure in 1831:

It is not to the scarcity of provisions alone that the present want is owing. No; while I am writing this letter, the town of Ballina, in which three hundred families are crying out for food, is busy with the bustle of corn traders, and the public roads are covered with the crowded conveyances of its exports. It may, then, excite your ... wonder ... that the people should be starving while the markets are stocked with provisions. (MacHale 1888: 268)

Three years later, when Cobbett visited Ireland, he observed the same homeless thousands sleeping and living in the streets of Dublin that Kettle would comment on years later. But he knew that this was not even despite, but *because* of the enormous under-utilised agricultural potential of the Irish environment. He wrote in his *Political Register*:

I have now been over about 180 miles in Ireland, in the several counties of Dublin, Wicklow, Kildare, Carlow, Kilkenny and Waterford. I have, in former years, been in every county of England, and across every county more than one way. I have been through the finest parts of Scotland. I have lived in the finest parts of the United States of America. And here I am to declare to all the world, that I never passed over any 50 miles, in my life, any unbroken miles, of land so on average during the whole way, as the average of these 180 miles ... and yet here are these starving people! And this is only because they have *no law* [his italics] to give them their due share of the fruits of their labour! (Cobbett 1984: 93)

Cobbett felt obliged to observe that, since the union, there had been three major famines, during which Irish output had not diminished. On the contrary,

Hundreds of thousands of living hogs, thousands upon thousands of sheep and oxen alive; thousands upon thousands of barrels of beef, pork, and butter; thousands upon thousands of sides of bacon, and thousands upon thousands of hams; ship-loads and boats coming daily and hourly from Ireland to feed the west of Scotland; to feed a million and a half people in the West Riding of Yorkshire, and in Lancashire; to feed London and its vicinity, and to fill the country shops in the southern counties of England; we beheld this, while famine raged in Ireland amongst the raisers of this very food. (Cobbett 1984: 272)

Repeated often enough, however, the opinion that Ireland could not feed its own population effectively denied the contradictions of Ireland's colonial status. These were especially apparent in Tipperary, which "contained some of the finest agricultural land in Ireland" (Beames 1983: 265), yet where, as a Poor Inquiry Commissioner observed in the early 1830s, "the general feeling among farmers is not to break up pastures, but to get their land by degrees into grass on account of the low price of corn" (quoted in Beames 1983: 265). This would prove to be a major underlying cause of the pattern of assassination that became an important form of peasant resistance there (Beames 1983), so that, on the eve of the Famine, Foster observed that "The county of Tipperary has long possessed the notoriety of being a focus of outrage and disorder." The reason was clear. As he noted, "You have here the richest land and the most extreme poverty" (Foster 1846: 330).

This was precisely the kind of contradiction which Malthusian thinking obscured. Thus, it not only served in a general way to rationalise Irish underdevelopment; it also helped, as an ideological tool of English rule, to discount the legitimate origins of Irish resistance, which was reduced to little more than the disorderly conduct of a people so degraded by self-inflicted poverty that Thomas Carlyle would describe them as "human swinery" (1882: 201). Such resistance was bitterly regarded by English politicians and intellectuals, who saw it as an affront to the civilising effects of colonialism. As a result, the British government's response to rural unrest in a time of great distress was not to remove the sources of distress, but to introduce a coercion bill. The historian Thomas Babington Macaulay, MP for Leeds and staunch defender of the Reverend Malthus, who spoke in favour of the bill, was typical in seeing "In Ireland ... the spirit of Jacobinism at work, and an immediate threat to the social order, there and in England" (in Clive 1973: 232). It fuelled his contempt for the Irish to such a degree that he wrote in May 1833, a year after a great cholera pandemic had swept through the British Isles, "that he preferred the cholera to the moral pestilence now raging in Ireland" (in Clive 1973: 231). Such opinions were a dress rehearsal for England's response to the Great Famine a decade later, when Macaulay was paymaster general in Russell's cabinet (Knowles 1975: 224).

In the aftermath of the Napoleonic Wars, as the pace of clearances increased under pressure from grazing, rural Ireland had become a place of growing conflict, which came to a head in the decade immediately preceding the Great Famine (Beames 1983). With memories of the United Irishmen still fresh, the English had taken this seriously enough to impose a constabulary. It had little effect. Another option consisted of projects to get the Irish to emigrate, and here it was not only Malthusian logic but Malthus himself who was enlisted in their support. Testifying before Wilmot-Horton's Parliamentary Select Committee on Emigration in 1827, Malthus had been asked about Ireland's economic prospects. He replied "that it has very great capabilities, that it might be a very rich and a very prosperous country, and that it might be richer in proportion than England from its greater natural capabilities". When asked if this future prosperity would be more likely to develop if "a judicious system of emigration [was] put into force", he responded affirmatively (Select Committee on Emigration from the United Kingdom 1827: 549), although he clearly regarded it not as a solution for Irish poverty in itself, but as an adjunct to a process of agricultural modernisation along English lines (Ghosh 1963: 49) – which presumably meant consolidation and clearances.

In lending his support publicly to a general policy of Irish emigration (questioning only the expenses it would impose on the state) (Ghosh 1963: 49ff.), Malthus demonstrated how the "principle of population" could be deployed in a pragmatic and opportunistic way to serve specific national and class interests. In this case, the Irish had to leave their homeland, not because it was resource-poor, but because its resources were so attractive to the English. In other words, it was only resource-poor for the Irish, who were regarded as too backward to use resources productively. But it was important, then, for the Irish to be regarded as redundant, even if, as Michael Sadler suggested a decade later, an ordinary, rational person "Would think about preventing the undue emigration of corn, cattle, and pigs, rather than of promoting that of the people" (Sadler 1842: 71). In the end, however, neither emigration schemes nor constables proved capable of countering the endemic impact of colonial rule, and it took a famine to accomplish what no governmental policy or intervention could do: to clear Ireland of two million people within five years.

The Making of the Great Famine

In 1845, most of Western Europe was hit by *Phytophthora infestans*. Combined with a poor grain harvest in many parts of Europe, the failure of the potato added to a pattern of agrarian stress which would be a major factor in the riots, rebellions and revolutions that swept across Europe in 1848.

However, events in Ireland differed dramatically from developments elsewhere, where, at least, widespread starvation was generally forestalled. In the Swiss canton of Bern, for example, when a food riot broke out in October 1846, the reaction of the cantonal government was to acquire food grains from abroad to prevent wholesale food shortages (Pfister 1990: 283). The contrast between this response and England's reaction to pending famine in Ireland was due to the fact that Bern was in command of its own affairs, while Ireland's fate depended on the interests of a colonial power. Indeed, many of the leading figures in the British cabinet at the time – including Lord Palmerston, the Foreign Secretary, and Lord Clarendon, President of the Board of Trade and Lord Lieutenant of Ireland – were absentee Anglo-Irish landlords (Ridley 1970: 2–4, 321; Prest 1972: 237; Stephen and Lee 1921–22, Vol. 20: 347–50). And if they were not, their families often were: the Duke of Bedford, the brother of the prime minister, Lord John Russell, also owned substantial estates in Ireland (Prest 1972: 238).

Travelling through Ireland late in 1845, as the first potatoes were beginning to blacken in the fields, Thomas Foster wrote that he was "certain that some steps will be required to be taken to avert the horrors of a famine" (1846: 328–9). Those measures were never taken. The British government generally acted as if it regarded the famine as the only effective means of repressing the rebellion that was then rampant throughout rural Ireland. Russell, moreover, was especially possessed of "a Malthusian fear about the long-term effect of relief", while Clarendon believed that "doling out food merely to keep people alive would do nobody any permanent good" (Prest 1972: 271). Except, of course, the poor, whom such callousness ultimately condemned to death.

The relief programme, such as it was, was in the hands of Charles Trevelyan, who had been educated at the East India College at Haileybury, "where he had been greatly influenced by [Malthus's] lectures" (Clive 1973: 318; Stephen and Lee 1921–22, Vol. 12: 886–7; Vol. 19: 1135). His wife, Hannah, was the sister of the historian and politician Thomas Babington Macaulay, whose fervent Malthusianism (Trevelyan 1978: 116) had led him to challenge Sadler for a parliamentary seat because of the latter's anti-Malthusian views. Trevelyan's own forceful Malthusian attitudes were clearly reflected in his opinion that the famine was "a direct stroke of an all-wise and all-merciful Providence" (Trevelyan 1848: 201). His justification for meagre assistance for the Irish was that

> posterity will trace up to that Famine the commencement of a salutary revolution in the habits of a nation long singularly unfortunate, and will

acknowledge that on this as on many other occasions, Supreme Wisdom had educed permanent good out of transient evil. (Trevelyan 1848: 1)

But if Trevelyan thought it was a divine blessing, the divines thought otherwise. A year earlier, Bishop Hughes of New York had already written:

> they call it God's famine! No! no! God's famine is known by the general scarcity of food, of which it is the consequence; there is no general scarcity, there has been no general scarcity of food in Ireland, either the present, or the past year, except in one species of vegetable. The soil has produced its usual tribute for the support of those by whom it has been cultivated; but political economy found the Irish people too poor to pay for the harvest of their own labour, and has exported it to a better market, leaving them to die of famine, or to live on alms; and this same political economy authorizes the provision merchant, even amidst the desolation, to keep his doors locked, and his sacks of corn tied up within, waiting for a better price. (Hughes 1847: 21)

Nevertheless the argument that the famine was God's way of redressing a Malthusian imbalance between people and resources appealed to a British cabinet dominated by Irish absentee landlords. And, to the extent that it justified the barest minimum of relief, the argument that nature must be allowed to take its course also meant that aid would not confound the workings of the "market". As a result, one of the most perverse features of the famine years was that Irish exports – the reason, after all, that the island was a colony – were not only maintained throughout the crisis, but actually increased. In 1846 alone, almost half a million pigs were shipped to England – pigs that in a good year might have been eaten, but now had to go to pay the rent (O'Donovan 1940: 192). Even the London *Times*, which had little visible sympathy for the Irish, conceded that, "while England was avowedly feeding Ireland ... whole fleets of provisions were continually arriving from the land of starvation to the ports of wealth and the cities of abundance" (*Times* 1880: 45). Yet this was not widely appreciated in England, where the famine was simply a dramatic sign of how catastrophically the Irish had mismanaged their resources and of their failure to diversify their diet. As a letter-writer to the *Times* remarked:

> they inhabit a country a great part of which is at least equal in fertility to our own, with more that is capable of being made so. There is no reason, *except their own willful mismanagement* [my italics], why they should not grow as fine crops of wheat as are raised in the Lothians, and, after feeding themselves, export the surplus to our shores. (*Times* 1880: 14)

The real problem was that the food that Ireland was already exporting to England in such prodigious quantities was *not* surplus.

The Aftermath of the Famine: The Clearances Continue

Despite massive depopulation – as over two million people died or emigrated due to the famine (Ó Gráda 1972: 154) – and in spite of increasingly delayed marriage, the "permanent good" to which Trevelyan alluded never materialised, because the real problem of Ireland, British colonialism, had not gone away. And, far from leaving Ireland's future to God's will, Westminster quickly took advantage of the famine to enact bills which accelerated the very process of land concentration and eviction that had put rural Ireland at such peril in the first place (Kennedy 1973: 28–9). One of the most notable of these measures was the so-called "Gregory clause" to the poor-relief act of June 1847, named after William Gregory, the MP from Cork, who introduced it. This provision prevented anyone with more than a quarter-acre of land from being considered destitute and thus able to qualify for poor relief. Since many Poor Law guardians, who were responsible for administering local relief, were also landlords, it was inevitable that this measure was exploited to force impoverished tenants to relinquish their holdings (Donnelly 1975: 98; 1995: 159–60).

Through this and other pressures, as many as half a million people may have been evicted between 1846 and 1854 (Donnelly 1995: 155–6). The agricultural landscape was dramatically transformed.

> The market in evicted land was especially brisk during the famine and its immediate aftermath…. The wholesale clearances of the late 1840s and early 1850s allowed commercially ambitious individuals to acquire pasture ground at relatively cheap rates. On many estates the evicted land formerly held by subsistence tenants was consolidated into large pastoral holdings and relet to graziers and other men of capital. (Jones 1983: 392)

Between 1845 and 1851, the number of plots of less than one acre fell from 135,000 to 38,000, while those between 1 and 15 acres declined from 493,000 to 280,000 (Steele 1974: 3). Between 1841 and 1901, the percentage of all holdings between one and five acres fell from 45 to 12, but the proportion of those 30 and above rose from 7 to 32 (Kennedy 1973: 89). By the 1870s,

> half the country belonged to a thousand people with an average of around 10,000 acres each. Great and small, the landlords were, as a body, British, or Anglo-Irish, and Protestant. (Steele 1974: 3)

For decades, the main source of pressure on the small-scale Irish cultivator remained precisely what it had been in the years preceding the famine, the expansion of pasturage, only now it occurred with an unprecedented intensity. The proportion of Irish agricultural land being cultivated declined from one-third in 1851, in the immediate wake of the Great Famine, to less than one-fifth in 1881. It had fallen to one-seventh by 1926 (Kennedy 1973: 91–2), at the time of partition. All this was to meet a growing demand for beef in Britain, which was reflected in the dramatic price differentials between grain and meat that characterised the post-famine period:

> From a low point in 1850, the last Famine year, the prices of cattle at the Ballinasloe October fair, the "greatest" fair in the west of Ireland, doubled by 1855 and then continued to rise steadily at an average of 2 pounds per year until 1880.... In contrast, grain prices fluctuated wildly after the Famine, wheat prices being 21 per cent lower nationally in 1876 than in 1840. (Jordan 1987: 326)

Irish exports of cattle rose from almost 202,000 in 1846–49 to about 558,000 by 1870–74 (O'Donovan 1940), a development that was facilitated by the establishment of the Irish railway network in the second half of the nineteenth century (Jones 1983: 377). By 1880, it could be written that

> agriculture of most other kinds has been steadily dwindling down; 519,307 acres out of a total tillage area of 5,500,000 had gone out of cultivation in ten years. The wheat culture was ruined.... The breadth of land even under oats had declined by 320,000 acres ... 50.2 percent of the entire surface area of the country and two-thirds of its wealth were devoted to the raising of cattle. (Dublin Mansion House Relief Committee 1881: 2)

In the province of Connacht alone, total crop acreage declined from 744,263 in 1869 to 694,708 a decade later, while land in meadow and clover – a sign of grazing – soared by 30 percent from 200,766 to 262,095 acres (House of Commons 1870: 756–7; 1880a: 848–9). By then, cattle and sheep graziers, who occupied almost half the land of Ireland, were the dominant political force in the country (Crotty 1981: 111–13). One of the worst hit parts of Connacht was County Mayo, where the post-Famine increase in pasture had been especially rapid.

> Between 1847, the first year for which reliable are available, and 1851 the number of cattle in Mayo rose from 79,148 to 116,930. There were 173,596 cattle in 1876 and 191,497 in 1900, representing an increase of 142 per cent over the fifty-three years. The number of sheep rose 225 per cent over the same years. In order to graze this livestock the amount of land in Mayo devoted to grass, meadow and clover increased from 485,651 statute acres in 1851, or 38.8 per cent of the total acreage of the county, to 595,843 acres, or 44.9 per cent of the total, in 1900. (Jordan 1987: 327)

Because much of this expansion involved the conversion of cropland and a process of land consolidation, typically effected through evictions, the result was that many remaining subsistence cultivators in the most fertile regions of the county were forced either to relocate in peripheral areas or to emigrate (Jordan 1987: 327–30). As early as the 1860s, a Poor Law Inspector reported from Mayo that

> Amongst the small farmers or occupiers of land, [deprivation] is everywhere in the barony severe; but in the electoral districts, already alluded to, I am convinced it is intense. Many families there are, I believe, utterly without means. The whole of their stock of potatoes and corn is gone; it has barely sufficed for their own support up to the present time, and been inadequate for that of their cattle, which have died of starvation and cold. Such families are now without means of supporting themselves or cultivating their farms. They find that if they surrender them, and go into the workhouses, they become paupers for life; and, in most cases, they will die sooner than adopt such a course. (in Day 1862: 37)

By 1870, the expansion of cattle and sheep grazing had considerably worsened conditions for small-holders and rural labourers. In Mayo, where as few as nine landowners owned over one-third of the land and most were disinclined to rent their land to anyone but large graziers (Jones 1983: 395), families which still depended on potato cultivation were under increasing pressure (Jordan 1987: 334; cf. Crotty 1981: 111). As cattle and sheep pushed tillage onto worse soils, not only did total crop acreage decline, but productivity fell as well.

The Crisis of 1879: Famine and Protest

The pattern of increasing land monopolisation and the expansion of grazing which spurred it were only a part of the problem, however. By the late 1870s, a great agricultural crisis had embraced much of Western Europe and severely affected the British Isles. In large part, this was due to horrendous weather, which made European agriculture especially vulnerable to new developments in the international market. As Lamb has noted,

> The decline of English agriculture, which lasted for fifty years, dated from this time. The harvests had been affected by difficult seasons from 1875, and the impact of competition on Britain's free trade market of cheap North American meat from the prairies was beginning to be felt. 1879 turned the decline into a collapse. (1982: 245)

The situation in Ireland was especially grim for the near-landless who depended on the potato, the average yield of which fell from 4.7 tons in 1876 to 2.0 tons in 1877 (Solow 1971: 121). There was a slight, patchy recovery in 1878, but climatic conditions worsened the following year and average yields declined further to about 1.3 tons per acre – "half a ton below the last recorded *famine* [her emphasis] year (1872)" (Solow 1971: 122).

One of the normal safety-valves in times of rural distress, seasonal employment in England (Kerr 1943; Green 1956: 116; Johnson 1970: 236–8), was limited now by the general agricultural depression and by increasing mechanisation (Royal Commissioners on Agriculture 1881: 668), which had significantly reduced English farmers' demand for Irish labour. At the same time, imports of cheap and abundant grain and meat from the United States, whose vast interior plains were being opened up by new advances in long-distance transport (Royal Commission on Agriculture 1881; Ross 1980: 198–204), were not only filling the vacuum created by crop failures throughout Europe (Solow 1971: 122–3), but undercutting local prices. The price of Irish ham in Ireland was actually three pence higher than that of imported US ham (*Sligo Independent* 1879: 3). It is little wonder that 1878 was regarded by some as the least profitable for the agricultural economy of Ireland for thirty years (Moody 1981: 273).

As a result, many small and moderate-sized farmers and cottiers were in debt to merchants and landlords (Moody 1981: 283) and, as few landlords were prepared to countenance non-payment of rent, the number of "ejectments" rose nationally from 1,749 in 1878 to 2,677 in 1879. It was an increase of 53 percent in one year. The growing tide of anger and frustration which had been accumulating since the late 1860s began to be expressed in new forms of rural protest by the end of the 1870s.

Connacht, which was the most deprived region of the country, took the lead with 56 percent of all the so-called "agrarian offences" registered by the constabulary during 1879 and the first month of 1880. Of the 544 cases reported for that province alone, 36 percent occurred in Mayo, one of the counties hardest hit by evictions, although it only contained 29 percent of the province's population (House of Commons 1880b: 286–7, 349). Half of the protest meetings called within Connacht at this time, to build public pressure – "agitation" in official parlance – for land reform, were held in that one county alone (House of Commons 1880b: 292). Not unexpectedly, it was the home of the land agent for the Earl of Erne, Captain Charles Boycott, who gave his name to the mass resistance – "boycotting" – which he encountered when he attempted to evict his employer's tenants (Ellis 1972: 160; Marlow 1973: 13; Taatgen 1992: 170). And it was in Mayo that growing popular resistance gave birth to one of the most potent challenges yet raised against English rule in Ireland, the Land League, with its call for land reform. The challenge was perhaps the greater because, as Crotty has observed, although the majority of participants in the League were small-scale cultivators and rural labourers, one of its guiding forces was actually the graziers themselves, who no longer wanted to put up with "the sharing of profits from the booming livestock trade with an Anglo-Irish Protestant elite whose title to that share rested on the increasingly anachronistic grounds of conquest, confiscation and royal munificence in an increasingly distant and irrelevant past" (Crotty 1981: 111). To that extent, the League brought into question the very basis of English hegemony.

Modernisation and the Demise of Subsistence Agriculture

In Dublin, in October 1879, the Irish National Land League was established, consolidating regional groups from Mayo and elsewhere. Through 1880–81, however, the British government prosecuted and interned many of the League's leaders and activists, and eventually Gladstone's Liberal government passed the Land Act of 1881, which was designed both to blunt the movement's principal demands and to modernise Irish agriculture. As such, anticipating more recent global trends, modernisation meant favouring large commercial and grazing interests. As Crotty notes,

> The principal distributional effect of the 1881 and subsequent land acts has been to broaden, and thereby make more durable, the proprietorship of Irish land. They hardly transformed that proprietorship. Instead of 10,000 Anglo-Irish landlords owning all the land, now some 20,000 graziers own half of it and 95 percent of the people continue to own none of it. (Crotty 1981: 114)

Thus, far from highlighting the extent to which Ireland's "population problem" was a function of the dominant mode of production which under-utilised the country's agricultural resources, the famine of 1879 – like that of the 1840s – proved principally to be a means of reaffirming the established pattern of agrarian relations.

That, despite the decline in Irish population, the early 1880s found the west of Ireland, in the words of a report by the Dublin Mansion House Committee, one of the chief relief agencies, "emerging from another famine, surrounded by the same phenomena of a fruitful soil and a starving population, a war of classes, a stain of crime, and the self-same prostration of national energy attributed to the self-same causes" (1881: 77), underscores the extent to which the role of classic Malthusian pressures within the Irish rural economy was exaggerated. Yet Malthusian thinking was so pervasive – and so convenient at a time when the last vestiges of subsistence agriculture were being exorcised –

that the turbulent events of the late 1870s only served to reinvigorate the argument that Ireland was over-populated. Even as the 1881 Land Act was being passed, E.T. Wakefield, an English barrister who owned land in Ireland, wrote, in a pamphlet called *The Disaffection of Ireland: Its Cause and Its Cure*, that the physical misery which afflicted so many people in Ireland was "the direct result of over-population, that is, population beyond the available resources of the country" (1881: 3).

Among the reasons he cited for this, few were new: "unfavourable climate", "unproductive soil", "early marriages" and "inaptitude for commerce" (Wakefield 1881: 4). Echoing the conventional wisdom, he argued that Ireland was not destined to be peopled by small-scale cultivators, for "we know that the climatic, geological and geographical conditions of Ireland have in the main determined her to be a grass-growing, cattle-rearing country" (Wakefield 1881: 7). This, of course, contrasted with the earlier "wisdom" of landlords during the Napoleonic Wars, when Ireland not only had been highly regarded as a grain-producing country, but was actually considered "the granary of Great Britain" (Ó Gráda 1972: 152). It is the task of colonial enterprise to make its agenda "natural", rather than consistent. But, if Ireland was to be little more than a cattle farm for England, then there was little room for the Irish. The expansion of grazing over the preceding three decades had done much to prove that. For those who were left, Wakefield (1881: 5) revived the suggestion that they emigrate to underpopulated parts of the British Empire.

The irony is that, by the time of Wakefield's proposal, the decline of agriculture had already forced such draconian reproductive strategies on rural Irish households that the age at marriage and the rate of celibacy were both on the rise, until they were among the highest in Western Europe (Kennedy 1973; O'Reilly 1986: 222–3; Scheper-Hughes 1979). Yet rural Ireland, depopulated, was still being asked to populate the rest of the Empire. This, again, underlines the fact that, despite a dramatic reversal of the demographic trends to which Malthusians had ascribed the Great Famine and notwithstanding the subsequent decline in Irish population, the subsistence sector would remain precarious and problematical as long as Ireland remained a constituent of the wider English economy. As grazing continued to expand, emigration – a matter not so much of policy as of personal necessity – became a way of life for rural Ireland, its preeminent role in the international division of labour. It continues so even now.

As with many developing countries today, this outflow of Irish population reinforces the popular view, shaped by over a century and a half of Malthusian thinking, that the country is perennially characterised by excess population. But, as we have seen, that idea has been little more than the product of Malthusian ideology applied to the imperatives of colonial rule, which, in Ireland as in many other parts of the world, created an economy that has tended to export labour in the absence of the productive means to employ it. Any "surplus" population from which Ireland ostensibly suffered was the result, not of Irish reproductive habits, but of livelihood and survival strategies which were impelled, first, by English landlords and a British Parliament which steadfastly refused to accommodate Irish demands for autonomous development, and which are now perpetuated by an Irish state (within the framework of the European Union) which serves the interests of large farmers and cattle interests.

In 1805, Thomas Newenham (1805: 336) noted that the Irish themselves ate little meat, as most of the beef and pork which they produced at that time went to England. In 1995, the value of Irish beef sales amounted to $2.6 billion, of which 83 percent was derived from exports (Associated Press 1996). Much of this meat still goes to Britain, but Scandinavia, South Africa and Russia are among the new markets (MacConnell 1996). The development policies that led to this way of using Irish land have not in themselves brought about a decline in the number of rural Irish poor, however. If there are fewer of them, it is because they have left the country. So, the west of Ireland today is a land of dying communities, characterised by "celibacy, childlessness, and ageing of the Irish farm population" (Scheper-Hughes 1979: 39), all induced by an ongoing process called "modernisation" (Scheper-Hughes 1979: 42–4). In this, Ireland pioneered the pattern that dominates the late twentieth century, when capitalist agriculture, with its diminishing need for human labour, is forcing millions of people to seek a living far from home.

3

Malthusian Transformations: From Eugenics to Environmentalism

The underdevelopment of rural Ireland produced a steady flow of Irish emigrants into the new industrial urban centres of Britain and the United States. In England especially, all the attitudes about the inferiority of the Irish that had incubated through centuries of colonial domination came to justify their relegation to the most menial jobs and the worst habitations – in the "Little Irelands" as they were often called – where they became a focal point for more general ideas about the nature and origin of poverty.

Such ideas developed in counterpoint to the emergence of new forms of working-class solidarity, for which one of the principal catalysts was the introduction of the Corn Laws and the subsequent rise in the price of bread. Popular protest provoked repressive measures from the government – the highpoint of which was the famous "Peterloo" massacre at a large public meeting at St Peter's Fields, Manchester, in 1819 – which, in turn, led to a further heightening of working-class consciousness (Morton 1979: 362–6; Thompson 1963: 683ff.). The 1820s were surprisingly quiet, but they culminated in the Chartist movement in the 1830s, many of the leading figures of which were Irish-born or of recent Irish extraction.

But Chartism's enduring impact was limited. The proto-fascist Orange Order in England and Scotland played a role in many manufacturing districts, fomenting working-class disunity along religious and ethnic lines in an effort to suppress such radicalism (House of Commons 1969). And, as we have seen, the Whig reforms of the 1830s and 1840s also helped to contain Chartism's influence. A period of economic prosperity, reflecting England's increasingly globalised economy, helped as well, as Engels observed, by making English workers more bourgeois (Morton 1979: 440). But Chartism had reached political limits, too,

because its leaders failed to develop a coherent appreciation of a capitalist system in rapid transition from an agrarian to an industrial mode
of production (Strachey 1936: 357–67). A more sophisticated analysis
of the contradictions of capitalist development was required, and it
emerged chiefly through the efforts of Marx and Engels, even as the
Chartist movement, which they had supported, declined.

But the deepening misery of the industrial workforce in England not
only inspired the founders of modern, scientific socialism: it also impelled the heirs of Smith, Ricardo and Malthus to devise new and more
creative rationalisations for the poverty that capitalist development engendered. In the end, however, no matter how elaborate or clever the
economic model, nothing could compare to blaming the poor themselves.
All that was needed by the second half of the nineteenth century was to
give this view the intellectual legitimacy that an age of science required.

The idea that the poor were primarily victims of their own moral
shortcomings never ceased to enchant the well-to-do, the most vocal of
whom seemed, like Malthus, to write from a clerical vantage point.
Edinburgh's Reverend John McFarlan observed in his *Inquiries Concerning
the Poor* in 1782 that

> in tracing the causes of poverty, I have endeavoured to show that the greatest
> number of those who are now objects of charity are either such as have
> reduced themselves to this situation by sloth and vice, or such as, by a very
> moderate degree of industry and frugality, might have prevented indigence.

Malthusian arguments had added to such sentiments the idea that profligate fertility was just another cause of their indigence. By the beginning
of the nineteenth century, this idea was helping to justify the conviction
that the poor had an urgent need for moral improvement, under duress
if need be. It was especially prevalent in the writings of individuals such
as James Kay(-Shuttleworth) and Edwin Chadwick, whose policies played
a prominent role in structuring the lives of the English working class, not
only in the nineteenth century, but up to the present day.

Chadwick is the more famous of the two. A barrister, he was the
protégé of the utilitarian philosopher Jeremy Bentham (Watson 1969:
3–5), who had himself been trained as a lawyer. Bentham's family was
wealthy, however, and he never needed to practise law. After his father
died in 1792, he inherited a fortune, which enabled him to turn his
attention to the same issue that was also engaging his contemporary,
Thomas Malthus: the poor laws. Chadwick met Bentham in 1829, became his private secretary and lived with him for the last year of
Bentham's life (Watson 1969: 3). Under his influence and as the secretary of the Poor Law Commission, Chadwick was the principal author

of the *Report of the Royal Commission for Enquiring into the Administration and Practical Operation of the Poor Laws*, the recommendations of which were translated into the Poor Law Amendment Act of 1834 (Watson 1969: 6–7, 16–17), that embodiment of utilitarian and Malthusian reasoning which presumed that the poor required harsh incentives to lead productive lives and provided these by offering them a choice between derisory wages or entering the poor-house, where they were subjected to a deliberately barbaric and humiliating regime.

Since local poor law guardians were responsible for appointing doctors to administer to their charges, Chadwick routinely reviewed medical reports and was eventually led to make certain generalisations about the relationship between poverty and health. By 1842, he had written the *Report on the Sanitary Condition of the Labouring Population of Great Britain*, which is still regarded, uncritically, as the high point of the nineteenth-century public-health movement (Ross 1991). Interestingly, however, it virtually never refers to employment and wages. It is, in fact, less about the *causes* of poverty than about the "moral condition" of the poor. Thus, one of its principal themes is that many of the problems of the poor, such as disease, are the result, not of inadequate income, but of what Chadwick called "domestic mismanagement". It is a theme which still dominates the field of health education.

Chadwick was quite clear that he regarded disease, not primarily in terms of poverty ("destitution"), but as a function of "intemperance" and other immoral forms of behaviour. He believed that people who grew up in poor conditions tended to be worse off physically and to be "less susceptible of moral influences".[1] He wrote of how "these adverse circumstances tend to produce an adult population short-lived, improvident, reckless, and intemperate, and with habitual avidity for sensual gratification". In turn, "these habits lead to the abandonment of all the conveniences and decencies of life, and especially lead to the overcrowding of their homes, which is destructive to the morality as well as the health of large classes of both sexes." Chadwick and his colleagues regarded such habits as a cause of labour unrest. But, reflecting the interests of manufacturers, their response was to recommend the establishment of an effective constabulary – not higher wages (Commissioners 1839).

James Kay, born in Rochdale, Lancashire, and trained at Edinburgh as a physician, is usually regarded as the father of English public

---

1. It must be said that, in this period, even Engels expressed similar sentiments about the Irish living in the slums in England, writing of "those who have not yet sunk in the whirlpool of moral ruin which surrounds them, sinking deeper, losing daily more and more of their power to resist the demoralising influence of want, filth, and evil surroundings" (Marx and Engels 1972: 38; Engels 1958: 104ff.).

education. His introduction to the subject began when Chadwick invited Kay, then an Assistant Poor Law Commisioner, to investigate the question of educating pauper children (Watson 1969: 23). But Kay had already established his views on the essential needs of the poor in his 1832 pamphlet, *The Moral and Physical Condition of the Working Classes Employed in the Cotton Manufacture in Manchester*. In that work, he noted, "It is melancholy to perceive how many of the evils suffered by the poor flow from their own ignorance or moral errors" (Kay 1969: 5–6).

Rather than acknowledge that workers in the Manchester factories might be underpaid, he observed that

> The wages obtained by operatives in various branches of the cotton manufacture are, in general, such, as with the exercise of that economy without which wealth itself is wasted, would be sufficient to provide them with all the decent comforts of life – the average wages of all persons employed in the mills (young and old) being from nine to twelve shillings per week. *Their means are too often consumed by vice and improvidence* [my italics]. (Kay 1969: 44)

He admitted that there were some workers who had an "exceedingly meagre" wage, despite working long hours, but

> They consist chiefly of Irish, and are affected by all the causes of moral and physical depression which we have enumerated. Ill-fed – ill-clothed – half-sheltered and ignorant, weaving in close damp cellars, or crowded workshops, it only remains that they should become, as is too frequently the case, demoralized and reckless, to render perfect the portraiture of savage life. Among men so situated, the moral check has no influence in preventing the rapid increase of the population. (Kay 1969: 44)

The Malthusian bias is clear. But while one may talk of population pressing on the means of subsistence, as if it were a general principle, the real argument is the same one routinely made by pre-Malthusian moralists such as McFarlan. If most Malthusians believed that poverty was caused by over-population, it was because they also believed – as we have seen in regard to Ireland – that the poor exhibited no *moral* check on their sexual behaviour. This gave rise to the view, so well expressed in Kay's writings, that moral instruction might provide the key to civilising the unrestrained passions of the masses. The thought that education might serve to give the poor new opportunities for remunerative employment was never considered.

The Irish were a particular target of Kay's. It was not just that he regarded them, as we have seen, as morally and physically debased. He had a thorough contempt for them and, like many in England, sought to blame them, rather than employers, for the low wages which English workers received – not least, because of their mere numbers.

The existence of cheap and redundant labour in the market has, also, a *constant* [his italics] tendency to lessen its general price, and hence the wages of the English operatives have been exceedingly reduced by this immigration of Irish – their comforts consequently diminished – their manners debased – and the natural tendency of manufactures on the people thwarted. We are all well convinced that without the numerical and moral influence of this class [i.e., the Irish], on the means and on the character of the people who have had to enter into competition with them in the market of labour, we should have had less occasion to regret the physical and moral degradation of the operative population. (Kay 1969: 44–5)

Kay's ultimate solution for the improvement of the condition of the working class was better public education, with the specific purpose of moral and political indoctrination. His ultimate aim, however, was social and political stability. He wrote in a time of great social upheaval which, within a few years, would culminate in the Chartist movement, and it was to guard against such turmoil that Kay envisaged the aims of education for the poor:

The preservation of *internal peace* [his italics], not less than the improvement of our national institutions, depends on the education of the working classes.... The education afforded to the poor must be substantial. The ascertained truths of political science should be early taught to the labouring classes, and *correct* [his italics] political information should be constantly and industriously disseminated amongst them. Were the taxes on periodical publications removed, men of great intelligence and virtue might be induced to conduct journals, established for the express purpose of directing to legitimate objects that restless activity by which the people are of late agitated.... The poor might thus be almost made to understand their political position in society, and the duties that belong to it. (Kay 1969: 98)

Malthusianism would play a role in helping the poor, not only to comprehend their place in a society of extreme differences in access to resources and power, but to understand that their position was not the result of how society was organised. This was the view which Place, another of Bentham's disciples, was advocating. Rather than agitate, workers must learn to accept that their lot in life was based on their own inadequacies. At best, Neo-Malthusians would suggest that the poor should limit their family size in the faint hope that this might bring about a rise in wages.

The Emergence of Eugenics

It was in the second half of the nineteenth century that the ruling class began to give up the idea that the poor could be educated to appreciate and accept the appropriateness of their poverty. In the face of the increasing immiseration of the poor and their apparent unwillingness to accept its inevitability, a more deterministic theory emerged which defined the poor as the product of heritable deficiencies.

It was a view which, despite deep historical roots, really came into sharp focus in the 1870s and 1880s, with the work of Francis Galton, who coined the term "eugenics" in 1883 in his work *Inheritance of Human Faculties* (Searle 1976: 3). Galton, a cousin of Charles Darwin, conceived it as the means by which the physical and moral attributes of a population might be improved by selective breeding which favoured the increased genetic representation of those who were considered to possess more of what he variously called "natural ability" and "civic worth". It was taken for granted by Galton and other eugenicists that such qualities generally were distributed throughout the population in a manner which reflected social classes, and that such classes themselves reflected the intrinsic character of their members, rather than the historical development of political and economic relations.

There had always been in Malthusianism an implicit presumption that the poor were not really the equals of the more privileged. Malthus had created the basis of a demographic determinism which rationalised poverty as the result of the poor having too many children. But his writings and those of many of his followers had always implied that one of the reasons for this was that the poor lacked middle-class virtues such as prudence, foresight and the capacity to manage their affairs in a rational manner. Eugenics went the next step in drawing the conclusion that these moral deficiencies were innate, that the poor were inherently inferior to the well-to-do and therefore incapable of manifesting such traits. The implication was no longer that the poor were a threat to social order simply because they were too numerous. They were dangerous on an even more fundamental level, because their excessive fertility was considered to be the cause of the deterioration of the nation's "racial stock". At the same time, it was obviously important for the fertility of the "better types" somehow to be enhanced.

The necessity for eugenic theory was also the result of the failure of neo-classical economics effectively to resolve or, at least, to dispose of the question of the origins of poverty. The condition of the working class in the industrial countries had deteriorated through the nineteenth century, but a succession of prominent European economists, including Marshall, Walras and Pareto, had only managed to make poverty marginal to their analysis of how markets maximise societal welfare. Like many of his contemporaries, Alfred Marshall, the most eminent of the Cambridge economists, dealt with the issue in part by dismissing the merits of Marx as a serious critic of capitalism (Hobsbawm 1964: 245–9). And, in the end, Pareto would endorse Mussolini and the birth of Italian fascism (Gouldner 1970: 149). To a large extent, it was simply an implicit tenet of their thought that the poor had different wishes and desires than the rich; and that economic theory only needed to explain and countenance the behaviour of those who had the competence to compete rationally in the marketplace. Individual failure was primarily a reflection of personal incapacity, rather than of any inherent defect in the economic or social system.

Even when poverty was obviously related to low income, the eugenicists took comfort in the view, expressed by Leonard Darwin, the President of the Eugenics Education Society between 1911 and 1929, that "The rate of wages may be made to offer some indication of the innate qualities of the wage-earner." Such a generalisation solved many problems for the neo-classical economist at the turn of the century. Even Keynes, the most prominent of Marshall's students, had strong eugenical views that in part reflected his being a member of England's so-called "intellectual aristocracy", which played a prominent role in the emergence and advocacy of eugenics. He was an officer of the Cambridge University Eugenics Society and delivered the Galton Lecture in 1937 (Searle 1976: 13, 121), by which time the racialist Nuremberg Laws of Germany (issued in September 1935) (Shirer 1960: 233) should have left little doubt about the imminent implications of eugenical theory.

The eugenic perspective also clearly built on Malthus's antipathy to the emergent public health ethos (Ross 1991), a hostility which increasingly infected the medical community itself. Malthus's own views about medical intervention had been clearly expressed in his opposition to Jenner's work on the smallpox vaccine. To Malthus, it had been sufficient to suggest that such developments would only lead to more people surviving and, hence, according to his theories, greater population increase and more misery. But to the eugenicists, one of the most serious liabilities of public health measures was that they were blind to inherent differences and therefore ensured that people survived regardless of their "civic worth". By the end of the nineteenth century, it was common to find statements such as that of Dr John Berry Haycraft, author of *Darwinism and Race Progress*, that "Preventative medicine is trying a unique experiment, and the effect is already discernible – race-decay" (in Wohl 1983: 334).

But what most united Malthusian thinking and that of the eugenicists, beyond the appearance of having scientific laws on their side, was their anti-democratic stance, their scarcely concealed contempt for and fear of the poor. For their "excess population" one can always simply read "the majority". Thomas Macaulay is an excellent example. In 1831, as a Whig MP, he spoke against universal suffrage in the debate on the Reform Bill. Acknowledging that many working people lived in misery, he expressed fear that the vote would render them a real danger to social order and especially to the rights of private property (Kirk 1954: 171). A year later, taking advantage of the fact that the Reform Bill had enfranchised many of the new industrial towns (if not most of their citizens), he was elected MP from the northern city of Leeds. He had run against Michael Sadler, largely because the latter had written so critically about Malthus, but also because Sadler was a champion of the Poor Laws, which the Malthusians sought to abolish. Soon after, Macaulay became secretary of the Board of Control, which presided over the administration of India, and, even as he spoke in Parliament on the benefits which English rule conferred on the sub-continent and alluded to the "honourable poverty" which characterised the English who served there – overlooking myriad examples of those who, though a pale reflection of the great Clive, had enriched themselves during their service (Calder 1981: 692–700) – he was preparing to go there himself as a member of the new Supreme Council of India, at a splendid annual salary of £10,000 a year (Dutt 1940: 493). But he had no intention of extending to such a lucrative colony the blessings of representative democracy. On the contrary, he observed that India should never expect "free government. But she may have the next best thing – a firm and impartial despotism" (quoted in Dutt 1940: 271). Macaulay's principal legacy would be the imposition of a system of education through which "Westernization should eradicate the traditional culture of India" (Kirk 1954: 169).

As a great believer in the value of English bourgeois values and in the significance of the "Glorious Revolution" of 1688, when the Whigs installed William of Orange as king (who then proceeded to undertake a new conquest of Ireland) (Morton 1979: 280–89), Macaulay was an arch foe of any form of popular government. Such elitism was an obvious source of his affection for Malthusian thinking, and the merger of the two was clearly evidenced toward the end of his life when he wrote to the American Henry Randall that American democracy would work only so long as there was enough unoccupied land. But that would not continue for ever:

> The time will come when New England will be as thickly peopled as old England. Wages will be as low, and will fluctuate as much with you as with us. You will have your Manchesters and Birminghams, and in those Manchesters and Birminghams, hundreds of thousands of artisans will assuredly be sometimes out of work. Then, your institutions will be fairly brought to the test. Distress everywhere makes the labourer mutinous and discontented, and inclines him to listen with eagerness to agitators who tell him that it is

a monstrous iniquity that one man should have a million while another cannot get a full meal. (in Schuster 1940: 332)

So we see the early appearance of the idea that it was population pressure
which created poverty that led, in turn, to the poor being so susceptible
to "outside agitators" for change.

Macaulay then argued that Malthusian pressures required undemo-
cratic institutions to guarantee social stability. In England,

> In bad years there is plenty of grumbling here, and sometimes a little rioting.
> But it matters little. For here the sufferers are not the rulers. The supreme
> power is in the hands of a class, numerous indeed, but select; of an educated
> class, of a class which is, and knows itself to be, deeply interested in the
> security of property and the maintenance of order. Accordingly, the malcon-
> tents are firmly, yet gently restrained. The bad time is got over without robbing
> the wealthy to relieve the indigent. (in Schuster 1940: 332)

What was most important was that, where political power was concentrated in the hands of a few, it could effectively protect private property
against demagogues and discontents. For Macaulay, the worst thing he
could imagine was a day when "a multitude of people, none of whom
has had more than half a breakfast, or expects to have more than half
a dinner, will choose a Legislature" (in Schuster 1940: 332).

Fourteen years after he wrote this, it would have seemed as if his
worst fears had come come true, when France's military defeat by Prussia
in 1870 led to the establishment of the Paris Commune. The Commune
– which the great anarchist Bakunin saw as the "first striking and
practical demonstration" of revolutionary socialism, as "a bold, clearly-
formulated negation of the State" (Dolgoff 1972: 263–4), which was to
become the reference point for the left for many decades to come –
made even some of the most liberal minds of Europe tremble. But it
also galvanised the forces of conservatism into new forms of reaction.

The brutal repression of the Commune, which left 10,000 dead in
the space of several weeks, demonstrated the kind of genocidal fury
which the European elite was capable of directing against the organised
working class. The decimation of European workers in the First World
War nearly fifty years later would underscore even more dramatically
the general contempt with which the lives of the working class were
regarded. It was also a terrible culmination of the endemic disdain with
which their participation in national political life was viewed by their
so-called superiors. Just two years before the outbreak of the war,
William Inge, Dean of St Paul's, had mocked democracy as "perhaps
the silliest of all fetishes that are seriously worshipped among us" (in
Searle 1976: 68). Such views, however, did not prevent working-class

men from being called upon to die in its name. Few of the hundreds of thousands of soldiers who died at the Marne, on the Somme, at Verdun or Ypres were given a second thought. But in Britain during the years after the war, myriad novels and histories would emphasise how the war had decimated the ranks of the men of the upper class, the ones whom eugenical thinking considered to have been the least expendable, even though "such casualties were but a small fraction of total British war losses" among the more than six million English, Welsh, Scots and Irish who served in arms (Winter 1977: 465, 450).

However, in the decades between the Commune and the Great War, it was not just the poverty in which the working class lived, or their disposability in the wars of colonial expansion that occupied virtually every year of Queen Victoria's reign, enriching British industry, that truly reflected the attitudes of the upper and middle classes toward the poor. One must also look at the economic and social theories that contrived to legitimise both poverty and war.

The writings of Place and those who followed him make it abundantly clear that "Neo-Malthusianism" was not just a campaign for birth control. Nor was it, despite its claim, a campaign for the betterment of the lives of the poor. When the Malthusian League – one of whose vice presidents, a former prime minister of Holland, Dr Samuel Van Houten, seems to have first coined the term "Neo-Malthusian" – was founded in 1877 (D'Arcy 1977: 429; cf. Ledbetter 1972), it was explicitly to spread knowledge about "the law of population, of its consequences, and of its bearing upon human conduct and morals". The connection with the earlier concerns of Kay and Chadwick is obvious. Life in the industrial slums was interpreted in terms of its apparent moral disorder, and one of the principal symptoms and causes of the immorality of the poor was the way they were densely packed together in such urban settings (Treble 1979: 174–5). The reference to "overcrowding" had a Malthusian flavour, but ignored the fact that the poor simply could not afford accommodation in less populated, more sanitary surroundings.

It was also implied that it was the immorality of the poor, rather than their good judgement, that inclined them toward socialism. The poor must learn, as Kay had suggested, that they were the cause of their own poverty; and that it was only by having fewer children, rather than by attacking capitalism, that they could improve their material circumstances. By 1913, the president of the Malthusian League, Charles Drysdale, would tell the National Birth-Rate Commission, a private organisation, that "The population difficulty is the principle cause of the labour unrest of the present day" (in Ledbetter 1976: 101). It was a stance which would become more vociferous after the Russian Revolution and which, in the first years after the Second World War, would find a place in modernisation and demographic transition theory, when population pressure would be regarded as the main source of unrest in developing countries and the ultimate source of the conditions that attracted peasants to communism.

By 1920, in the 42nd Annual Report of the Malthusian League, it was being observed that "the harassed taxpaying and employing classes and all who wish to avert revolution, would be well advised to support the Malthusian League to the utmost of their powers and means". The problem for Malthusians, however, was not just that population pressure caused poverty, but that the poor were so fertile because of what was seen as their innate inferiority. At the same time, evidence suggested that it was not workers who used birth control the most. While there is ample reason to believe that working-class women were often desperate to limit their child-bearing (Davies 1915), this was an aspiration that often had to be compromised because children continued to make an invaluable contribution to the survivorship of working-class households well into the twentieth century. As a result, Neo-Malthusians came to regard voluntary contraception as limited in its potential and actually dysgenic.[2] It had to be more systematic and selective. Initially, this was proposed to prevent certain categories of the ill or disabled from continuing to affect the quality of the so-called national gene pool. But it rapidly came to be viewed as a way of dealing with a broader spectrum of social ills.

How many people could this be extended to? By the turn of the century, it seemed that numbers could be grabbed out of the air. The category of the "feeble-minded" seems to have first been used in 1876 by Charles Trevelyan, then a member of the Council of the Charity Organization Society (Simmons 1978: 388). In the years just before the First World War, the term became a convenient explanation for a wide variety of social problems, including prostitution, vagrancy and petty crime. Havelock Ellis

> quoted an investigation at Pentonville Prison, where, even after prisoners too mentally affected to be fit for prison discipline had been excluded, eighteen per cent of adult prisoners and forty per cent of juvenile offenders were found to be feeble-minded. Another authority ventured the opinion that only four to five per cent of criminals came from parents who were "really sound". Groups on the fringes of society who were especially likely to find themselves in prison, like prostitutes and tramps, were also thought to contain a very high proportion of the feeble-minded. (Searle 1976: 31)

---

2. That is, it would encourage the reproductive contribution of individuals regarded by Neo-Malthusians as socially, politically or physically "inferior".

By 1909, when the Poor Law Commissioners in England endorsed the view of "The Royal Commission into the Care and Control of the Feeble-Minded", it was obvious that the hardships faced by the poor evoked little compassion. On the contrary, inspired by eugenic and Malthusian thinking, policy-makers were increasingly entranced by the assumption that science had demonstrated that poverty was primarily the result of physical and moral debility (Simmons 1978: 394–5). This seemed to call not for social justice, but for special measures of control. One of those who subscribed to this view was Winston Churchill, the Home Secretary in 1910–11. Churchill came from a distinguished lineage: in 1689, his ancestor John Churchill, the first Duke of Marlborough, had set fire to the Irish city of Cork in the name of King William (Newby 1987: 123). Winston had inherited his ancestor's spirit of tolerance. He was particularly inspired by the work of Dr Alfred Tredgold, who had been a medical expert to the Royal Commission (Searle 1976: 117; Simmons 1978: 392–6). In 1910, Churchill endorsed and circulated among the cabinet an article which Tredgold had published in the *Eugenics Review* the previous year, entitled "The Feeble-Minded – A Social Danger". A cabinet colleague, W.S. Blunt, wrote that Churchill was "a strong eugenist. He told us he had himself drafted the Bill which is to give power of shutting up people of weak intellect and so prevent their breeding. He thought it might be arranged to sterilize them" (in Searle 1976: 108).

Such ideas were especially risky in the hands of a man who not only had strong political prejudices – chiefly against socialists – but also happened to be the Home Secretary. Once the view became fashionable that diseases were generally the result of hereditary factors and that many social problems were actually "medical", unacceptable political beliefs could easily be described as symptoms of mental disorder. To someone such as Churchill, it required very little for the phrase "people of weak intellect" to include socialists. Then, the policy of selective sterilisation as a strategy for the enhancement of societal well-being took on ominous political implications.

Immigrants and Radicals

It was especially after the Russian Revolution that eugenicists in the United States tended to conflate the genetically inferior with political radicals. Both seemed to be disproportionately comprised of people of immigrant origins. A major writer on this subject was Lothrop Stoddard, a Professor at Harvard University and the author of *The Rising Tide of Color Against White World Supremacy* (1920) and *The Revolt Against Civili-*

zation; *The Menace of the Under Man* (1922). In the latter work, Stoddard wrote of evolution as a process of "ever-increasing inequality". Hence, the idea of social and political *equality* was, in his mind, "one of the most pernicious delusions that has ever afflicted mankind" (1922: 45). That it "should have been actually attempted in Bolshevik Russia" was an unforgiveable offence against nature, as well as his class. Such thinking had led Stoddard naturally into the role of director of the American Birth Control League (Gordon 1976: 283).

The introduction to *The Rising Tide* was written by Madison Grant, a lawyer, member of the upper class of New York, treasurer of the second and third international congresses of eugenics, in 1921 and 1932 respectively, a co-founder of the Galton Society, a president of the American Eugenics Society and a member of the Immigration Restriction League. In his own book, *The Passing of the Great Race* (1918), Grant wrote of the threat to Nordic peoples from what he called the "inferior races", in particular the Jews and the Irish, and of the need to curb their reproductive urges by virtually any means, including sterilization and castration. These methods could eventually

> be applied to an ever widening circle of social discards, beginning always with the criminal, the diseased and the insane, and extending gradually to types which may be called weaklings, rather than defectives, and perhaps ultimately to worthless race types. (in Chase 1977: 172)

By 1931, J. Landman, of the College of the City of New York, would state unequivocally in the *Eugenical News* that

> There are 10,000,000 or more of socially inadequate people in the United States who are a constant menace to our country and race. They are the mentally diseased such as the manics and the dementia praecoxes, the dependants such as the deaf, the blind and the deformed, the delinquents such as the wayward and the criminals, the mentally deficient such as the morons and the idiots, the degenerates such as the sadists and the drug fiends, and the infectious such as the tuberculous and the syphilitics. (Landman 1931: 111)

Grant is also notable for having been, at the same time that he vented his eugenical opinions, a founder of the New York Zoological Society, which ran the Bronx Zoo. Like Stoddard, who was a director of the Save the Redwoods League (Chase 1977), he anticipated the right-wing environmentalism that would emerge in the decade after the Second World War. Indeed, he was its effective god-father, for, as we shall see later, the author of one of the landmark books of that movement was his disciple.

Grant and Stoddard's vision, like most such philosophies, embraced a violent antipathy to democratic society. In this respect, they merely

brought to the fore feelings which Malthus had harboured more dis-
creetly, in his efforts to defend property and privilege against the claims
for a more egalitarian system. Macaulay had begun to give vent to such
thoughts. But the writings of Stoddard, Grant and their contemporaries
represented, more overtly than ever before, a rabid conviction that the
poor, indeed all who questioned the social origins of poverty, represented a threat to their very concept of civilisation.

From the late nineteenth century onward, this view was being expressed with equal fervour in much of Europe (Stein 1987; cf. Banister
1901), where eugenic ideas were also fuelled by fears of declining domestic birth-rates. In France especially, where such apprehensions had
been expressed since it lost the Franco-Prussian War, they were exacerbated by the devastating human losses of the First World War. This, in
turn, inspired not only pro-natalist and nationalist groups (Glass 1966:
223), but also French demographers such as Arsène Dumont, author of
Dépopulation et civilisation, who were preoccupied with the social consequences of fertility decline (Winter 1989: 126).

Given such conflicting currents, it is not surprising that, although
individuals such as Stoddard and Grant recognised birth control as an
instrument of social policy, most eugenicists at this time still tended to
regard it with considerable ambivalence. First, it seemed to be used
disproportionately by the people whom they did not want to limit
fertility, that is, the middle and upper classes. This had engendered a
preoccupation with what was called "race suicide", the idea that the
upper classes (as if they alone were "the race") were failing to reproduce themselves (Robinson 1933: 48). Secondly, it was still widely
advocated by the left. Up until the First World War in the United States
and Europe, many of the leaders in the fight to popularise the knowledge and use of contraception were more or less associated with the
socialist movement, including Margaret Sanger, who had coined the
phrase "birth control" in 1914 (Fryer 1965: 226).

The Russian Revolution was a turning point, however. After 1917,
socialists throughout the West suddenly seemed to pose an imminent
threat. In the United States, where the government launched a witch-
hunt against the left, the birth control movement quickly moved to
distance itself from its socialist allies, shifting toward the eugenics camp
and becoming more closely associated with establishment interests,
including most notably the medical profession (cf. Hartmann 1987: 95–
6), with its history of moralistic resistance to the popularisation of
contraception (Gordon 1976: 170). Sanger more than anyone epito-
mised this general transformation, which echoed the earlier efforts of
Francis Place in situating birth control within the institutional and ideo-

logical framework of capitalism. By 1919, she was writing in her *Birth Control Review*: "More children from the fit, less from the unfit – that is the chief issue of birth control" (in Chase 1977: 55; cf. Hartmann 1987: 97). In 1921, when the American Birth Control League was founded, she became its first president, with Stoddard its director. Five years later, she was commenting favourably on the new US Immigrant Act of 1924, with its racial quotas, observing that

> while we close our gates to the so-called "undesirables" from other countries, we make no attempt to cut down the rapid multiplication of the unfit and undesirable at home ... it now remains for the United States government to set a sensible example to the world by offering a bonus or a yearly pension to all obviously unfit parents to allow themselves to be sterilized by a harmless and scientific means.... There is only one reply to a request for a higher birth rate among the intelligent, and that is to ask the government to first take off the burdens of the insane and feebleminded from your backs. Sterilization for these is the remedy. (Sanger 1926: 299)

By the early 1930s, concerns about differential fertility had taken on an apocalyptic tone, as evidenced in the words of the American economist Joseph Spengler:

> The steady decline in the birth rate threatens Western civilization both from within and without. Decline in numbers and multiplication of the unproductive age will of necessity undermine the materialistic base upon which the industrial civilization of Western Europe and America rests. A thinning of ranks may expose the social superstructure of non-growing nations to *the onslaught or the overflow of the swarming people* [my italics]. (in Mass 1976: 34)

Eugenics, Birth Control and the Decline of Midwifery in the United States

In the United States, such views flourished with the fusion of eugenics and the medical establishment. One of the rarely noted consequences was the disappearance of midwives, who embodied an alternative, democratic use of birth control. In the decades before 1935, as US medicine was transformed from a popular art into an elitist profession, midwives (as well as homeopaths and other "irregular" medical practitioners) were almost wholly displaced by doctors and hospitals. The conventional argument that this represented an improvement in care is not borne out by evidence which, on the contrary, suggests that "midwives were as competent and clean birth attendants as local physicians", and were often better (Declercq 1985: 124).

The decline in midwifery in the United States contrasts with its survival in England, where, as we have seen, eugenic ideas were no less popular. The explanation lies in the fact that, from the mid-nineteenth century onward, English midwifery was increasingly practised by middle-class women who found support among male doctors of the same class. According to Donnison (1977: 177), they "aimed at making midwifery a suitable profession for educated women, and sought state registration as a means to that end". In the United States, meanwhile, midwives had little in common, socially or economically, with doctors. They were largely working class and foreign-born, their ranks continuously renewed by immigrants (Declercq 1985). This in itself ensured that midwives played a major role in obstetrical care well into the early twentieth century. According to Litoff,

> At the turn of the century, midwives and physicians attended about an equal number of births ... conservative estimates indicate that as late as 1910 at least 50 percent of all births were attended by midwives. (1978: 27)

But midwives' principal clients were overwhelmingly the poor, including rural blacks and urban immigrants. Thus, "A 1908 study revealed that 86 percent of all Italian-American births in Chicago were reported by midwives" (Litoff 1978: 27; cf. Declercq 1985: 125). Immigrant women felt comfortable being attended by women who were themselves to a large extent foreign-born and could probably speak their own language.

However, it was also precisely this that exposed midwives to pressure from a medical establishment which was rapidly being transformed into a professional elite that reflected the interests of the dominant class. One concern at this time was to Americanise immigrants into a productive and compliant workforce. As the educational system evolved toward this end (Bowles and Gintis 1976), so too did US medicine. The high point of the transformation of American medicine was the Carnegie Foundation report by Abraham Flexner, which spearheaded the move to systematise, standardise and centralise medical training – a process which also had the effect of bringing considerable class uniformity to the medical profession.

In this context, immigrant midwives were not only widely regarded as an obstacle to Americanisation. As a source of popular gynaecological and obstetrical advice for those very people of whom doctors and eugenicists most disapproved, they were perceived as a major impediment to the way that access and use of contraception were coming to be regarded, as a form of bio-social control. And not to be underestimated as an issue, midwives were closely identified with foreign-born communities which were regarded as a source of radicalism. It was no coincidence that one of the great left-wing figures of this period, the anarchist Emma Goldman, was a midwife (Drinnon 1961: 64–5).

Toward a Eugenic State

In 1939, the American Birth Control Federation was established. The following year, at its annual conference, Henry Fairchild, a former president of the American Eugenics Society and author of *The Melting Pot Mistake* (1926), spoke favourably of the growing amalgamation of the eugenics and birth control movement (Hartmann 1987: 97). By 1941, the Federation was sponsoring symposia with such titles as "Race Building in a Democracy". On Sanger's advice, the organisation hired Guy Irving Burch, Director of the Population Reference Bureau and of the American Eugenics Society, and a leader of the racist Coalition of Patriotic Societies (which was indicted for sedition by a Federal court in 1942, along with the Ku Klux Klan) (Chase 1977: 367), to use his Bureau to campaign for birth control as a means of reducing the population of blacks and immigrants in the USA.

But nowhere did eugenic thinking have such an impact as it did in Germany, where it became almost an obsession in a country that was only a few decades old, whose centuries of disunity had nurtured deep anxieties about the survival of the German "race". These ideas came to the fore toward the end of the nineteenth century, when the rapid rise of industrial capitalism in Germany engendered an intensive anti-socialist drive by the ruling class that was not dissimilar to what was occurring at the same time in France, Britain and the United States. In the 1890s, restrictive laws and government propaganda systematically sought to inhibit the electoral advance of the left (Hall 1976).

The First World War changed many things, including German socialism. In the aftermath of a war which had devastated much of Europe, the threat of revolution in Germany seemed imminent from the very moment that the Weimar Republic was born in November 1918. Lenin and Bukharin were among those who expected (and hoped for) a revolution in Germany – indeed, Bukharin had conferred with Karl Liebknecht, a leader of the German communists in October in Berlin (Cohen 1980: 82). Shirer writes that

> revolution was in the air in Berlin. The capital was paralyzed by a general strike. Down the broad Unter den Linden, a few blocks from the Reichstag, the Spartacists, led by the Left Socialists Rosa Luxemburg and Karl Liebknecht, were preparing from their citadel in the Kaiser's palace to proclaim a soviet republic. (Shirer 1960: 52)

It was the reaction to such events that doomed Weimar to fail as a putative liberal democracy. When the Social Democrat leader Philipp Scheidemann proclaimed a Republic as a pre-emptive measure, the Army leaders Ludendorff and Hindenberg were happy in such circumstances to empower the Social Democrats to take all the responsibility for Germany's surrender to the allies and ultimately for the subsequent peace treaty. This made it possible for Hitler, mounting the Munich beer hall putsch just five years later, to label Scheidemann's group "the November criminals". But long before this, an alliance was covertly forged between the Social Democrats and the army, in which the government would "put down anarchy and Bolshevism and maintain the Army in all its tradition" (Shirer 1960: 54), while the Army would lend its support to the state. By mid-January 1919, the Army had crushed the Spartacists. Luxemburg and Liebknecht were murdered. By July, the Republic had "normalised", with a liberal, democratic constitution which reflected all the proper traditions of the European Enlightenment. But the country was still controlled by the old forces: by the Army, with its Prussian background, and large industry.

One of the instruments of repression of the German left – in particular of the soviet government which took over Munich in 1919 – was the so-called Freikorps. Perhaps because, by then, German medicine, much as in Britain and the United States, had absorbed eugenic and racialist ideas which, at least in the case of Germany, seemed to embody their passionate concerns about national survival, many graduates of the Freikorps went on to become doctors. But there was a more general tendency here as well, as "Physicians became Nazified more thoroughly and much sooner than any other profession" (Kater 1989: 4–5). As a result, even before the establishment of the Third Reich with its eugenic laws, such doctors, having the power to act in the interest of what they defined as a greater social good, were already beginning to sterilise selected patients at their own discretion. In the early years of the Nazi regime, such sterilisation soon evolved into a programme of euthanasia directed toward what the Prussian Ministry of Justice called "valueless life". Such "medical killing became a pilot scheme for the holocaust" (Weindling 1989: 546, 548).

As early as 1878, George Drysdale's pamphlet *State Remedies for Poverty* had suggested that government would have to assume responsibility for curbing fertility. Fifty years later in Germany, his suggestion – and many of the eugenic ideas which Stoddard, Grant, Sanger and Birch had promoted – had become national policy, and "state remedies" had been transformed into mass murder on an unprecedented scale.

From Eugenics to Environmentalism

As a result, in the midst of the Second World War, the American Birth Control Federation considered it appropriate to change its name to the more benign Planned Parenthood Federation of America. None the less, Margaret Sanger was its first president and its board of directors included former presidents of the American Eugenics Society and the Race Betterment Conference. In 1948, it became the US chapter of the International Planned Parenthood Federation, which was formed at Sanger's instigation with initial funding from the British-based Brush Foundation, which had been previously associated with eugenic work, and the Osborn family of New York, which was also strongly identified with the eugenics movement (Gordon 1976: 344, 397).

But the war necessarily brought about an important shift in the way that eugenic ideas were actually expressed. As eugenic concerns were muted in the shadow of the Third Reich, environmental catastrophism became the principal vehicle for Malthusian fears. The publication of Fairfield Osborn's *Our Plundered Planet* (1948) marked the beginning of this new shift. But bearing in mind Stoddard and Grant's environmentalist credentials, and that the Osborn family had established the American Museum of Natural History, this was not a wholly surprising development. It was one which reached its high point in 1968 when the Sierra Club published Stanford biologist Paul Ehrlich's *The Population Bomb*, which it had commissioned (Sierra Club 1997).

The Political "Tragedy" of the Commons

When environmental degradation is chiefly attributed to the poor – sometimes to their lack of opportunities, but more often to their tendency to reproduce for short-term advantage, to which their poverty itself was largely attributed – ecologists such as Ehrlich who want to comment on societal ills have readily found laws in nature to explain them without recourse to the complexities of political economy. When an eminent biologist simply and unashamedly writes that "ecology's first social law should be written: 'All poverty is caused by the continued growth of population'" (Colinvaux 1978: 222), it is self-evident that Malthus has found new allies in the modern environmentalist movement.

According to Colinvaux, the "best essay" on the "evolutionary basis of the human predicament" (Colinvaux 1978: 242) was "The Tragedy of the Commons", a short article written the same year as Ehrlich's book by the American biologist Garrett Hardin. In it, Hardin revived the ideas of William Lloyd, to argue that only a system of private ownership could prevent the degradation of environmental resources by imposing the constraints required to curb individual fertility. Against the backdrop of events in the developing world, such a view was (and remains) intensely ideological. It was published and largely received as credible science.

Hardin's article provoked a new research genre (cf. McCay and Acheson 1987) on the nature of common property resources, which has effectively exposed the largely polemical character of his metaphorical portrayal of the commons. This research has demonstrated that, as in eighteenth-century England, such systems generally manage local resources in a way which tends to balance individual rights against collective needs, according to complex regulations and requirements which curb the kind of excesses which private ownership – *not* the commons – tends to favour. Although such research underscores how Hardin grossly over-simplified the nature of a commons, historical research which would have been readily accessible to Hardin at the time could have made this same point just as well (cf. Gonner 1966). But Hardin's original essay is actually devoid of any real empirical content. This alone suggests that it was largely a political tract. That it was accorded any scientific respect is explicable only in terms of the acceptability of the general message it carried and the extent to which much of what he actually said was conveniently disregarded.

Because Hardin's article has been cited endlessly and is undoubtedly one of the most widely known modern essays on the relationship of population and environment, it is worth considering its significance more fully. This means examining it not in isolation, but as the culmination of ideas that Hardin had been expressing far less metaphorically in other work since the end of the Second World War. Only from that perspective can one can see how "The Tragedy of the Commons" embodies all of the cardinal qualities of Cold War Malthusian thinking: it is anti-socialist, anti-democratic and eugenic. It is simply a hypothetical model to justify the political message that common ownership and use, in the face of population pressure, is inevitably destructive – an implicit argument against land reform in developing countries – and that the only viable alternative is a form of private ownership. Any commons, in this view, must be privatised, even if this implies an infringement of personal liberty, especially in regard to the "freedom to breed" (Hardin 1975: 14).

Readers of the essay have frequently portrayed Hardin as extremely reasonable for saying that, when personal liberty needs to be circum-scribed in this way, it could be through what he termed "mutual coercion, mutually agreed upon" (Hardin 1975: 15). Some have written as if this were, after all, no more than what representative democracy is all about. But that is a seriously misinformed generalisation. In fact, unless the distribution of resources and the power and privileges which they yield is equitable, which it is not, even in the Western industrial "democracies", then coercive legislation can never be "mutual". In actual practice, freedom is curtailed in *different* degrees for *different* groups of people. Even in Malthus's day, Edmund Burke had conceded that the English Parliament was an institution for the defence of hereditary property. As such, it would be a gross distortion of history to argue that the enclosure acts initiated by that Parliament – the very acts which privatised the English commons – were undertaken on everyone's behalf, for the good of all. Quite the contrary, as E.P. Thompson rightly observed:

> Enclosure (when all the sophistications are allowed for) was a plain enough case of class robbery, played according to fair rules of property and laid down by a Parliament of property-owners and lawyers. (1966: 218)

But Hardin, of course, as he made even clearer in subsequent publications (e.g., 1985), was not actually concerned about pastures, but about virtually all circumstances where, *in his view*, individuals collectivise costs but privatise advantages. However, he has also been forced to concede that he was not talking about any particular historical or material reality, but about the commons as a hypothetical model where it was unmanaged under conditions of scarcity (1993: 178–9). This is a major – and one might almost say fatal – concession, but the fact is that it still distracts us from the principal theme in the original essay. In that article, Hardin proceeded to extend the concept of the commons to freedom and, in particular, to the freedom to breed. In so doing, he made one of the most critical and revealing pronouncements of the entire piece:

> To couple the concept of freedom to breed with the belief that everyone born has an equal right to the commons is to lock the world into a tragic course of action. (Hardin 1975: 14)

The crucial idea here, again, is that only the private ownership of crucial resources and an inegalitarian distribution of rights in reproduction (or otherwise) can prevent the "tragedy" which Hardin envisaged as the inevitable outcome of a democratic and egalitarian society. Much as for Malthus, the sanctity of private property for Hardin was threatened on a fundamental level by the idea that everyone had rights in society. The message, therefore, was simple: some people have powers and privileges, but we do not need to ask by what means, fair or foul, they acquired them. It is simply the case, now, that these cannot be redistributed and that those who seek equity must understand – much as Kay had suggested that the poor must understand the "ascertained truths of political science" – that our collective future security depends, not on social or economic justice, but on reducing *their* numbers, coercively if necessary. In this sense, the central argument of "The Tragedy of the Commons" was merely a clever defence of private property and an argument against the "welfare state", phrased in terms of the environmental and demographic concerns of the world in which it was published.

But there was something more insidious in the essay as well which embodies the way in which post-war environmentalism became a vehicle, not simply for the more ideological aspects of Malthusian thinking, but also for eugenic convictions. The actual concern about what Hardin called "a commons in breeding" was that the poor had too many children and – recall the argument about the English poor laws – made excessive claims on public resources.

> If each human family were dependent only on its own resources; if, the children of improvident parents starved to death; if, thus, overbreeding brought its own "punishment" to the germ line – then there would be no public interest in controlling the breeding of families. (Hardin 1975: 14)

Precisely what Hardin had in mind can only be appreciated in terms of his earlier writings. In 1949, he had published a textbook entitled *Biology: Its Human Implications*. In it, while the ovens at Auschwitz and Dachau were barely cool, he staked out an unambiguously eugenic position. He asserted that the problem of population was as much qualitative as quantitative, and that people with superior IQs were unfortunately having fewer children than those with lower IQs. Like others who had made this claim before him, Hardin attributed the problem to the nature of a democratic system which made insufficient allowance for what he regarded as intrinsic and heritable differences. In the terms that he would later employ, Hardin was concerned that the survival of too many of the genes of the wrong people would degrade the genetic commons. Thus, in the 1951 edition of his book, echoing Malthus's criticisms of public health measures, Hardin asserted that "Every time a philanthropist sets up a foundation to look for a cure for a certain disease, he thereby threatens humanity eugenically" (Hardin 1951). This view, which encapsulated the grimmest aspect of the Malthusian message, that all ameliorative efforts are falsely conceived – unless they privilege the rich over the poor – was to become a popular one over the next decades, in the writings of those who regarded "over-population" as the paramount threat to global security and who could only view efforts to reduce mortality in developing countries as exacerbating that threat.

For Hardin, every act of charity, every aspect of public welfare, was not merely a threat to the concept of private property, but had potentially dysgenic consequences. But what could these be, unless one assumed that poverty was the result not of historically constructed systems of production – systems which could be challenged and changed – but of intrinsic and largely unalterable characteristics of the poor themselves? Thus, like most eugenicists, Hardin was not solely concerned about the quality of the gene pool, which was a fairly unknowable factor, open to all kinds of polemical assumptions. More important was the way that eugenic arguments defended the status quo by blaming the victims of injustice as carriers of dubious inborn traits which not only retarded their own prospects, but threatened the entire social order.

Perhaps one of the most revealing symptoms of Hardin's stance was the list of "selected references" for the last chapter of the 1949 edition of his biology textbook. One of the works cited was a book which had been published two years before by Guy Irving Burch and Elmer Pendell, entitled *Human Breeding and Survival: Population Roads to Peace and War* (1947). It is one thing to cite books because they are recent. But Pendell, an economist, was a member of Birthright, Inc., a eugenic group working for surgical sterilisation, while Burch, as noted earlier, had links to the most dubious racist organisations (Chase 1977: 366–7).

Such associations were of less concern to Hardin than was the menace of communism. His book *Nature and Man's Fate* makes clear how saturated his thinking was with Cold War passions. Following the standard chapter on eugenics is one entitled "Liberalism and the Specter of Competition", which is primarily an assault on the ideas of all those who, as Hardin put it, possessed a "fear and hatred of competition". Anyone critical of the Social Darwinist ethic was dismissed as "utopian", because "the struggle for existence ... cannot be escaped", either in biology or in culture (Hardin 1959: 219). This was more or less the view that had so recently infused the ideology of National Socialism (Stein 1987: 253–7).

Hardin clearly regarded competition, not merely as Malthus's "stimulus to industry", but as an essential characteristic of Nature generally and of human nature in particular. As Malthus had derived capitalist relations of production from divine necessity, Hardin, in a tradition that reaches from the Social Darwinists to contemporary sociobiology, viewed them as a manifestation of biological reality. This is an extremely arguable point. As Gould (1991: 334ff.) has noted, one can just as well find selective advantage in co-operative behaviour. It is none the less a consistent theme in Hardin's writings that one can adduce certain features of something conveniently designated as "human nature", and include among them competitiveness and envy, which are precisely the behavioural tendencies that he regards as leading to the "tragedy of the commons" and ensuring the fallibility of socialism. For, as Hardin would make clear years later, he regards "commonism" and "communism" as more or less equivalent (Hardin 1993: 214 ff.).

Thus, Hardin would write that competition – for him, an innate and immutable feature of all life – was

> the specter that haunts communism. This is the specter that haunts most of what has been called "liberalism" in the past century and a half. This is the demon that cannot be exorcised by verbal incantations of "brotherly love," "cooperation," "togetherness"... (1959: 220)

For Hardin, Malthus and Lloyd, the very idea of a "commons" was simply an affront to their shared conviction that human nature was compatible only with a competitive system based on private ownership. To the charge that poverty was an unacceptable failing of such a system, the Malthusians countered that it was chiefly population pressure which impoverished environments and peoples. From that, the argument would be developed, by Hardin and others, that environmental degradation was primarily a local process, for which developed countries were not responsible.

The central point in "The Tragedy of the Commons" was that only private property could protect the environment against over-population. Hardin's more recent publications, which I will refer to in the last chapter, have only served to underscore that argument, which has now become a cardinal tenet of contemporary neo-liberal dogma. The passion with which this conviction has been embraced today by conservative policy institutes and multinational corporations is evidence that it is not really an argument to conserve nature or even, in the end, to limit population, but a means of legitimising an unrelenting process of privatisation and enclosure.

4

Malthusianism, Demography and the Cold War

Uncritical and ahistorical reflection on the demise of the Soviet Union will doubtless give undue credence to the view that socialism is incompatible with "human nature". With time, moreover, few people will question the popular Western view that the Cold War was primarily the result of communist aggression or, at least, that "the postwar drawing of lines between the Communists and the Western powers ... probably had a historical inevitability to it" (Halberstam 1972: 132), and therefore requires little more to be said. But what we have come to know as the Cold War had its origins long before the Second World War, in the growing conflict between capital and labour, of which the crushing of the Paris Commune in 1871 was just one shattering illustration. If, however, one must fix a more precise and recent time, it was when American, British, French and Japanese troops invaded Russia in 1918, to try to defeat a revolution which they saw as a real threat – and as a concrete alternative model of development – to their economic security (Hobsbawm 1994: 63–70; Foglesong 1995; Bradley 1968).

While the priority of the new Soviet leadership in the waning days of the First World War was peace at virtually any price, including the ceding of vast Western territories, "it was the West which was on the offensive, not the Soviets" (Fleming 1961: 31). Intervention failed to obliterate the new Soviet state, but it transformed what had been a surprisingly bloodless revolution into a wasteful civil war (Fleming 1961: 16–35), forced the USSR to adopt a strategy of immediate survival, rather than one of long-term planning, and distorted the subsequent course of Soviet political development (Hobsbawm 1994: 64). As Fleming observes:

> It is difficult to conclude that the originally pacifist Reds would or could have created a powerful new war machine without the early and persistent intervention of the West. When they were encircled with Western-armed forces on

all sides there was nothing to do except to go to war, and to make the war total.... They had to do so in order to survive. In the fires of this grim testing time they also hammered out the machinery of the totalitarian state.... Evolution in the Soviet Union would have proceeded much more slowly and, in all probability, with much greater moderation, without the scourging compulsion of Western intervention. (196: 31–2)

Intervention revealed much about the nature of the Western governments. In Britain, Lloyd George's coalition government was counter-revolutionary and, ideologically, its chief strategists behaved in a way that "was always in counterpoint to the danger from the Left as they perceived it, attacking and counterattacking as political opportunities arose" (Scally 1975: 11). Lloyd George himself described his post-war reconstruction programme as "a cheap insurance against Bolshevism" (in Foster 1976: 33), so it was not out of character for his government to send troops into Russia against the Bolsheviks. Meanwhile, despite the high moral arguments that Woodrow Wilson would launch at Versailles, the United States not only sent its troops into Russia. A few months after a general strike brought Seattle to a halt, Wilson's Attorney General, A. Mitchell Palmer, unleashed a domestic assault on "reds" (Landau 1988: 27; Zinn 1980: 366–9). The glittering prosperity of the USA in the twenties was just the thin veneer of a decade which began with the severe repression of progressive forces, saw the execution in 1927 of Sacco and Vanzetti, two Italian anarchists framed on a murder charge in Massachusetts, and culminated in the Great Depression.

The Birth of the Official Cold War

The 1920s intensified many contradictions in the process of capitalist development (Dobb 1963: 321ff.) and the symptoms of economic prosperity that have defined this era in our collective cultural memory were variable and precarious at best. In Weimar Germany, an artistic efflorescence obscured an emerging alliance of capital and militarism. In Italy, Mussolini's Fascists had taken political power by 1922. And in Britain, many parts of its industrial heartland were already suffering from severe recession during the "roaring twenties". The British General Strike of 1926 (M. Morris 1976) predated the collapse of the US stock market by three years.

During the thirties, throughout much of Europe, unprecedented crisis in the capitalist economies and the threat of social upheaval encouraged fascist tendencies – that particular combination of populism and corporatism – whose origins can be traced to patterns of nationalist and anti-socialist politics that arose in the second half of the nineteenth century (Müller 1976; Eley 1983; Hall 1976). Even the United States was not immune to such tendencies (Williams 1969). But it was Germany, poor in overseas colonies, seeking to colonise Europe (Dobb 1963: 374–5), that began what would soon prove to be a second world war.[1]

By the time the United States and Britain had been forced finally to engage Germany in military struggle – less from conviction than necessity – it was clear that such a war was regarded as a distraction from the long-term objective of destroying the Soviet Union and eliminating the socialist challenge to Western capitalist power. It might even be the means of achieving that end. As Landau notes,

> Washington did not recognise the Soviet government until 1933. At the Locarno Conference of 1925–1926, British and French diplomats sought to involve Germany in an anti-Soviet bloc; at Munich in September 1938, British prime minister Neville Chamberlain gave Germany a "free hand" to invade Russia. (1988: 44)

Whatever else it was, at least fascism was counter-revolutionary. So by the time that war against Germany was inevitable, an alliance with the Soviet Union was largely opportunistic. The West pursued the war with a dual intent – of defeating Germany and, with any luck, of seeing an end to the USSR. Well into 1942, Churchill, who had helped to engineer the British invasion of Russia in 1918 (Hitchens 1990: 191–7), took the view that Russia was an "'expendable' ally" (Wirth 1964: 356). So when Hitler invaded the Soviet Union, the opening of a second front, to take pressure off the Soviets, was never a priority. It emerged as a tactical reality only when it was clear that the Russians were unilaterally turning back the German forces (Landau 1988: 30). But, even then, Churchill argued for the Allies to invade "the soft underbelly" of Europe from the south, chiefly to have Western armies in the Balkans before the Russians could reach there (Fleming 1961: 154). In much the same way, the invasion of Normandy was designed to get Western troops into Germany before the Russians could invade Hitler's domain – and especially Berlin, the symbolic prize – on their own (Fleming 1961: 167; Wirth 1964: 844ff.).

In this vein, many of the West's tactics during the war can only be understood in terms of a desire to exploit German aggression in order

---

1. Of course, one must also see the rise of German fascism as a historical process. Although Hitler would make much of the fact that the Versailles settlement over-burdened Germany, even Keynes, in his work, *The Economic Consequences of the Peace* (1919) referred to it as a "Carthaginian peace" (Keynes 1971: 22–3). While one of Keynes's principal fears was that the treaty might lead to the kind of revolution that had occurred in Russia, he was right to anticipate the adverse social consequences of such a settlement.

to defeat the Soviet Union or, after that had failed, to rely on the Red Army to bear the brunt of the effort to defeat the Germans and to exhaust itself in the process (Fleming 1961: 155–60; Cronin 1996: 18–19). Which it undoubtedly did. The USSR lost as many as 25 million people in the war and suffered immense economic losses (Thompson 1981: 58; Cronin 1996: 16; Wirth 1964: 847, 885–6). Yet, despite the pivotal role that the Russians had played in the defeat of fascism – which Truman and others had willingly conceded in mid-1945 (Landau 1988: 35) – any doubts that they had always been the principal enemy quickly vanished, as the West moved to revive a vanquished Germany, while adopting an increasingly belligerent stance toward the Soviets, whose own priority was to ensure their future security and to undertake the essential tasks of reconstruction (Cronin 1996: 19).

Nevertheless, hostility on the part of the West was even more imperative than it had been in 1918. At that time, the United States and Western Europe had recognised that the prosperity of capitalism depended upon external markets (cf. Hobson 1902). But the Second World War hastened the disintegration of the colonial empires that had guaranteed them. Moreover, the Soviet Union seemed to offer a clear socialist alternative for developing countries now striving for independence. Thus, the post-colonial era presented many insecurities for the West and strengthened the resolve of men such as Churchill, Truman and Dulles to resume their old adversarial attitude toward the Soviet Union at a time when the war had incapacitated the Russian economy and the United States possessed two-thirds of the world's industrial capacity (Landau 1988: 34).

Even before the end of the war, there had been intimations of a renewal of the pre-war anti-communism which had been such an integral feature of fascism itself. Right after VE Day, the USA cancelled lend-lease shipments to the USSR, even though the Russians were due to enter the war against Japan (Wirth 1964: 885). But more than anything else, it was the deployment of the atomic bomb – in August 1945 – that served unambiguous notice on the Soviet Union that Roosevelt's policies were dead and that, under Truman and Churchill, the Western capitalist powers had no intention of transforming a war-time alliance of convenience into post-war coexistence. By the autumn, the USA had already effectively decided to keep German war reparations to a minimum, in order to transform at least the American zone of occupied Germany into "a barrier to Russia, the Left, and socialization, and a region fully oriented toward the larger United States goals for Europe" (Kolko and Kolko 1972: 114). In March 1946, Churchill – who, at the anniversary gathering of the Anti-Socialist and Anti-Communist Union in 1933, had described Mussolini as a political leader who had "established a centre of orientation from which the countries involved in a hand-to-hand struggle against socialism should not hesitate to be guided" (Melograni 1976: 233) – gave his famous "Iron Curtain" speech in Fulton, Missouri. As he publicly revived his pre-war hostility toward the USSR, President Truman, who, as a senator, had been among those who "had seemed to welcome the heavy loss of both Russian and German lives as serving American interests" (Thompson 1981: 58), applauded from the platform (Williams 1962: 260). In the summer, the USA terminated reparations to the Soviets from the Western zones of divided Germany (Williams 1962: 260).

By the time that the Rockefeller Foundation president, John Foster Dulles, became Eisenhower's Secretary of State in 1952, Western aims were fairly clear. Dulles, the son of missionaries, who had advocated an alliance with Germany and Japan as early as the 1920s and who had "labored diligently as late as 1939 to work out a broad understanding with Nazi Germany and a militarized Japan" (Williams 1962: 275), based on the conviction that the Soviet Union was the real and common enemy, announced just before assuming office that he would liberate the Russians and the Chinese from "atheistic international communism" (Williams 1962: 275–6).

As early as 1941, however, the Americans and the British were already engaged in efforts to create a post-war international order based on the long-term financial stability of the global capitalist economy. The institutional framework for this was established in the summer of 1944 at Bretton Woods, New Hampshire, with the creation of the so-called Bretton Woods institutions, which included the International Monetary Fund and the International Bank for Reconstruction and Development (the World Bank). Within thirty years, the contradictions and the limitations of this institutional arrangement would be revealed. But in 1947, as the policies of these new institutions took shape, the agenda of the World Bank, under the direction of John J. McCloy, a close associate of the Rockefeller family, quickly came to reflect the Truman administration's view that US security depended on a firm anti-communist line. As a result, the Bank's first loan went to France, to stabilise a war-torn economy believed to be under immediate threat from the left (Bird 1992: 290–91).

In the meantime, it was the Marshall Plan which was designed to restore a market for America's post-war surplus and so prevent another depression (Williams 1962: 271–2). But the point of ensuring that Europe's recovery was comprehensive and rapid cannot be understood without reference as well to the US policy of containment of the Soviet

Union. That policy was first publicly formulated in July 1947, in an anonymous article by George Kennan[2] entitled "The Sources of Soviet Conduct", which appeared in *Foreign Affairs*, the journal of the Council on Foreign Relations (CFR) (Stephanson 1989: 1989: 73). As the CFR is one of the most crucial club-like links between major corporate and financial interests and government (Domhoff 1970: 112ff.)[3] and the article was written by a senior member of the Foreign Service who would soon become US Ambassador to the USSR (Kennan 1951), it must be regarded as representative of establishment views. And although it has become fashionable in recent years for Kennan to be represented as having been a voice of moderation, his view that communism was a "malignant parasite which feeds only on diseased tissue" (Kennan 1978: 63) was neither moderate nor atypical of the times. In 1931, two years before he was posted to Moscow, he had not only expressed the same Manichaean views that would distinguish some of his more extreme contemporaries in Washington before and after the Second World War, but could envisage no common ground for compromise between the USA and the USSR, maintaining that "the two systems cannot even exist together in the same world unless an economic cordon is put around one or the other of them" (in Stephanson 1989: 7). By the late thirties, such views left little room for an objective assessment of the imminent dangers presented by Nazi Germany. And, indeed, Kennan thought Soviet fears about German expansionist designs were exaggerated, while he regarded any anti-fascist co-operation with the USSR as unwarranted (Stephanson 1989: 11, 21). His views in the immediate post-war period were scarcely more broad-minded, and, in 1948, as the Director of State Department Policy Planning, he argued that "It is better to have a strong regime in power than a liberal government if it is indulgent and relaxed and penetrated by Communists" (in Landau 1988: 33). This was the so-called voice of reason in Washington. Not surprisingly, "Kennan's warnings about Soviet intentions were immediately seized upon by [Secretary of Defense] Forrestal as intellectual and historical evidence of the great struggle ahead" (Halberstam 1972: 134). According to Lincoln Gordon, who worked on the Marshall Plan and was later US ambassador to Brazil, Kennan's idea of contain-

---

2. The article, published under the pseudonym "X", was an elaboration of the so-called "long telegram" which he had sent to Washington in February 1946 when he was Chargé d'Affaires at the US Embassy in Moscow (cf. Kennan 1978).

3. Among the roles of the CFR, which was established in 1921, was "to provide a revolving door through which candidate members of future and present establishments may circulate, and a fish tank of talent from which incoming Presidents and Secretaries of State may select (Hitchens 1991: 306; cf. Horowitz 1971: 144–6). Despite this, it affects an air of studious neutrality, not least through the publication of its journal *Foreign Affairs*.

ment was taken to refer as much to the possibility of national communist party victories as it was to any actual Soviet expansion (United States Information Service 1997). As such, it was justified by the ostensible need to ensure that the war-time devastation of the European economy would not provide any opportunity for such parties to come to power, especially in France, Italy and Greece (Leffler 1992: 194–8; Carew 1987: 6–18).

It is useful to recall that, even in the early 1950s, the French Communist Party was being described by a leading US journalist as "the most valuable piece of property Russia owns within the Atlantic world" (White 1953: 346), and that the situation in Italy was regarded as even more alarming (Allen and Stevenson 1974: 8–10). The significance of the role of US aid in confronting this state of affairs was regarded as so great that, well over a decade later, people such as Gordon (who would later help to orchestrate US support for a military coup against the elected president of Brazil) (Colby and Dennett 1995: 442; Langguth 1975: 90–91) were still citing the post-war rejuvenation of the Italian economy as an example of how to eradicate poverty in the Third World (e.g., in the poverty-stricken northeast of Brazil) in the face of communist resistance to what he called "the free road to development" (Gordon 1963: 23–5).

Such an assessment is particularly ironic when one considers the condition of contemporary Italy. During the three decades since the end of the war, household income distribution after tax had hardly changed. That is to say, the so-called "economic miracle" which Italy experienced in the late fifties and early sixties, founded as it had been on cheap labour, had hardly advanced the conditions of the working class (Moss and Rogers 1980: 168, 171). In 1980, many rural communities continued to suffer from "material inequalities ... at least as great as a quarter of a century ago", while, in urban areas, which had attracted a great wave of migration from the countryside, numerous households lived on "low-paid and clandestine employment" (Moss and Rogers 1980: 176, 180). Fifteen years later, the official unemployment nationally was over 12 percent.

In retrospect, Italy may be adjudged an even more instructive example for the developing world than Gordon and others imagined, not only in terms of the problems it presented, but the solutions it was offered. But in early 1947, it had seemed that the Italian Communist Party – the largest in the world outside of the Soviet Union (Blum 1986: 23) and one which had gained much genuine support during its years of resistance to fascism – would win the general election the following year. Even when it did not, the threat of communist influence seemed to persist – and it is not difficult to understand why. It was the Marshall Plan which, above all, helped to shift the political balance toward the Christian Democrats, despite the fact that it was a party that was "riddled through with collaborators, monarchists and plain unreconstructed fascists" (Blum 1986: 24). But this was not done with financial aid alone. Working within the framework of the Economic Cooperation Administration (ECA), which ran the Marshall Plan, was the newly formed Central Intelligence Agency (CIA), which engaged in covert operations in both France and Italy, where it subsidised anti-communist newspapers and trade unions (Bird 1992: 302; Pisani 1991: 81–121). The National Security Council in Washington authorised the CIA to subvert the normal electoral process in these countries (Leffler 1992: 196). As a result, the centre-right steadily consolidated its power. In Italy, the Christian Democrats would remain in power for the next thirty years.

More importantly, however, the Marshall Plan – whether justified in humanitarian or anti-communist terms – helped the United States to establish its influence in the rebuilding of capitalist society in post-war Europe, which was regarded as essential to the health of the US economy. It had emerged, among other things, out of a paper co-authored by David Rockefeller (Hitchens 1990: 311), while the final draft of the Economic Cooperation Act which established the Plan was largely the product of a committee chaired by Secretary of Commerce, millionaire Averell Harriman, and composed of individuals drawn substantially from the Committee for Economic Development (CED). This organisation had been founded soon after the United States entered the war, with the deliberate aim of raising and resolving issues about post-war planning (Eakins 1969: 144–5, 164). Not only did the CED's chairman, Paul Hoffman, become the head of the ECA, but the "top officials of ECA were largely recruited from the CED staff and officers" (Eakins 1969: 166). The Plan was clearly the child of the liberal corporate community in the United States.

At the same time, it also suggests how the Malthusian creed first became part of the rationalisation of Western programmes to inhibit the influence of revolutionary forces throughout the developing world. As early as 1951, an article in the US publication *Senior Scholastic* highlighted the increasingly popular view that "over-population creates a breeding ground for communism ... [because] Communist propaganda thrives on poverty and discontent" (in Wilmoth and Ball 1992: 646). It was Italy, however, which was one of the first targets of such assumptions – for no other reason than it was the Western European country regarded as most vulnerable to communism (Phillips 1948). High levels of unemployment, which were hardly unexpected, and an equally unsurprising post-war baby boom, served to fuel the argument that Italy was over-populated. The US encouraged Italian emigration – as did the Christian Democratic government (Pacciardi 1954: 445) – and, according to the chief of the ECA mission to Italy, Marshall Plan funds helped to rebuild Italy's merchant navy in order to provide transport for emigrants (Pisani 1991: 114–15). The ECA even "suggested that 'sympathetic consideration' be given to Italian requests for loans from Export–Import Bank or International Bank 'for specific projects of economic development in Latin America which could absorb large numbers of Italian emigrants'" (Pisani 1991: 116).

Broadly, then, the Marshall Plan not only assumed the task of postwar reconstruction in Europe but did so in a way which effectively created the dominant pattern of US foreign assistance, where "dollar aid abroad solved the foreign trade problem, which in turn solved the problem of full production at home" (Eakins 1969: 166). In the process, it also established development aid as an instrument of the emergent Cold War. It began to do the same with Malthusian thinking. But this process had actually begun several decades earlier, as demographic thinking came under the patronage of the US corporate elite at a time when it was emerging as one of the principal influences on the shaping of US foreign policy.

Notestein, the Demographic Transition and the Cold War

As the Caldwells have pointed out, the "population field" in the United States arose within a framework which was largely determined by eugenic interests (1986: 4ff.). It was "the differential rate of reproduction by social class and supposedly related inherent characteristics of intelligence and even character that had brought most of the real professionals to the study of fertility" (1986: 7). This had manifested itself primarily in concerns about the relative fertility of immigrant groups. In the 1880s, Francis Amasa Walker, a professor of political economy at Yale, at one time the president of MIT, head of the American Economics Association and Commissioner of Indian Affairs (MIT Libraries 1995; Folbre 1994: 184), had harnessed Malthusian thinking to the idea of the closing of the US frontier. He suggested that, as the opportunities for continental expansion had come to an end, large-scale immigration could no longer play a favourable role – especially if they were no longer the northern and western European immigrants of an earlier period. Now, according to Walker (1896), the majority of immigrants were representatives of a "degraded peasantry ... beaten men from beaten races; representing the worst failures in the struggle for existence", who were depressing the general standard of living in the United States and thereby having a negative impact on the birth-rate of the white native-born population.

Over the next two decades, concern about a decline in family size among the so-called "best" stock, that is, the upper and upper-middle classes, became an obsession among people as diverse as Teddy Roosevelt and E.A. Ross, a president of the American Sociological Society, who was one of the leading figures in the emergence of a modern sociology that reflected the interests of late-nineteenth-century corporate capitalism (Smith 1970: 77–8; Hofstadter 1955: 171). But it was Walker, writing at a time when immigrants were increasingly regarded as a threat to the economic and political security of the very people whose income was derived from their labour, who especially voiced the concern of that elite that such foreigners were engendering a class conflict that otherwise would not have existed (Folbre 1994: 184).

It was portentous that someone with Walker's ideas was appointed the superintendent of the Ninth and Tenth US Censuses (in 1870–72 and 1879–81 respectively) (MIT Libraries 1995), from which vantage point he could talk with apparent authority. Although it was not until the 1920s that the government actually restricted such immigration, the census data themselves prompted prominent figures such as Woodrow Wilson – who, as president, would advocate the self-determination of peoples – to echo Walker in expressing concern that the wrong kind of European immigrant was contaminating the "sturdy stocks" from northern Europe with whom they both identified the vitality of the United States. "Now", wrote Wilson,

> there came multitudes of men of the lowest class from the South of Italy and men of the meaner sort out of Hungary and Poland, men out of the ranks where there was neither skill nor energy nor any initiative of quick intelligence; and they came in numbers which increased from year to year, as if the countries of the south of Europe were disburdening themselves of the more sordid and hapless elements of their population. (in Hitchens 1990: 130)

Such sentiments commingled with apprehensions about the equally sordid *ideas* that these new immigrants brought with them or were at-tracted to. For Walker, the new immigrants – Hungarians, southern Italians, Russian Jews – had "proved themselves the ready tools of demagogues in defying the law, in destroying property, and in working violence" (Walker 1896). This, rather than the exploitation of labour, would be described as the ultimate source of the labour unrest that characterised the first decade of the new century (Zinn 1980: 314–49; Cahn 1980; Banister 1925). It was an echo of Macaulay, but also a taste of what would come, after the Russian Revolution gave the issue of immigration a political edge that would enlarge the eugenics agenda.

But before that, in 1888, Columbia University's Mayo-Smith, one of the first teachers of what could be considered modern demography, had written of the need to restrict immigration into the United States to prevent the country from being overwhelmed by the "depraved dregs of European civilization" (in Hodgson 1983: 18). One of his most renowned students was Walter Willcox, who taught "applied ethics" and then "social statistics" at Cornell University. Willcox, like his teacher, identified enough with eugenic thinking that at one time he served on the Advisory Council of Charles Davenport's Eugenics Society (Hodgson 1983: 18–19; Ryder 1984: 6–7). It would be a student of Willcox, Frank Notestein (1902–83), who came to be regarded as "one of the architects of modern demography" (Ryder 1984: 5) and who, through the 1940s and 1950s, played a critical role in transforming eugenic and Malthusian concerns into an instrument of Cold War political thinking.

A major figure in Notestein's rise to eminence was Frederick Osborn (Ryder 1984: 7), a member of a prominent New York family whose American Museum of Natural History was a major focal point of the American eugenics movement and the home of the Galton Society. It had sponsored the Second International Congress of Eugenics in New York in 1921 (Osborn 1974), whose 300 delegates included Henry Fairfield Osborn (the museum's president, Congress president and Frederick's uncle), Madison Grant, Harry Laughlin, Lothrop Stoddard, and the future president of the United States, Herbert Hoover (Mehler 1988). Frederick Osborn himself had retired from business before the age of 40 and had undertaken studies at the Museum with the anthropologist Clark Wissler, a prominent figure in Galton Society circles (Ross 1985). Osborn went on to be a delegate to the First International Population Conference in 1927 and was among a small handful of North American and British population scientists who sought to promote differential reproduction within society, based on their ideas about the relative genetical value of different classes. By the late 1930s, he had become secretary of the American Eugenics Society (Mehler 1994), and in 1937, despite a reputation for being less conspicuously racist than his uncle Henry, was one of the founders, along with textile millionaire Wickliffe Draper and Harry Laughlin, of the Pioneer Fund, which remains a unique source of financial support for academic racism (Mehler 1994).

Osborn and his close colleagues played a key role in the development of a modern field of demography that began with an interest in eugenic questions surrounding differential fertility (Caldwell and Caldwell 1986: 7–8) and which, especially after the Second World War, would be transformed under their financial aegis to give a new impetus to Malthusian thinking in Western development policy. One of the first sources of funding for such research was the Milbank Memorial Fund, which had been founded after the First World War. In the late twenties, one of the Fund's trustees, Thomas Cochran of the powerful Morgan Bank, proposed that the Fund's ongoing work in public health should continue only on condition that it focused on birth control as well. This led to the creation of the Population Research Office in 1928 under the initial direction of Edgar Sydenstricker, an economist with whom Notestein co-authored his first publication, "Differential Fertility According to Social Class" (Gordon 1976: 307). Sydenstricker was soon joined there by Notestein and Clyde Kiser (Caldwell and Caldwell 1986: 10; Notestein and Sydenstricker 1930).

After obtaining his doctorate, Notestein had gone to work for the Milbank Fund. But in 1936, Osborn persuaded the Fund, of which he was a trustee, to establish an Office of Population Research (OPR) in Princeton's School of Public and International Affairs (a school his father and Albert Milbank had helped to found in 1930) and which would also be supported by the Rockefeller Foundation (Gordon 1976: 396; Leitch 1978). Notestein became its director. Over the next decade, the OPR

> became a kind of sanctuary for eugenicist demographers. Kingsley Davis, Clyde Kiser, Frank Notestein, Dudley Kirk, and Frank Lorimer[4] all worked there. When Rockefeller financed the Population Council, these five men moved to it immediately. (Gordon 1976: 396)

It is clear that Notestein was enlisted to help legitimise the issue of birth control as a critical element of Cold War development thinking – and equally clear who his patrons were. During the 1940s, the Milbank Memorial Fund and the Rockefeller Foundation (both of which had demonstrated interests in China since the late 1920s), had become increasingly concerned about the potential impact of demographic growth in developing countries. In late 1948, it sent Notestein and others to the Far East, to visit Japan, China, Indonesia and the Philippines. One of Notestein's conclusions from the trip was that there was a need to develop a suitably cheap and effective method of contraception. "We doubt", he wrote, "that any other work offers a better opportunity for

---

4. Kiser was a president of the American Eugenics Society in the 1960s (Osborn 1974: 123); Lorimer, who represented the Planned Parenthood Federation of America in the International Committee on Planned Parenthood, which was established in 1948 and which became the International Planned Parenthood Federation in 1952 (Katz 1995), had been on the staff of the Eugenics Research Association in Washington in the 1930s (Lorimer 1931: 99); and Davis was on the Steering Committee of the World Population Emergency Campaign in the 1960s (Katz 1995).

contributing to Asia's and the world's fundamental problems of human welfare" (in Caldwell and Caldwell 1986: 19). The peasants struggling for land in China, the Philippines, Indochina and India would have disagreed. But, clearly, birth control was about to become one of the instruments of Western development policy.

The Chinese Revolution and the Perils of Modernisation

The victory of the Chinese communists in 1949 had a profound effect not only on the Rockefeller Foundation and specifically on John D. Rockefeller 3rd, but also on the Ford Foundation (see Chapter 6). In their history of the latter in the field of population, the Caldwells only regard the increasingly global perspective of Ford after 1949 as a reflection of a "rapidly increasing belief in Third World development", coupled to a growing concern about the potential impact of population growth in developing countries (Caldwell and Caldwell 1986: 21). They neglect not only the way that the Ford Foundation was to reflect the West's Cold War ideology, but also the fact that its immense resources were rapidly to become an instrument of US geo-political policy. However, in more practical terms, in the summer of 1952, Rockefeller convened a special "crisis conference" on population at Williamsburg, Virginia (Caldwell and Caldwell 1986: 25), and it was Notestein who formulated the agenda (Ryder 1984: 13). Later that year, Rockefeller established the Population Council, which drew financial support from the mid-1950s onwards from the Ford Foundation and, after 1958, from the Rockefeller Foundation (Barnes 1973: 662).

Notwithstanding the recent defeat of the Nazi eugenic state, the Population Council showed unmistakable signs of eugenic sympathies during its first decade. It provided funding for the American Eugenics Society (AES) (Osborn 1974: 122), and in 1955 it offered to support the *Eugenics Quarterly* for a period of three years if matching funds could be found (Gordon 1976: 396). Neither effort is surprising, considering that Frederick Osborn, the Council's first head, was an officer of the AES almost continuously from 1935 until his death in 1973 and president of the Pioneer Fund until 1956 (Mehler 1994).

Around 1961, Notestein succeeded Osborn as president of the Population Council (Barnes 1973: 662–3; Ryder 1984: 11). Under both men, the Council played an important role, not merely in theoretical research on interesting population questions, but (in keeping with Notestein's conclusions after his 1948 trip to the Far East for the Rockefeller Foundation) in the development of new birth control techniques. Some of these – including Norplant – would prove quite controversial, as they were used particularly within the framework of Western-sponsored population-control programmes which provided the means for Third World women to limit their fertility under circumstances that were rarely voluntary in the full meaning of the term (Hartmann 1987: 196–200). Osborn continued to maintain that such devices would contribute to eugenic ends (Meehan 1996). But Notestein had moved on to larger questions of how birth control could be applied in the defence of the political and economic interests of the West in an age of decolonisation and revolution.

Most notably, during the Second World War, Notestein and his colleagues at Princeton, who did considerable work for the State Department over these years (Szreter 1993: 678), began to rework the concept of the "demographic transition"[5] as a way of understanding the evolution of patterns of human fertility. Judging from their book *Future Population of Europe and the Soviet Union*, it was also a way of formulating policy to reconcile the decline in European population growth with an increase among potential competitors. As Notestein and his co-authors wrote:

> The fact is that the nations of Northwestern and Central Europe are at the end of their period of population growth. Other peoples will increase more rapidly, and the spread of industrial techniques will bring them growing power. Successful policy depends on recognition of that fact ... the shifting balance of world population will put new strains on fixed economic and political arrangements ... neither justice nor peace can be maintained unless orderly ways are found for adapting such arrangements to the needs of a changing world. Practically policy must be directed toward relieving mounting population pressures at their source. (in Ryder 1984: 12)

With this, Notestein reflected the increasing pressure to revise demographic theory to allow for the fact that rapid modernisation might not lead to fertility decline before it produced a threatening level of social and political instability. On the eve of communist victory in China, he had helped to provide the theoretical basis for the development of

---

5. The idea of the demographic transition was based largely on the perceived experience of Western Europe and, as such, unquestioningly reflected much of the received wisdom about the emergence of modern Europe. The prevailing view was that this had coincided with the appearance of a new mode of rationality, which had manifested itself economically in the development of capitalism and socially in a decline in family size. Both trends were taken as signs of a transition to a less tradition-bound, more individualistic ethos (cf. Stone 1977). Most importantly, they were regarded as unique to Europe, and to a Europe, moreover, that was envisaged as having an economic and social existence that was largely independent of the rest of the world. The result was that this transition was readily conceptualised as the product of peculiarly European conditions and that the problem of "modernisation" became one of how Europe could export its achievements and make them take root among "traditional" societies.

birth control as an instrument of Western policy in the period after the
Second World War.

By 1954, Eugene Staley, a senior international economist at the
Stanford Research Institute, highlighted the importance of Notestein's
views in his book *The Future of Underdeveloped Countries: Political Implications of Economic Development*, a work that was published by the Council
on Foreign Relations. Recalling the views of Macaulay eighty years earlier,
Staley made it clear that the American establishment was now willing,
in Notestein's words, to attribute "political explosion, and the economic
disorganisation which accompanies it", to unchecked population growth,
rather than to social injustice or inequalities in resource distribution.
Thus, he posed the crucial question:

> Can birth rates be reduced within a peasant society, as a means of facilitating
> its transformation into an industrial society, instead of waiting for birth rates
> to fall as a delayed consequence of such a transformation? (Staley 1954: 284)

The perils of modernisation and the threats it presented to the interests and security of the West would continue to preoccupy Western
leaders and intellectuals for the next thirty years. But during that time,
the frustrations it entailed in "facilitating its transformation" along
desired channels would turn many academics and technocrats into im-
patient pragmatists in the pay of the government and the corporate
elite. One of the most illustrious of them was Robert McNamara, who
left a brief tenure as head of the Ford Motor Company to become
Kennedy's Secretary of Defense. McNamara, who knew nothing of life
in the developing world, nevertheless referred to modernisation as "the
difficult transition from transitional to modern societies" and worried
about how a "sweeping surge of development ... has turned traditionally
listless areas of the world into seething caldrons of change" (in Shafer
1988: 80). Later, when he was about to assume his next role as president
at the World Bank, when he still knew comparatively little about the
developing world, except that it had enormous capacities to challenge
its oppressors, he published an account of his years as Secretary of
Defense, *The Essence of Security*, in which he wrote that the Soviet Union
and China "regard the modernization process as an ideal environment
for the growth of Communism" (1968: 147). Of course, it was the West
primarily that had taken this view, at least since the end of the Second
World War. As a result, it was Western leaders who had come to the
general conclusion that, if modernisation was inevitable, it was best to
pass through it as rapidly as possible and to manage its destabilising
excesses firmly, even aggressively, to prevent it from becoming a source
of "opportunities" for the Soviet Union.

In that same spirit, in the late fifties, Staley had moved on from abstract questions – such as whether birth rates could be reduced in order to enhance the process of modernisation – to more practical tasks. He reviewed the final manuscript of India's Planning Commission's popular presentation of its Second Five-Year Plan, in which the Ford Foundation had played a significant role (India Planning Commission 1958: vi, viii). And a few years later, as president of the Stanford Research Institute, he showed what an economist could really do to modernise a peasant society. In June 1961, Staley headed an official mission to Vietnam to assess the need for the USA to assume more of the costs of South Vietnam's war efforts (United States Defense Department 1971: 62–3). His report's starting point was a classic statement of Cold War paranoia, which wholly failed to appreciate how the specific historical problems of the region had given rise to a nationalist peasant insurgency. "Vietnam", it said,

> is today under attack in a bitter, total struggle which involves its survival as a free nation. Its enemy, the Viet Cong, is ruthless, resourceful, and elusive. The enemy is supplied, reinforced, and centrally directed by the international Communist apparatus operating through Hanoi. To defeat it requires the mobilization of the entire economic, military, psychological, and social resources of the country and vigorous support from the United States. (in United States Defense Department 1971: 63)

The report not only recommended that the USA commit itself to a significant increase in military forces in Vietnam, but endorsed a proposal, known thereafter as "The Staley Plan", for the resettlement of Vietnamese peasants into "strategic hamlets" (Scheer 1995: 153), where, surrounded by barbed wire and troops, they would be isolated from Vietcong influence. This was controlled modernisation with a vengeance.

In even more formidable fashion, the economist Walt Rostow, whose most notable book, *The Stages of Economic Growth* (1952), was subtitled "A Non-Communist Manifesto", who (echoing Kennan's metaphor in his long telegram) had described communism as "a disease of the transition to modernity", became the Director of Policy and Planning in Kennedy's State Department and then Johnson's chief adviser on Vietnam (Frank 1969: 28; Marr 1995: 211). Bringing to his task a definition of communism which set no apparent limit to what he would inflict on the Vietnamese in the name of Western modernisation, Rostow – who had gloated to his Washington staff over the murder of Che Guevara (Halberstam 1972: 197) – was the most persistent and unwavering supporter of the repressive puppet regime in the south. Calling him "the biggest Cold Warrior I've got", Kennedy sent him on the administration's first fact-finding mission to South Vietnam, an initiative that suggested not only the new president's hard-line views, but also the close relationship of policy-makers and modernisation theorists such as Rostow.

In the long run, however, the Vietnam War was to prove to people such as McNamara – although not to Rostow (Rostow 1996) – that a military strategy could escalate indefinitely without any significant results. The logic of the systems analysis that he loved eventually would suggest that it was time to devise more effective ways to control and direct the process of modernisation toward desired ends. A wide variety of measures eventually needed to be enlisted in this cause. International birth control programmes, which the World Bank under McNamara endorsed, were one. For those who regarded birth control as too problematical, however, there were the more virile options of covert operations and counterinsurgency, which began to play a key role in US policy during the Kennedy years (Metz 1995). And there was the Green Revolution, to which the World Bank, beginning during the tenure of one of McNamara's predecessors, Eugene Black (a former senior vice-president of Chase Manhattan), had lent its weight, with the backing of the Ford and Rockefeller Foundations (see Chapter 6). Many of the same premises that informed Wolf Ladejinsky's advocacy of capitalist land reform (see Chapter 5) were incorporated into the strategy of the Green Revolution. As such, it would turn out to be less about actually enhancing the food security of the poor in developing countries than about securing the economic interests of the United States, by enhancing the role and influence of multinational capital and helping to control the uneasy course of change in agrarian societies (cf. Galli 1978, 1981).

Militarising Malthus: The Career of William Draper

From that perspective, it is not surprising that what Mass describes as "the first official body of the US government to advocate Neo-Malthusian policies" (1976: 41; Piotrow 1973: 36ff.; Caldwell and Caldwell 1986) was the President's Committee to Study the United States Military Assistance Program (Zlotnick 1961: 685). This committee, chaired by General William H. Draper, Jr, was subsequently known as "The Draper Committee". Draper himself would come to play a conspicuous role in national and international population policy-making, eventually becoming the head of the fund-raising arm of Planned Parenthood (Chase 1977: 383). When he died in 1974, an obituary appeared in the *Population Index*, written by Frank Notestein (1975).

An understanding of Draper's career is crucial to tracing the way in which population issues gained prominence in US government strategic planning during the post-war years. But, first, it is important to appreciate the general role of the Draper Committee and similarly appointed groups in the world of US policy-making and strategic thinking. As Domhoff has noted, they "are almost without exception headed by members of the power elite and staffed by the employees and scholars of the foundations, associations, and institutes" such as Rockefeller, Ford, Carnegie, Rand, the Council on Foreign Relations, etc. In this way, the views of important economic interests within US society are elevated to a higher level, as they are recast as the recommendations of special committees (1970: 134–5).

A precedent had been established with the Gaither Committee – officially, the Panel of the Office of Defense Mobilisation Science Advisory Committee – which Eisenhower convened in 1957 to examine the question of military preparedness (Bird 1992: 465). Its chair, H. Rowan Gaither, was a San Francisco lawyer, banker and a prominent member of the Ford Foundation. As it happened, he was also a close business associate of Draper in one of the first "venture capital" firms in California – Draper, Gaither and Anderson – established in 1958. A decade earlier, moreover, Gaither had headed the committee whose report had defined a new global role for the Ford Foundation (Rosen 1985: 6–7) (see Chapter 6). And he had already been a pivotal figure in the emergence of the RAND Corporation, a non-governmental think-tank with special interest in weapons system development and strategic planning.[6]

Created by Douglas Aircraft for the US Air Force (at that time still the Army Air Force) in 1946, Project RAND (an acronym for "*R*esearch *an*d *D*evelopment"), as it was originally called, was re-established with Ford Foundation assistance as an independent corporation the following year. While it remained closely associated with the Air Force (Smith 1966), it developed into a crucial link "between the military services and the intellectual community in the name of national security" (Yergin 1978: 361; cf. Freedman 1986). As a result, the Gaither Committee in 1957 was "heavily peopled and supported by RAND intellectuals" (Morris 1988: 140). By the sixties, run by trustees who represented major US corporations (Mobil, Standard Oil of California, Citicorp, among others) and who were often also members of the

---

6. Gaither maintained an indirect continuing association with RAND through his partner, Frederick Anderson, who was a RAND trustee into the early 1960s (Domhoff 1970: 125).

Council on Foreign Relations, RAND had become one of a very limited number of select organisational mechanisms through which the American elite helped to define and operationalise US foreign policy (Domhoff 1970: 123–7).[7] The systems analysis which was one of the specialities of RAND became the governing intellectual paradigm in McNamara's Defense Department, which recruited many high-level personnel from RAND (Morris 1988: 179–83). The Ford Foundation, meanwhile, remains a major sponsor of RAND research in the area of national security and thereby maintains the links that the Foundation forged fifty years ago with the military and intelligence communities (RAND 1997).

The formation of RAND's Labour and Population Program in 1967 would underscore the extent to which population concerns had become a part of national security policy over the preceding decade since the Draper Committee, primarily constituted "to appraise the military assistance program and the relative emphasis the United States should place on economic aid" (Packenham 1973: 57–8), had been enjoined to include "the population problem" within its terms of reference (Piotrow 1973: 37–8). But it is the composition of this ten-person committee which reveals how seriously this must be regarded. Its chair was not only a partner of Rowan Gaither; nor only the chairman of the Mexican Light and Power Company (Piotrow 1973: 37), a relatively inconspicuous company whose board of directors happened to include General Lucius Clay, under whom Draper had served in the US zone of occupied Germany, and the Mexican banker Ortiz Mena, the first head of the Inter-American Development Bank. Most importantly, for most of his professional life, Draper had been an investment banker at Dillon, Read and Co., one of several prominent firms whose members occupied major roles in government with beguiling regularity, when they were not representing prominent industrial and financial corporations (Kolko 1969: 19, 22).

---

7. The first head of project RAND was General Curtis LeMay (Nieburg 1970: 246), who later became famous for his advice during the Vietnam War to "bomb the Vietnamese back into the stone age". Within a short time, however, it was considered advantageous to reestablish RAND independently of Douglas and the Air Force, and in 1948 it became a non-profit organization, with initial funding from the Ford Foundation (Nieburg 1970: 246). By 1963, RAND was 45 among the 500 largest military prime contractors for "experimental, developmental, test and research work" (Melman 1965: 328). By the end of the decade, while the bulk of its work was still for the Air Force, its agenda had broadened considerably, to include "brainstorming future generations of weapons and 'paper' analyses of new strategic and tactical doctrines" (Nieburg 1970: 202, 246). It was while he was at the RAND Corporation, for example, that Herman Kahn wrote his notorious work *On Thermonuclear War*.

One of Dillon, Read's senior figures, James Forrestal, had been Secretary of the Navy under Roosevelt and then the first Secretary of Defense under Truman. Among the small handful of men who set the early tone for the Cold War and the individual who most influenced Kennan to publish his essay on containment (Lafeber 1980: 64), sponsored him in Washington and introduced him to George Marshall (Schaller 1985: 86–7), Forrestal was a tense, paranoiac man who, perhaps more than any of his powerful and anti-communist contemporaries, had a deep-seated and irrational fear of the Russians, which brought his life to an abrupt end when he jumped out of a hospital window, convinced that communists were pursuing him.

Some of Forrestal's Manichaean views about the Soviet Union also characterised his business associate Paul Nitze, who had entered investment banking as a protégé of Clarence Dillon, the firm's founder. As it had been Forrestal who brought Draper, then a vice-president of Dillon, Read, to Washington to be under-secretary of the Army (Schaller 1985: 85), it was Draper, then an aide to General George Marshall, who invited Nitze to Washington (Nitze 1995), where he became director of the financial division of Nelson Rockefeller's Office of the Coordinator of Inter-American Affairs (CIAA) (Colby and Dennett 1995: 115) (see Chapter 7). (It would be Kennan, however, who brought Nitze onto the staff of the Policy Planning unit [Stephanson 1989: 204].) Nitze spent most of the rest of his life in government and, by the 1980s, was renowned as one of Washington's most pre-eminent arms control negotiators. But for forty years he had advocated an aggressive posture toward the USSR. In 1950 he had been the principal drafter for the Policy Planners of National Security Council Memorandum 68 (NSC-68), which had counselled against negotiating with the Russians, advocated development of the hydrogen bomb, favoured massive increases in US military expenditure, and generally helped to implement the policy of containment (Blight and Welch 1989: 11; Landau 1988: 56–7). He also had been the principal author of the Gaither Committee Report, which "came up with a broad-scale surprise attack program ... with a price tag of $44 billion" (Morris 1988: 141). In 1962, when he was Assistant Secretary of Defense, he was among Kennedy's most hawkish advisers during the Cuban missile crisis (Blight and Welch 1989: 11, 139–51 *passim*).

Yet another prominent member of the firm was C. Douglas Dillon, son of the founder, a trustee of the Rockefeller Foundation (Colby and Dennett 1995: 337), who served in the Eisenhower administration as Undersecretary of State (Divine 1981: 147; Lafeber 1980: 210) and would later be appointed by Kennedy as Secretary of the Treasury.

These were among Draper's principal colleagues at Dillon, Read, and they testify to the collective influence of a firm which in the 1930s had figured prominently in helping to finance the Third Reich (Kolko 1968; Kolko and Kolko 1972: 113), and which immediately after the war played an important role in the Japan Lobby, a combination of people in government and industry who sought "not simply the revival of the Japanese economy, but a reconstitution of its ties to the Asian mainland as well" (Cumings 1990: 176). It is noteworthy, then, that men such as Draper and Forrestal, who had been so influential in guiding the firm, came to play a prominent role – along with Kennan and others – in shaping US Cold War policy in a way which sought the rehabilitation of German and Japanese industry in order to contain the Soviet Union (Schaller 1985: 88). It was the pre-war strategy of the West revived.

Draper served with Forrestal in Washington until he moved to Germany to head the economics division in the post-war administration of General Lucius Clay (Borkin 1978: 158), whose command over the American sector was roughly on a par with that of MacArthur in post-war Japan (Halberstam 1986: 124). One of Clay's major initiatives was to end Western Germany's reparations to the USSR, a major event in the evolution of the Cold War (Fleming 1961). More generally, the US wanted to create a Western Germany[8] which was strong enough economically to act as a bulwark against the Soviets. As one of Clay's chief aides, Draper "had in effect ended one program, that of denazification of West German politics and the breaking up of the old German cartels, and started a new one, that of strengthening German industry" (Halberstam 1986: 125; cf. Schaller 1985: 85).

In the summer of 1947, Draper was appointed Undersecretary of the Army, with special responsibility for occupied areas (Schaller 1985: 111). In that capacity, he came to play a similar role in Japan where initially, under MacArthur, US policy had treated Japan as a country that had lost a war of aggression. Among the measures which had been enacted was an anti-monopoly law – the Law for the Elimination of Excessive Concentration of Economic Power (Yanaga 1968: 35) – which was designed to break up the *zaibatsu*, the giant industrial combines such as Mitsubishi which had dominated the Japanese economy since the Tokugawa era and through the Second World War. Early in the US occupation, the dissolution of the *zaibatsu* had been regarded as essential for the curbing of future Japanese militarism. But there were many

---

8. But not a united Germany, although it would later blame the division of Germany on the Russians.

reasons why this policy was reversed (Halliday 1975: 177–8, 181–2). In Japan itself, communist influence within the trade union movement was regarded as a major threat (Halberstam 1986: 120–25). But, even more, the communists looked as if they would soon take power in China, war in Korea seemed likely, and a strong Japanese economy, able to dominate Asian trade on behalf of long-range US policy objectives, seemed increasingly more important. As a necessary adjunct to these goals, "US economic policy for Japan directly gave an impetus to remilitarisation. Draper, one of the architects of restoration, was a major exponent of Japanese rearmament" (Halliday 1975: 197).

On the Draper Committee was another old colleague from his days in Berlin and a member of the earlier Gaither Committee (Bird 1992: 465), John J. McCloy, the prominent Wall Street lawyer and a former assistant secretary of war (1941–45), who had gone on to become the second president of the World Bank, succeeding Eugene Meyer, who had only served in that job for six months (Mason and Asher 1973: 41–50). McCloy himself had left the Bank after two years (Mason and Asher 1973: 49–62) to replace Draper's boss, General Lucius Clay, in Germany as the first civilian US High Commissioner for Western Germany. In that role, one of his most notable acts was to reverse the conviction for war crimes of the Nazi industrialist Alfried Krupp (Manchester 1968: 749–70).[9] At the time of his appointment to the Draper Committee, McCloy was the chairman of Chase Manhattan Bank, a trustee of the Ford Foundation and "a major figure in the Republican Party and a staunch conservative who was considered one of the architects of the Cold War" (Hersh 1983: 163; cf. Domhoff 1970: 117; Scheer 1974: 59; Mass 1976: 41).[10]

Collectively, then, the members of the Draper Committee were the supreme embodiment of the major forces that directed the course of US foreign policy and that had revived the anti-Soviet posture of the West which had been suspended briefly during the war. That such a committee became so interested in the threat that over-population might present – or be said to present – to the political stability of countries that were of strategic importance to US defence and security interests, especially in the Western hemisphere, marks it as a distinctive moment in the political evolution of Malthusianism.

---

9. It is not just that Krupp was an early member of the Nazi Party. His firm – which owned 55 percent of Ruhr coal and 90 percent of German steel production – was the heart of the Nazi war machine. The company had also employed Auschwitz prisoners in its factories (Manchester 1968: 4, 443, 696).

10. He would later serve on the Warren Commission, which presented the official interpretation of the assassination of President Kennedy.

But it also reflected wider currents. Draper himself was particularly susceptible to the influence of an old friend, Hugh Moore, a US millionaire whose fortune was based on Dixie cups and whose Hugh Moore Fund had entered the field of population control in the early 1950s with its pamphlet *The Population Bomb*. A few years later, Paul Ehrlich would borrow this phrase as the title for his own book (Lader 1971: 1, 5). But in 1958 Moore targeted the Draper Committee as an unprecedented opportunity to advance the cause of population control as what Neo-Malthusians were labelling "the greatest menace of our time" (Ehrlich 1971). In a speech at Moore's memorial service fourteen years later, Draper openly acknowledged Moore's influence on the committee's work (Draper 1972: 16). As a result, it had focused considerable attention on the "population problem" and recommended government financing of population research as part of security planning. And it inaugurated a new role for Draper, which, in retrospect, seems a perfectly natural progression. From having played such a prominent role in the emergence of US Cold War policy, he went on to ensure that Malthusian concerns became a fixture in Western development policy, where they remain today (cf. Saunders 1986).

The result was that population policy began to fulfil some of the expectations of Hardin's writing, as a component of US policy in the defence of its international interests. Thus, when the situation in the severely deprived Northeast of Brazil looked increasingly volatile in the early sixties, as peasant leagues seemed to present a serious challenge to established patterns of landownership and power in the region (Page 1972, Scheper-Hughes 1992: 46–8) and *The New York Times* reported that "the makings of a revolutionary situation are increasingly apparent across the vastness of the poverty-stricken and drought-plagued Brazilian Northeast" (in Page 1972: 12),[11] Draper was among those who were sent there on special mission. He reported that conditions in the Northeast were as bad as those in India, where the Ford Foundation had already invested millions of dollars in family planning campaigns.

As far as Brazil was concerned, events proved to be moving too fast. In response to developments in the Northeast and what were regarded as policies hostile to the interests of international capital on the part of Brazil's nationalist president, João Goulart, the US government was also

---

11. About which US economist Herman Daly, writing in 1970, argued that it was largely their excessive birth-rate that "maintains the masses in a state of hopeless impotent poverty" (1970: 568), because their "unlimited reproduction" created a highly competitive labour market and hence kept wages low (1970: 546).

pursuing a more covert strategy. The US Consulate in Recife, the principal city in the region, had been expanded and its political section had become home to the CIA (Page 1972: 125–8; Colby and Dennett 1965: 424). Through its activities there and elsewhere in the country, the USA monitored and supported plans for a military coup which finally took place on 1 April 1964 (Bird 1992: 553; Colby and Dennett 1995: 442). As a result, Brazil became "a much more willing and efficient participant in international capitalism" (Hewlett 1975), even if the price for this was a marked decline in social and economic equity, and one of the highest degrees of repression in Latin America.

Meanwhile, in 1964 the Alliance for Progress, which was a major fixture of the US response to the Cuban Revolution, opened an Office of Population. It was funded by USAID, whose missions in Latin America were formally advised the next year that population control was "a priority area" (Colby and Dennett 1995: 475; Mass 1976: 43–6). The head of the Alliance at the time was Thomas Mann, brought back from his ambassadorship in Mexico. A brief scan of his career puts his Malthusian concerns, like Draper's, into proper perspective:

> Mann's experience included running the Bolivian desk at the State Department during the grim days of Indian tin miners' strikes in 1942 ... heading up petroleum affairs at the postwar embassy in the Venezuela of Creole Petroleum and other oil companies, assisting the CIA's new dictatorship in Guatemala as U.S. consul in 1954, and promoting U.S. big business in Latin America first as assistant secretary for economic affairs and then as acting assistant secretary for Latin America. (Colby and Dennett 1995: 422–3)

The establishment view, as articulated in an essay in *Foreign Affairs*, was that "Time is not with us in Latin America. The pressures of population and revolution are increasing" (Lodge 1966: 197). But, of course, it was not just Latin America. Three years later, having become the national chair of Moore's Population Crisis Committee (Lader 1971: 44),[12] Draper testified before the US House of Representatives' Committee on Banking and Currency that "unless and until the population explosion now erupting in Asia, Africa and Latin America is brought under control, our entire aid program is doomed to failure" (quoted in Mass 1976: 46). That same year, the US Foreign Assistance Act earmarked $35 million for population programmes under a special "Title X" amendment. By 1971, the annual Agency for International Development (USAID) population allocation was up to $100 million – much of

---

12. When he retired from this position, the speakers at the testimonial dinner in New York included General Lucius Clay, John D. Rockefeller 3rd and Paul Hoffman (Lader 1971: 48).

it channelled through the International Planned Parenthood Federation (IPPF)[13] in various countries (Mass 1976: 49), as a result of Draper's lobbying efforts (Lader 1971: 44–5). This was far more than it appropriated for healthcare, but that was a contrast which, in Malthusian terms, was inevitable.

Toward the end of the 1960s, in part through the efforts of Draper and John D. Rockefeller 3rd, the United States had begun to shift its population strategy to a wider, global stage (Green 1993: 308–9) where the question of population pressure was rapidly assuming a pivotal role as an explanation of social and economic problems in the developing world and as a rationale for the Western development strategies that were proposed to address those problems. By 1968, in his inaugural speech at the World Bank, Robert McNamara emphasised the central importance of curbing population growth, a position which has remained central to World Bank development policy.[14] A year later, US president Richard Nixon emphasised his view that "the United Nations, its specialized agencies, and other international bodies should take the leadership in responding to world population growth" (in Mass 1976: 63). The United Nations Population Division had been established as early as 1946, with Notestein as its director. In 1954, there was the UN Population Conference in Rome and in 1955 the Bandung Seminar. One result was the setting up of three regional centres for demographic training, in addition to one already established in Delhi. These centres, in Bombay (1956), Santiago (1957) and Cairo (1963),

> were sponsored by a combination of UN and Population Council (involving Ford Foundation) funds. In all this, the influence of Notestein and his two powerful patrons, John D. Rockefeller 3rd and Frederick Osborn, was ubiquitous. (Szreter 1993: 681)

In 1967, the UN established its Population Trust Fund, with most of its financial support coming from the United States. With an ominous inevitability, the US delegate to the UN Population Commission was General William Draper, personifying all the corporate interests of his colleagues, men such as Nitze, Forrestal and Dillon, who had helped to shape the discourse and policies of the Cold War. Draper lobbied strenuously to expand the resourcing and the efforts of the Fund, which was reorganised in 1969 as the United Nations Fund for Population

---

13. The IPPF had been formed at an international conference of birth control organisations held in Bombay in 1952 (Caldwell and Caldwell 1986: 41).

14. McNamara's predecessor, Eugene Black, joined the board of directors of Planned Parenthood (Gordon 1976: 398). The current president of the Bank, James Wolfensohn, is a trustee of the Population Council (The World Bank 1996).

Activities (UNFPA). It would be supervised by the UN Development Programme, which was then directed by Paul Hoffman (Johnson 1987: 58) and later would be headed by Draper's son, himself a prominent venture capitalist, and advised by a special panel which, of course, included John D. Rockefeller 3rd (Mass 1976: 62).[15] From such respectable heights, Malthusianism would justify one of the most influential Western development strategies of the post-war period: the commercialisation of Third World agriculture which came to be known as the Green Revolution. It would play a central role in subduing demands for land reform, which, as events in China had proven, could be a major impetus for systemic social change. It was not a coincidence therefore that the man whom Hoffman appointed to be the first executive director of UNFPA was Rafael Salas, former executive secretary of the Philippine government, close friend of the dictator Ferdinand Marcos, and a man who had helped to establish the Green Revolution in rice production in his country (Bonner 1987; Owen 1998).

---

15. Since then, it has consistently adhered, at the highest levels and in most of its official publications, to a Neo-Malthusian position (e.g., UNFPA 1991). When a cyclone wreaked havoc in southeeastern Bangladesh in April 1991, the headline of the UNFPA's bulletin, *Population*, declared: 'Bangladesh cyclone a Malthusian nightmare' (*Population* 1991: 1).

5
The Life and Death of Land Reform

> Unrest will smoulder, and perhaps ignite, as long as the land problem is not solved.
>
> Erich Jacoby (1949)

In the decades just after the end of the Second World War, peasants everywhere were demanding land. While they sought access to unused and under-utilised lands in the hands of large landowners, it was one of the tenets of Western policy toward agrarian change – a view that would rationalise the emergence of what would be called the Green Revolution by the 1960s – that there were no new lands on which to expand food production and that, in light of mounting population pressure, the only solution to the Malthusian spectre was to enhance output per unit of available land through technological means. Moreover, the proclaimed urgency to increase food production was said to require an efficiency which only large commercial farms could provide. In this way, the Malthusian fears which propelled the logic of the Green Revolution effectively helped to put land reform on hold as a central feature of agrarian development and even reversed it in many parts of the world. It therefore set the interests of the governments of the United States and Western Europe squarely at odds with millions of peasants around the world who sought to reclaim precious cultivable lands that colonialist powers and their descendants had, over the centuries, appropriated for non-subsistence production. In the process, it provided unprecedented opportunities for the intensification of capitalist relations of production in Third World agriculture. And it defused – but only for a time – the threat of peasant insurgency.

Wolf Ladejinsky and Pre-emptive Land Reform

There was a brief period, however, when an argument was made for land reform as a part of the Cold War strategy of the West. One individual who embodied this position more strenuously than anyone else was the agricultural economist Wolf Ladejinsky. His efforts, their motivations and their eventual marginalisation by the Green Revolution provide useful insight into the complex interrelationship of ends and means which characterised US thinking in the decade after the Second World War.

Born in 1899 in the Ukraine, Ladejinsky left the new Soviet Union in 1921, reaching the United States the following year, where he was to harbour a life-long distaste for communism and a reverence for the land-reforming zeal of Tsar Alexander II. Learning English, studying economics, he eventually secured a position in the Department of Agriculture's Office of Foreign Agricultural Relations in the Roosevelt administration (Walinsky 1977: 4–5). There, as early as 1939, he wrote a study on the "Agricultural Problems in India", which reached the Malthusian conclusion that

> rural India cannot solve all its many problems by tilling the soil, no matter how efficiently. Villages are over-crowded It is not certain how large the surplus farm population is but, if the view of India's agricultural experts that the lowest limit of an economic holding in that country is 15 acres is accepted, "in British India alone ... as much as 44 percent (or 36 million) of the total workers on the land were superfluous." In order to find even a partial outlet for these millions, India must be industrialized. (Walinsky 1977: 38)

The apparent precision of such an estimate of rural population surplus recalls the efforts of eugenicists to define the number of feeble-minded. But most important is how such a Malthusian vision was already preparing to legitimise the rural clearance which the Green Revolution eventually would effectuate. What it neglected to point out, however, was that there was an implicit alternative to defining so many people as surplus on the grounds that their holdings were too small and uneconomical: land redistribution.

Without abandoning his Malthusian assumptions, Ladejinsky played a prominent role in helping to place the issue of land reform specifically and pragmatically within the context of the Cold War. Drawing on what he saw as the principal lessons from his Russian past, he regarded rural poverty as an increasing source of discontent which tempted people to turn to what he regarded as the "deceptively simple solutions of the Communist line" (Walinsky 1977: 205). If people were attracted to communism because it embraced the cause of agrarian change, the West had to preempt that cause "as a necessary part of the conditions for Western survival" (Walinsky 1977: 206). As Ladejinsky wrote in 1950,

> we must realize how serious a threat an agrarian revolution could be at this point of history.... The only way to thwart Communist designs on Asia is to preclude such revolutionary outbursts through timely reforms, peacefully before the peasants take the law into their own hands and set the countryside ablaze. (Walinsky 1977: 132)

These ideas, which echo the attitude of Macaulay and others toward the "outbursts" of the Irish in the first half of the last century, had informed Ladejinsky's work in developing land reform in early post-war Japan. With the victory of the Chinese communists imminent, American authorities were anxious to prevent the extremely influential Japanese Communist Party from consolidating political power. The land reform programme was clearly directed toward that end. As Ladejinsky himself noted, under the existing system of land tenure in Japan,

> The Japanese village was full of unrest. Under the influence of Communist propaganda, it could have been a very serious political situation during the aftermath of the war. (in Cary 1962: 19)

The agricultural economist Laurence Hewes, who worked in Japan with Ladejinsky, was quite open about the way land reform was meant to forestall such trouble. "Almost the entire history of Japanese Communist activity", he wrote, and

> most of its aims and ambitions, centered on agrarian reforms. In fact, land reform had for long been the special political property of the Japanese Communists. If the reform were successfully accomplished, it would pull the rug out from under the entire Communist position in Japan. Finally, such a reform conducted in non-Marxist terms and stressing individual rights, private property, and auxiliary capitalist concepts could embarrass the Communist position throughout the world. (Hewes 1955: 88)

The reforms which Ladejinsky and his colleagues helped to effect are still regarded as the policy which above all "established a still-persisting pattern of electoral support by farmers for the ruling Liberal Democratic Party and destroyed the rural appeal of the Japanese Communists" (Prosterman and Riedinger 1987: 122). Yet, as would be shown by the case of Guatemala, where land reform would be thwarted by the United States just a few years later, the essential issue was not always land reform itself, but who controlled it. It was always better if it conformed to US objectives, rather than to an agenda set by the people of the country in question. In Japan,

The program as finally designed accented destruction of the institution of tenancy but explicitly discouraged any fomentation of class conflict. Again and again, Occupation personnel had pounded home the point that the program must bring about a release but not a revolution. The purpose was adjustment, not disruption. Pent-up forces of change and progress must be freed, but the essentially stable qualities of village life must be preserved. (Hewes 1955: 87)

In 1949, Ladejinsky went to China and Taiwan to assist the Joint Commission on Rural Reconstruction which had been set up by the US government and the Nationalist Chinese of Chiang Kai-shek. Before it could do very much, however, Chiang had been forced to evacuate to Taiwan, where he was finally persuaded to undertake the land reform he had never supported when he had controlled the whole of China (Stross 1986: 214). However, the communist victory in China made Ladejinsky more fervent than before about the positive political benefits of a pre-emptive land reform programme. In a popular essay in the *Saturday Review of Literature*, published in 1950 after his return from Taiwan and Szechuan, he attributed the "age-old wretchedness of the Asiatic peasant" to the Malthusian problem of "too many people, too little land" (Walinsky 1977: 131). He underscored how the West must prevent agrarian revolutions where peasants "take the law into their own hands and set the countryside ablaze", since such a course favoured communist interests (Walinsky 1977: 132). And he developed the argument that China had been and India remained crucial in this respect, because decades earlier the Soviet leadership supposedly had targeted them for a major role in their global strategy. As he wrote:

Toward the end of his life Lenin ... visualized the final conflict between a Communist East and a capitalistic West. In this struggle China and India were to join Russia as the forces of Communism ... Stalin developed a program for those countries consisting of three stages: a struggle against foreign imperialism, an agrarian revolution under the leadership of the Communist Party, and finally a proletarian dictatorship. The key step was to be the wooing of the peasants. (Walinsky 1977: 131)

Ladejinsky, therefore, emphasised "the urgency of taking the wind out of the Communist sails in a peasant ocean" (Walinsky 1977: 134). But he could never see that such reform, if left to the kinds of rulers who were allied with the West and who were the inheritors of dying colonial regimes, could never be effective and convincing enough to contain the aspirations and resentments of those who had been dispossessed.

None the less, it was with such ideas that Ladejinsky eventually arrived in Saigon with the US aid mission, in January 1955. He was to stay there for over six years (Walinsky 1977: 215), during a critical time in the history of Indochina. The previous May, French colonialist forces had been decisively defeated at Dien Bien Phu. The peace conference in Geneva temporarily divided Vietnam, pending elections, but France and the United States began to develop plans to resist them by creating a client state in the South, where the Emperor Bao Dai had appointed Ngo Dinh Diem as prime minister (Fitzgerald 1972: 102). These plans included Washington's sending Lieutenant Colonel Edward Lansdale to Saigon "as head of a military advisory mission" in June 1954 (Walinsky 1977: 215).

In fact, Lansdale was CIA. He had acquired a legendary reputation in the Philippines just after the war, when he helped to defeat the Huk communist insurgency (Halberstam 1972: 155–8). The Hukbalahap (People's Anti-Japanese Army) had originated, as its name suggests, during the Japanese occupation. Under Marxist leadership, it had continued after independence in 1946, first attempting to play a role in the new electoral system and, after being rebuffed (Blum 1986: 39), waging a guerrilla war against an agrarian order in which landowners, many of whom had collaborated with the Japanese (Mills et al. 1949: 69), were organising private armies to restore pre-war privileges. The old order was also endorsed by the fact that, by the early 1950s, US military forces, which had never vacated the islands, were training battalions of the Philippine Army in counter-insurgency (Blum 1986: 40).

Lansdale played a central role in developing many of their techniques. According to Putzel,

> There were two main thrusts in Lansdale's work during this period. The first was to launch a reform of the military and a programme of rural reform and psychological warfare. The objective was to undermine the Huk guerrilla movement and to create a reformist alternative in the countryside. The second thrust, linked to the first, was to groom then Defense Minister and long-time friend of the U.S., Ramon Magsaysay, to run on a popular reform programme as an alternative to what was now seen as a corrupt Liberal Party government under Quirino. (Putzel 1992: 88; cf. Marchetti and Marks 1974: 50–51)

After helping to engineer Magsaysay's election victory in 1953 (Blum 1986: 42), Lansdale briefly returned to Washington, but was soon sent to Saigon

> on assignment from [CIA director] Allan Dulles to act as the head of the military mission and then as CIA chief of station for domestic affairs. He met Ngo Dinh Diem just after the premier's arrival in Saigon, liked him, and shifted the weight of CIA to his support. (Fitzgerald 1972: 104)

He was also among those who put pressure on the Diem government to institute a national land reform programme as a major element in its campaign to defeat the Vietminh. After Ladejinsky was assigned to Saigon (Putzel 1992: 99), Lansdale introduced him to the dictator, for whom Ladejinsky became a personal adviser on land reform (Walinsky 1977: 215; Putzel 1992: 99). Unconcerned by Diem's lack of democratic impulses, arguing that "The overwhelming majority of the people in South Vietnam are not affected by the regime's authoritarianism" (in Fitzgerald 1972: 120), and even hinting that Diem's governance might have been "in close cooperation with divine Providence" (in Scheer 1995: 138), Ladejinsky's advocacy of the land reform programme was no more based on a sense of social justice than Lansdale's. It reflected the same political expediency that had worked so well in Japan. The fact was that the French had bequeathed the southern part of Vietnam a legacy of being a "landlords' country", with a high degree of landlessness and rural poverty (Hodgkin 1981: 179). A study by Ladejinsky in the Mekong Delta area found that 2.5 percent of the population owned half the cultivated land, while 70 percent owned less than 12.5 percent. Even "the American ambassador concurred with the French high commissioner that the Viet Minh land reform program posed a significant threat to the future of the Saigon government" (Fitzgerald 1972: 202).

The Ladejinsky perspective on land reform persisted through the 1960s. It can be seen in Bredo and Shreve's consultancy report for the Republic of Vietnam and USAID (1968) and it was still being advocated, in precisely the same terms, by Bredo in the mid-1980s with regard to Central America. Writing in the *Journal of Political and Military Sociology*, he would observe:

> Domestic political instability invites Soviet destabilization efforts. The most common source of disaffection in a country is the over-concentration of land ownership which frustrates the landless and the land poor and leads them to violent insurgency. Soviet intervention, seeking to aid the insurgents, is the tool for introducing Marxist socialism and establishing hegemony in the encroached areas. (1986: 280)

As it happened, however, when Diem did institute land reform, it only had the reverse effect to what Ladejinsky wanted, by actually worsening conditions for many of the peasants who had benefited from earlier Vietminh reforms (Wolf 1969: 197). Attempts to regulate landlord–tenant relations, for example, included the setting of a ceiling on rents. But in many cases, this limit was ignored by landlords, and even where it was accepted the fact was that, under the Vietminh, peasants generally had not had to pay any rent at all (Prosterman and Riedinger 1987: 123; Scheer 1995: 144). And while Diem seems to have given some serious consideration to the need for land redistribution in order to create a bulwark against communism (Post 1989: 107), he was obviously more reluctant to alienate the landowning class. As a result,

> the cumulative result of all the program as of the end of 1967 was the distribution of some 275,000 hectares of land to 130,000 families. This represented less than one-eighth of South Vietnam's cultivated land, with benefits going to barely one-tenth of those who had been wholly or substantially dependent on farming land as tenants. (Prosterman and Riedinger 1987: 126)

In contrast, in the North, the communist government had completed a process of land reform begun by the Vietminh; while in the South, the Vietcong – successors to the Vietminh – maintained earlier land reforms in areas under their control (Prosterman and Riedinger 1987: 126). As a result, "the mass of South Vietnamese peasants saw the Vietminh and Vietcong land reforms as dealing far more effectively with their basic needs and basic grievances than anything the Saigon government had to offer" (Prosterman and Riedinger 1987: 127). Naturally, then, the Vietcong had little difficulty finding recruits (Prosterman and Riedinger 1987: 127–8). While that was the case, there remained a view among certain Americans that support for the communists could only be turned into support for Diem (or similar governments elsewhere) on the basis of some meaningful land reforms. But none of them considered the possibility that, if the communists were the only ones capable of making such reforms a reality, then Diem and others like him were the wrong side to be backing.

The USA knew which side it wanted to back, and that inevitably made any land reform programme wholly ineffectual in terms of peasant needs. Ladejinsky's compromise position was what he called a "minimum programme", which would not jeopardise established power structures, but would undermine communist initiatives in the countryside. But that position revealed the limits and inconsistences of the "liberal" strategy. As Putzel observes,

> Ladejinsky's collaboration with Diem and Lansdale offers two important insights into the liberal approach to redistributive reform. First, Ladejinsky was willing to settle for the implementation of a "minimum programme." Secondly, he demonstrated on many occasions his willingness to work with dictatorial regimes to implement his model, an attitude not unlike that of supporters of the liberal approach in Taiwan and South Korea. The conclusion that can be drawn is that the strategic objective behind his work was first and foremost the consolidation of states friendly to the U.S. and only secondly the resolution of the plight of the rural poor. (1992: 100)

Ironically, despite the fact that his advocacy of land reform had been reformist and anti-communist, Ladejinsky was actually forced out of the US Department of Agriculture early in the Eisenhower administration as a result of McCarthyite pressures. It was a move which signalled that the USA no longer would be "championing the cause of agrarian reform and placed its efforts primarily on developing a military response to 'communist insurgency' and economic and technical aid, without challenging the status quo in rural power structures" (Putzel 1992: 98–9). At the end of a six-year stint in Saigon, Ladejinsky moved to the Ford Foundation, and from there, in 1964, to the World Bank. At both, the focus of his attention was India.

Meanwhile, in Vietnam, it had become clear that the autocratic Diem could never initiate the kind of rural development that would diminish the power of wealthy landlords. His acceptance of the need for some reform came only under persistent US pressure, but it was reform which only served to affirm the legitimacy of landlordism (Scheer 1995: 143–4). In the end, a more practicable strategy was one which simply eliminated the communists' potential client population and simultaneously consolidated and enhanced the position of wealthier land-holders. So, in South Vietnam in the mid-1960s, land reform gave way to what was called the "strategic hamlets" policy, designed to contain peasants within communities that were turned into a multitude of mini-concentration camps, where they presumably could be insulated from communist influence. This policy, which was largely devised by Lansdale, was carried out in conjunction with USAID under its then director, David Bell, who would later become the head of Population Studies at Harvard University. It would also prove ineffectual, and, almost twenty years after Dien Bien Phu, the United States was driven out of Vietnam, and US policy toward insurgent peasantries was once again transformed in the face of otherwise insuperable realities.

The Philippines, Land Reform and the Cold War

As Prosterman and Riedinger have observed, the Philippines had long been one of a number of critical countries where "The landownership issue has been central to episodes of large-scale violence, short of successful revolution" (1987: 11). Half-hearted attempts at land reform began in the Philippines in the 1950s as part of the campaign to suppress the Huks, whose influence predominated in the rice- and sugar-growing areas of Central Luzon, not far from Manila, where an increasing pattern of tenancies since the turn of the century had caused mounting tensions between absentee landlords and a growing population of sharecroppers (McMillan 1955: 27). When one considers that one of the main advocates of land reform had been Edward Lansdale, it is hardly surprising that such reforms never amounted to anything.

Ladejinsky himself had, from the beginning, regarded land reform principally as a way of suppressing a major source of political radicalism in post-war Japan, where he had pushed what was, relatively speaking, the "liberal" view that land reform was necessary in order to ensure political stability. After 1948, "he began to argue that land reform was a crucial element in the fight against Asian communists" (Putzel 1992: 75). By then, he also had acquired some influence at the top level of the State Department (Putzel 1992: 76). Within a short time after the Chinese communists came to power, in the brief period before McCarthyism began to constrain any residual liberal impulses in the Truman administration, the highest levels of the US government began to commend land reform as the least unacceptable option.

In the introduction to a volume of papers from an International Conference on Land Tenure and Related Problems in World Agriculture at the University of Wisconsin in 1951, Kenneth Parsons wrote of the choices facing the Western capitalist nations:

> The central question of world tenure policy therefore is this: Will the revolution on the land which is building up over so much of the world go the way of the West toward freedom – roughly the road of the French Revolution – or the way of the Marxist Russian Revolution? (in Putzel 1992: 76)

This is especially ironic, since, as I suggested earlier, the response through the West to the French Revolution – with its claim to place the "rights of man" before those of property – was not very different from the later reaction to the Russian Revolution. Only by contrast and, one imagines, only in principle did the French Revolution seem commendable.

So, the Japanese model of land redistribution was extended to other strategic areas. Foremost among them was the Philippines, whose strategic position had long been recognised. Shortly after the USA had acquired the islands from Spain, Senator Albert Beveridge had observed:

> The Pacific is our ocean.... Where shall we turn for consumers of our surplus? Geography answers the question. China is our natural customer.... The Philippines give us a base at the door of all the East. (Beveridge quoted in Zinn 1980: 306)

After the Second World War, a secret report of the US National Security Council had described them, along with Japan, as "our first line of defense and in addition our first line of defense from which we may seek to reduce the area of Communist control" (in Putzel 1992: 84). In 1952, a report for the US Mutual Security Agency by Robert Hardie, who had worked with Ladejinsky on land reform in Japan,

proposed a land reform programme that included all the essential components of the model outlined by the liberal reformers in Japan. His definition
of land reform corresponded to Ladejinsky's and emphasised land redistribution while also instituting measures to increase agricultural productivity. (Putzel
1992: 85)

But while such proposals might be made, the reality was that, whereas
the USA had enormous influence over Japanese policies during the
years of occupation, the power of Philippine landlords remained too
deeply entrenched and could thwart any meaningful process of land
redistribution, even if the government truly supported it. Moreover, as
soon as the Huk movement was suppressed, landlords who had been
willing to allow some change in the land tenure system rapidly reversed
their position (McMillan 1955: 32).

From 1955 onward, no matter how much the ceiling for large
holdings was reduced,

> most of the land expected to be available for redistribution evaporated into
> thin air; far fewer landlords than anticipated, it seemed, "owned" more than
> the amount permitted to be retained, whether it was three hundred, seventy-
> five, twenty-four, or seven hectares. Cumulatively, fewer than 20 percent of
> the roughly one million tenant families on rice and corn land have become
> amortizing owners. (Prosterman and Riedinger 1987: 182–3)

As Myrdal noted of the Land Reform Act of 1955, it

> created an organization to acquire estate land in excess of 300 hectares (or
> 600 hectares if held by corporations). This organization was empowered to
> act only if a majority of the tenants petitioned for subdivision. Implementa-
> tion of the act has been further impeded by the high compensation rates paid
> to landowners, since lands so acquired have often been priced beyond the
> reach of the occupying tenants. This land reform can be said to have been
> almost completely ineffectual. (1968: 1314–15)

A further effort at land reform in 1963 was equally unproductive, leading
a UN report to conclude that the law merely served as "an indication
... that the political power of landlords remains strong" (in Myrdal
1968: 1315).

But the ruling elite in the country was also severely divided. That,
combined with threats of peasant insurrection, gave Philippine president Ferdinand Marcos reason to declare martial law in 1972 and to
begin to centralise political power in the hands of his own faction. This,
as Bello et al. have suggested, seemed to forshadow a repeat of the
Brazilian "miracle" (1982: 28), especially as the Marcos group, according
to the World Bank, embarked on a "strategy of liberalization, export-
oriented industrialization, and a positive climate for foreign investment"

(in Bello et al. 1982: 32). In due course, the World Bank and the IMF became extremely influential in Philippine economic policy, especially as the country's foreign debt, the cost of the Marcos modernisation, began to soar (Bello et al. 1982: 50).

This strategy not only created new pressures on the rural poor, but gave renewed life to the Malthusian view that the main problem in the Philippines actually was over-population (cf. Paddock and Paddock 1967: 224–5). This position is readily apparent in the observation in 1955 by Robert McMillan of the US Operations Mission to the Philippines that "ownership of large areas of farm land tends to be concentrated among a few persons or groups", but that the main problem for small farmers none the less was population pressure. Although McMillan recognised that rural poverty created an urgency for land reform, he regarded population growth, causing rural–urban migration and under- and unemployment, as a major source of poverty, social tensions and demand for land. So, like Ladejinsky, he viewed "short-sighted landlords and large-scale farmers" as "sowing the seeds of revolution". Evolutionary land reform was far better (McMillan 1955: 25, 26, 32).

But as the land reforms of the fifties and sixties successively failed to amount to anything and as rural unrest continued, the population issue came to be seen in a different way. Two new strategies evolved in tandem, both sponsored by the Ford and Rockefeller Foundations. National and international interest in population control in the Philippines was growing and, early in 1962, Ford established an International Population Program at Cornell with an initial grant of $250,000. According to a Cornell press release, the programme was going to "involve research and training in the field of population, with particular emphasis on human fertility and migration, two factors of political as well as social importance to the countries of Latin America and the Far East" (Cornell University News Bureau 1962: 2).[1] In 1964, the Ford Foundation went further and approved funding for the Universities of Chicago and the Philippines to develop a Population Institute in Manila (Caldwell and Caldwell 1986: 107–8).

---

1. The Cornell programme was directed by J. Mayone Stycos, the director of Cornell's Latin American Program (Cornell University News Bureau 1962: 1). Stycos had supervised a Ford fertility survey in Puerto Rico in the late 1940s (Caldwell and Caldwell 1986: 24), at a time when the USA was interested in settling manufacturing industries there which would make use of cheap female workers (Hartmann 1987: 232). In 1954, Stycos published an article, "Female Sterilization in Puerto Rico", in the *Eugenics Quarterly* (Hartmann 1987: 341). By the late 1960s, his Cornell programme was active in Tegucigalpa, Honduras, just as a Malthusian perspective on social-political change in Central America was coming to dominate policy toward the region (see below).

By the time Marcos declared martial law, it was being commonly argued that, as a result of population growth, the Philippines had effectively run out of reasonably cultivable land. While this entirely side-stepped the question of how such land was being used, it was an argument that would eventually become, without a moment's pause for any consideration of political-economic relations, the principal explanation of environmental degradation, in particular, deforestation. Thus, the Neo-Malthusian writer Myers has recently written that the Philippines is a country

> where the agricultural frontier closed in the lowlands during the 1970s. As a result, multitudes of landless people began to migrate into the uplands, leading to a build-up of human numbers at a rate far greater than that of national population growth.... The result has been a marked increase in deforestation and a rapid spread of soil erosion. (1994: 57)

Despite the fact that such writers are always willing to admit that population is never the only factor and that land tenure patterns also play a role, in practice they disregard such matters. Here, Myers gives the clear impression that the availability of cultivable land in the lowlands simply ran out in the 1970s. This is a gross oversimplification – indeed, depoliticisation – of Philippine agrarian realities, but one which satisfactorily embodies what became the dominant view in the West, as it became clear that land reform was neither workable nor desirable.

Along with new initiatives in the field of population control, the Philippines also was targeted for the Green Revolution. As early as 1950, when the Philippine government was still busy combating the Huk guerrillas with US support, it had invited the Rockefeller Foundation to help develop national agriculture as part of a comprehensive package for thwarting revolutionary change. By 1958, when the subject had been raised at a meeting of senior Ford and Rockefeller officers of establishing a single international rice research centre somewhere in Asia which would give concrete expression to their efforts "to help solve the world food problem in such a way that [their] economic and political concerns about Asia would be allayed" (Anderson et al. 1991: 1), the Philippines was regarded as the best choice. And there were many reasons for this. Among them were the College of Agriculture of the University of the Philippines (UP) at Los Baños near Manila, and the fact that the Philippines was already a major site for US foreign investment, including Rockefeller oil interests. This was an important conjuncture. The College of Agriculture at Los Baños had become a "special project of Cornell University" (Pomeroy 1974: 106–7), and Cornell had long-standing associations with Rockefeller (see Chapter 6). In the 1950s, the Rockefeller

Foundation helped to establish Cornell's Southeast Asia Program, and the university's president, James A. Perkins, served as a director of Chase Manhattan Bank and of the Rockefeller family's International Basic Economy Corporation (IBEC) (Colby and Dennett 1995: 611, 789) (see Chapter 7). Such connections facilitated the UP entering into a joint research agreement with Rockefeller's Esso oil, which eventually became a major producer of the fertilisers that were applied to new varieties of rice (Pomeroy 1974: 106–7).

Cornell also had connections with Ford which would bear on such developments. Perkins had been a member of the Gaither Committee on US military preparedness, as well as a trustee of the Ford-sponsored RAND Corporation (which Gaither had helped to set up) (Domhoff 1970: 135; Colby and Dennett 1995: 474, 611). And in the mid-fifties, the university's former provost, Forrest Hill, became the vice-president of the Ford Foundation. As the Philippines acquired increasing importance within the Green Revolution system, and especially after Rockefeller and Ford established the International Rice Research Institute (IRRI) at Los Baños in 1960 – Hill would become the chair of IRRI's board of trustees (Anderson et al. 1991: 48) – Cornell naturally acquired a pivotal role which brought together the demographic and agricultural sides of the West's development strategy. One manifestation of that strategy was that "The problems of the large Asian rice farmer became the research projects of IRRI" (Vallianatos 1976: 59).

Not unexpectedly, Wolf Ladejinsky visited the Philippines in late 1962 on a mission for the Ford Foundation, visiting IRRI and talking with high-level officials (Putzel 1992: 119). He expressed his view that technical inputs depended on creating conditions which encouraged cultivators to invest in innovations (Myrdal 1968: 1257), but that he could not foresee how or why peasants would apply the new inputs if so much of the financial gain would probably end up in the hands of landlords, merchants and moneylenders (Putzel 1992: 118). But by then, the US position on land reform had significantly shifted toward the view that agrarian change should rely more on productivity measures than on redistribution (Putzel 1992: 119). While birth control programmes had the ostensible purpose of tackling one side of the population–resource equation, the Green Revolution seemed designed to deal with the other. The two together represented an integrated programme for a systematic restructuring of rural food production, at the heart of which was the use of higher yielding rice, not only to grow food without peasants, but to do so on less land, making more available for commercial crops for export. Ladejinsky was probably listened to with respect. But it was the story of the Irish potato all over again.

In support of the effort to introduce the new regime of fertilisers and irrigation, the World Bank made credit available for large irrigation projects, but for a long time the country continued to import rice (Bello et al. 1982: 69) as "cultivated land devoted to rice declined from 3.2 million hectares in 1960 to 3.1 million hectares in 1970" (Bello et al. 1982: 67). The Philippine countryside once again became a place of increasing political insurgency and resistance during the late sixties and seventies. As Bello et al. observe:

> Displaced and proletarianized by export agriculture and trapped by an oppressive and obsolete land tenure system, the Filipino peasantry, silent since the defeat of the Huk Rebellion in the early 1950s, began to throb once again with political activism in the late sixties. In the sugar fields of Negros and Panay Islands, sugar workers forged the National Federation of Sugar Workers despite massive landlord opposition and repression. Throughout Luzon and Mindanao, groups of smallholders began to affiliate with the Federation of Free Farmers, which advocated land reform and more coopera-tive production arrangements. In Central Luzon, the traditional bastion of rural rebellion, peasant organizations affiliated with the Marxist underground held demonstrations and marches for land reform. But the most significant development, and the most alarming in the eyes of the authorities, was the birth of the New People's Army (NPA), the armed wing of the Philippine Communist Party. (Bello et al. 1982: 69)

It was against this background that Marcos declared martial law in 1972 and attempted a new land reform, backed up by a national rural credit programme called Masagana 99 (M99). He was absolutely clear about the political purpose of the agricultural transformation it was meant to bring about, when he declared: "With the program – the integrated, intensive agricultural program – we stake the very nature of constitu-tional revolution" (in Bello et al. 1982: 77).

The programme, which was closely linked to new World Bank com-mitments which brought the Philippines about $1 billion for rural development projects over the next eight years, relied heavily on Bank advice. At the same time, the Bank's project funding was effectively supportive of the Marcos regime's agenda, which was, above all, to stabilise the countryside at the expense of small-scale cultivators. Thus, almost half of the Bank's funds for rural development in the country went into irrigation, a key component of the Green Revolution which was never likely to benefit most peasants. And, indeed, most of the increase in rice production since the seventies occurred precisely where land was irrigated. At best, some peasants might have gained and thereby entered into a new status as stalwarts of the regime. Most could not keep up with the increasing costs of requisite inputs, however, and by the mid-eighties rice output was in decline. But even before that happened, many poor Filipinos could not to afford to buy enough rice anyway (Putzel and Cunnington 1989: 30) – exactly the same situation that would be reported from India (see Chapter 6) and elsewhere.

The large dam projects which the Bank funded in Central and Northern Luzon also physically displaced thousands of peasants, forcing many into upland areas. There is no doubt, however, that such projects contributed to a period of increased national rice production as a result of new seeds, irrigation and a dramatic rise in fertiliser inputs, but increasing mechanisation, spearheaded by new technical innovations developed by the IRRI, also further marginalised a large number of landless agricultural workers, who were compelled to leave the countryside.

By the mid-seventies, the World Bank's *Poverty Report* observed that

A substantial portion of agricultural growth ... was concentrated in activities known to have substantial commercial content, and one could therefore argue that the benefits from the high level of agricultural growth may not have reached substantial numbers of the poor. (in Bello et al. 1982: 97)

But this was not just because the cultivation of new rice varieties offered few opportunities for poor farmers. The principal thrust of Philippine agrarian development over the last twenty-five years has been export crop production dominated by large land owners and multi-nationals. As a result, the Philippines is actually now forced to import vast quantities of rice from Thailand, Japan and China (Japanese Ministry of Agriculture, Forestry and Fisheries 1995), while it exports the labour that could have been the basis of food self-sufficiency. By the end of 1994, there were 6.21 million overseas Filipino workers, of whom 2.56 million were contract workers, 1.83 million were permanent residents abroad and 1.8 million were undocumented *(Philippine Reporter/Philippine News* 1995). Without any appreciation of the country's agrarian history, of the intransigence of the landed interests against which peasants have struggled over the last half-century, and of the way the national labour force of the Philippines became "surplus" at home and a labour reserve for the international economy, this could be taken as little more than a sign of over-population.

Land Reform and Counter-Revolution in Guatemala

While the United States was assuming a global counter-revolutionary role in the interests of the post-war expansion of multinational capital, taking over the lion's share of the cost of France's war to maintain its sovereignty over Indochina (Gettleman et al. 1995: 49) and campaigning against the Huks in the Philippines, the spectre of radical change was much closer at hand. In 1952, the Guatemalan government of Jacobo Arbenz introduced what was, up to that time, one of the most successful agrarian reforms in Central American history. So, in the same year that the French were defeated at Dien Bien Phu, the USA forcibly removed Arbenz on the grounds that he posed a "Communist threat" (Dunkerley 1988: 144–50).

In the second half of the nineteenth century, as commercial coffee cultivation had spread (to the detriment of subsistence production [Brockett 1988: 77]) through the Guatemalan highlands, the state facilitated the appropriation of communal Indian lands by large coffee growers (McCreery 1994: 181–6). Because coffee producers complained about the availability of Indian labour, especially at harvest time, they pressured the government to devise and enforce a system of legalised debt labour which "effectively turned the countryside into a forced labor camp for much of the Indian population" (Brockett 1988: 24; McCreery 1994: 186–94).[2] Alienated from their own lands as coffee drew Guatemala into the vortex of the world economy, the country's indigenous peasantry became a labour reserve at the service of an expanding export sector.

Then, toward the end of the century, US banana companies began to establish themselves in lowland regions of Central America. Acquiring great concessions of land and building (and controlling) the railways with which the bananas were shipped, United Fruit Company (UFC) and Standard Fruit contributed little to the local economies while wielding enormous political influence, and, with US government backing, ensuring the survivorship of authoritiarian regimes which perpetuated gross disparities in access to arable land (Brockett 1988: 28–35; Acker 1988). The companies exemplified and reinforced these inequalities:

> United Fruit's Costan Rican holdings in 1950, for example, constituted not only 4 percent of the country's entire territory, but also almost double the amount of land planted in the three basic food crops. Banana company holdings in Honduras in 1971 were estimated still to be around two hundred thousand hectares, which was about one-half of the total area planted at that time in the three basic food crops. Furthermore, the land controlled by the banana companies is usually among the most fertile in the region, yet over the years much of it has been left uncultivated; in Honduras in 1960, only 17.7

---

2. Early in this century, further expansion of highland coffee production was helped by Rockefeller efforts to eradicate hookworm (Morgan 1993: 18). They also did this in the American South, for the benefit of textile manufacturers whose profits were reduced because hookworm diminished workers' productive capacity.

percent of that land was under cultivation while another 11.1 percent was devoted to cattle pasture. (Brockett 1988: 77)

In Guatemala, although United Fruit was the largest landowner in the country, it only worked 15 percent of its holdings (Thiesenhusen 1995: 79; Mason 1986: 212–13), while thousands of peasant families had little or no land.

The Arbenz land reform programme sought to redress this imbalance. While it had the support, among others, of the Guatemalan Communist Party, Arbenz made it clear early in his administration that his government was committed to capitalist development (Parkinson 1974: 39). For that reason, the land reform programme was actually modest – "only uncultivated land could be expropriated and then only from large farms" – and, contrary to the ultimate aim of the Communist Party, the reform did not eliminate private property (Thiesenhusen 1995: 76; cf. Handy 1994: 87–9). As Handy observes,

> It focused on the prevailing preoccupation of the administration to attack "feudalism" in the countryside and to inspire both more productive and more equitable agricultural enterprises.[3] The law abolished all forms of *servidumbre* (which the administration defined as near slavery in the countryside) and latifundia with the essential objectives of developing the "capitalist peasant economy and the capitalist agricultural economy in general"; giving land to peasants, *mozos colonos* or resident workers, and agricultural workers who possessed insufficient land; facilitating the investment of new capital in agriculture through the rental of national lands; introducing new methods of cultivation to peasants; and increasing agricultural credit to all peasants and capitalist agriculturalists. (Handy 1994: 89–90)

It was a thoughtful, workable and cautious programme; but it had been devised by and for Guatemalans and implemented by a government with broad popular support (Parkinson 1974: 39). As such, it involved the Guatemalan government expropriating some 146,000 hectares from United Fruit. While such expropriation was eminently logical in terms of the needs of the country's peasants, it was not in Guatemala's favour that the former head of United Fruit's law firm, John Foster Dulles, was by then the US Secretary of State. The weight of Rockefeller interests, with their own designs on Latin America, was also opposed to Guatemala's reforms and their influence wove through the governmental corridors of power at the time, beginning, again, with Dulles:

---

3. The land reform decree explicitly stated that it aimed to replace "the feudalist modes and relations of production with capitalist ones" (in Berger 1992: 64). It is also worth noting that the Communist Party – actually called the Guatemalan Labour Party (PGT) – had only four deputies in the Guatemalan Congress at the time of the coup and no members in the Arbenz cabinet (Treverton 1987: 48–9).

Rockefeller Foundation chairman John Foster Dulles, as chief partner of the Sullivan Cromwell law firm in 1936, had personally drafted United Fruit's 1936 contract with the Ubico dictatorship that gave the banana company its ninety-nine-year lease with exceptional tax benefits. Nelson's former assistant at the State Department, John Moors Cabot, owned stock in United Fruit and had been U.S. Ambassador to Guatemala. His brother, Thomas C. Cabot, Jr., had briefly been president of United Fruit. John J. McCloy, as president of the World Bank, had denied Guatemala loans after reviewing its agrarian reform and liberal laws; within a year, as chairman of Chase [the Rockefeller Bank], McCloy would sit on United Fruit's board. John McClintock, Nelson's former chief of the CIAA's Basic Economic Division, was now United Fruit's vice president and chief troubleshooter for Central America. (Colby and Dennett 1995: 849)

Another influential figure was the liberal-minded corporate lawyer Adolf Berle, a former Assistant Secretary of State for Latin America in the Roosevelt administration, former ambassador to Brazil at the time of the military coup against Vargas (about whose nationalist posture Berle had great reservations), and a long-time close associate of Nelson Rockefeller, who introduced him into the Council on Foreign Relations in 1946 (Colby and Dennett 1995: 182–91). After resigning his ambassadorship that year, Berle also became the chairman of the American Molasses Company, whose principal creditor was Chase Manhattan. He would also become chairman of SuCrest, a major sugar refiner in pre-Castro Cuba (Colby and Dennett 1995: 191, 313).

In the early thirties, Berle had written or co-authored a number of books – among them *The Modern Corporation and Private Property* (1932) with Gardner Means – which had argued against the idea that the owners (as opposed to the managers) of major corporations had effective influence over how those enterprises advanced their interests. Since then, evidence of the intimate relationship of owners and government decision-makers – as in the case of US policy against Arbenz – has thoroughly discredited what Lundberg called "the Berle-Means fantasy" (1968: 291; cf. Domhoff 1970). But so did Berle's own career.[4]

In October 1952, when the Council on Foreign Relations – many of whose members had some relationship to United Fruit – had responded to events in Guatemala with one of its famous study groups, in this

---

4. Hofstadter has observed that Berle was just one of a number of prominent New Dealers, including David Lilienthal, the head of the Tennessee Valley Authority, who came to glorify the virtues of big business in the post-war period. Berle in particular "urged liberals to reconsider their former, and historically unjustified, antipathy to big business", arguing "that the contemporary business power system is governed by public consensus" (Hofstadter 1965: 227). Unfortunately, Hofstadter did not explore the kinds of associations – such as that between Berle and Rockefeller – which might account for the emergence of such views.

instance on the subject of "Political Unrest in Latin America" (Colby and Dennett 1995: 233), Berle was one of its members and it was led by Spruille Braden, a former Assistant Secretary of State for Inter-American Affairs and a consultant for the company. It was becoming increasingly clear by this time, however, that the protection of private corporate interests could not provide the public rationale for intervention. The argument was developed that Guatemala had come under Soviet influence – even though Arbenz had come to office in free elections, with 63 percent of the vote (Parkinson 1974: 39, 47; Black 1984: 14). More importantly, despite the fact that they were only a minor part of the ruling coalition and that there were only four communists out of fifty-six members of the Chamber of Deputies (Black 1984: 15), "those on the lookout for Communists in Arbenz's entourage could find them" (Treverton 1987: 49–50). While United Fruit directed a public relations campaign against what it described as a communist government in Guatemala (Landau 1988: 65), Berle proposed that the Arbenz administration should be characterised as "a Russian-controlled dictatorship". This was the position taken by the CFR, and it was the viewpoint that Berle expressed in a memorandum on the "precise problem of how to clear out the Communists" (in Treverton 1987: 59) to Eisenhower's International Information Activities Committee. As the focal issue, it successfully obscured the fact that US policy was guided principally by the corporate interests of United Fruit.

In June 1954, US-backed Colonel Carlos Castillo Armas led an insurgent force from neighbouring Honduras into Guatemala, triggering a coup (Dunkerley 1988: 149–50). Although he himself was assassinated in 1957 (Black 1984: 19), the Cuban revolution only a few years later made it important to ensure that what Washington had called "the Guatemalan 'Liberation' ... became a model for other such US operations in Latin America" (Jonas 1974: 57). That, in turn, required the USA to counter any impression that the coup had been anything more than an indigenous response to communist subversion; and, according to Berle, to convince people in other countries that the "United States is the acknowledged successful symbolic leader" for those seeking "to achieve social justice and improved economic conditions" (Berle 1960: 54). As part of the process of legitimation of US intervention, the CFR (whose chairman then was McCloy, whose vice-president was David Rockefeller, whose board included former CIA director, Allen Dulles, and the head of whose studies programme was Philip Mosely, who had a close working relationship with the Ford Foundation and the CIA) duly published *Social Change in Latin America Today* (Cumings 1997: 14–15; Council on Foreign Relations 1960). It was a book with contributions by a number of prominent US anthropologists with expertise in Latin America. In it, matching his analysis to the prevailing ethos of the Cold War, John Gillin, wrote:

> Communists and fellow travellers had succeeded ... in infiltrating and practically taking over the government.... In 1954, the late Colonel Carlos Castillo Armas led a maneuver from the neighboring republic of Honduras which forcefully ejected the Communists and their followers from positions of power in Guatemala. However, it is still widely believed throughout Latin America that the U.S. government or its agents engineered and financed this "liberación", and this belief has been exploited so successfully by Communist and other antagonists of the United States that the "Yankee Colossus" has suffered a severe loss of prestige. (Gillin 1960: 17–18; cf. Adams 1960)

Several years earlier, Gillin had already written about the coup in *Foreign Affairs*, describing Castillo Armas as "a modest and earnest man to whom both efficiency and practical idealism mean a great deal" (Gillin and Silbert 1956: 470). He had managed to overlook the fact that Castillo

> reversed the reform quickly, often with flagrant disregard for human rights. Some estimate that 9,000 persons were imprisoned, many of them tortured. The UFC union and the labor unionization movement were destroyed. Over 99 percent of the land distributed in the agrarian reform was returned to its owners.... Even the literacy programs were stopped on the grounds that they were tools of communist indoctrination. (Thiesenhusen 1995: 80)

Anti-communism was obviously enough proof of his idealism.

Meanwhile, Berle had published his own book for the CFR, entitled *Latin America – Diplomacy and Reality*. In it, he proposed that, when land reform was introduced, it should be in the "balanced" way that was represented by the Alliance for Progress (Berle 1962: 57). What that meant, in part, was that proper respect should be accorded the large land-owner, not least because "Under his management the land produces more per man and per acre than it does in the hands of the small farmer" (Berle 1962: 51) This assumption, as the work of the UN Economic Commission for Latin America (UNECLA) shows, was generally not correct. But, even more contradictorily perhaps, it also coexisted with the ideal image that Berle – like many of his New Deal contemporaries, notable champions of a liberal corporate model – took as his template for developing agriculture the Mid-Western American farmer who, in fact, had been disappearing since the end of the Second World War (Ross 1980: 212; Michie 1982). Ignoring that, he wrote:

> The ideal of every sincere agrarian reformer is to produce a situation something like that in the United States, where on a relatively small farm a family cannot only live but live in comfort. (Berle 1962: 55)

According to Berle, development toward this end would bring about an increased productivity which would inevitably reduce the need for so many farmers. At the same time, the prevailing view was that the "rapidly growing manpower of Latin America cannot be productively employed without massive industrialisation", which was "one of the explicit goals of the Alliance for Progress" (Gordon 1963: 27) and one which invited US capital investment. Thus, the proposed path of agricultural modernisation would actually intensify the problem of rural underemployment, while foreign investment would provide the work for the resulting reserve of cheap labour. However doubtful the merits or even the likelihood of this scenario, the main point was that the ideal image which Berle and others painted could not be the result of sudden or radical change; it would take "at least a generation" (Berle 1962: 57).

But the Guatemalan peasant, however patient, was never destined to emulate the Iowa farmer. In the real world, the overthrow of Arbenz had reversed the process of land reform (Dunkerley 1988: 434ff.), reestablished the dominant role of the banana industry – largely controlled since 1972 by a subsidiary of Del Monte, itself a unit of the US conglomerate R.J. Reynolds (Gardner 1991; Jonas and Tobis 1974: 131) – and inaugurated an era of increased foreign investment of precisely the kind that Berle and his associates advocated. By the late 1970s, North American capital invested in Guatemala exceeded national investment (Dunkerley 1988: 464) and the country was being opened up for the development of cash crops and cattle, which put further pressure on a land-hungry rural population:

> In the 1950s and 1960s, the U.S. Agency for International Development (AID), private banks and U.S.-led multinational development banks, such as the Inter-American Development Bank and the World Bank, provided cheap loans to transform Guatemala's "backward" economy into an efficient agro-export machine, producing one or two main crops for the international market. (Gardner 1991)

While peasants were being starved of the means to create a viable family-based agriculture, commercial farming – the link between the ruling class of Guatemala and the world economy – received substantial support and encouragement:

> Between 1956 and 1980, large-scale agro-export production received 80 percent of all agricultural credit, as land devoted to cotton increased by 2,140 percent, to sugar by 406 percent and to coffee by 56 percent. The next export boom came with cattle a few years later. From 1960 to 1978, grazing land increased by 2,125 percent (Gardner 1991).

More recently, as many of these exports have declined with changes in the global economy, many Guatemalan peasants have been encouraged to cultivate non-traditional vegetables, fruits and flowers for the European and North American markets, making extensive use of pesticides and chemical fertilisers which have had a deleterious impact on the health of the land and the people who work it.

Disregard for the welfare of the majority reflects the fact that growing social and economic inequalities have proceeded hand in hand with the commercialisation of Guatemalan agriculture. This, in turn, mirrors the general tendency since the early 1950s to attribute a disproportionate number of social and economic problems in Latin America to the "fact" that population was rising faster than food production (Gillin 1960: 48; Halperin 1956). There was little consideration of the way that agricultural production and productivity were suffering from the commercial development in the countryside.

By the late sixties, in their Neo-Malthusian work *Famine 1975!*, William and Paul Paddock explained the nature of Guatemala's food insecurity as follows:

> Land has been put into production which simply lacks the qualities needed to *maintain* production. The rising cost of food combined with the population pressures on the land have pushed farmers farther and farther up the hillsides and farther and farther out into the jungle. They are now tilling land which should never have been farmed. (Paddock and Paddock 1967: 46)

But the reason it was being farmed had nothing to do with peasant fertility. Especially after the ouster of Arbenz, good land was increasingly inaccessible. Just a few years after the Paddocks wrote, large landholders, who constituted less than 2 percent of the population, received almost 41 percent of all national revenues (Berger 1992: 2). Some forty years after the overthrow of Arbenz,

> Guatemala has the most unequal land tenure in all of Latin America, with less than 2 percent of the landowners controlling 65 percent of the farmland. At the other end of the scale, approximately 27 percent of the total population is landless and forced to work as part-time wage laborers. As more land has become concentrated in fewer hands in the last 30 years, the average size of small farms has declined from 1.71 to 0.79 hectares. (Gardner 1991; cf. Brockett 1988: 72–3)

One consequence was the emergence of populist insurgency. While the Paddocks's argument, that the problem of Guatemalan agriculture was chiefly demographic, was meant to provide an ideological defence against the legitimacy of popular struggle for access to land, the Guatemalan state – dedicated to the interests of a small privileged class and enjoying the logistical support of the United States (Thiesenhusen 1995: 84–5; Dunkerley 1988: 425–515; Adams 1970: 262ff.) – adopted more forceful measures, which became ever more terroristic as even the lands onto which peasants had been displaced or encouraged to colonise were targeted for mineral development (Mason 1986: 214) or cattle ranching (Faber 1993: 66, 134–5). By the 1980s, Guatemalans lived under one of the most repressive governments in the world (cf. Berger 1992: 1–2; Black 1984). That and the unresolved lack of access to land or productive employment has impelled an estimated 200,000 Guatemalans to seek refuge and work in Mexico, the United States or elsewhere (Faber 1993: 73).

Population, Cattle and Clearances in Central America

The intervention against Arbenz foreshadowed by half a decade US efforts to undermine the Cuban Revolution. But in that instance the USA was unsuccessful in its attempt to depose a popular progressive government by force. It was precisely that failure, however, which moved the Kennedy administration to devise alternative arrangements, includ-ing the Alliance for Progress, created in 1961 to forestall Cuban-style change throughout the Americas.

In 1960, just before the Alliance for Progress was initiated, the UN Economic Commission for Latin America had observed that one of the chief obstacles to increased food production was a land tenure system which denied millions of the poor access to adequate land of good quality, while a small number of large landowners (*latifundistas*) exercised monopoly control over high-quality land (UNECLA 1968: 335–6). Despite the predominant view among writers as diverse as Berle and the Paddocks that large farms represented optimum land use, the UNECLA noted that a high proportion of latifundia lands were under-utilised, causing rural labour underemployment – what Neo-Malthusians, however, typically described as a surplus rural population – which in turn maintained a reserve of low-waged workers (UNECLA 1968: 346). As a result, comparative statistics from seven countries in Latin America, compiled by the Inter-American Committee for Agricultural Develop-ment (CIDA), indicated that, "although in the aggregate the latifundios occupy 23 times as much land as the minifundios, the amount of cul-tivated land on the large estates was only about 6.5 times greater than on the small farms" (UNECLA 1968: 347). Much of the land on large estates was devoted to cattle grazing and a large proportion was fallow, even where soils were of sufficient quality for productive cultivation. As a result, "only 4 per cent of the total amount of land belonging to latifundios was planted with annual or permanent crops" (UNECLA 1968: 348). In contrast, small farm units not only devoted more of their acreage to producing food, but typically practised more intensive forms of cultivation (UNECLA 1968: 349).

It is little wonder, then, that the UN survey concluded that the prevailing system of land use in Latin America – which remains more or less the same today – wasted cultivable resources. It noted that

> From the point of view of the economy as a whole, this traditional system of land tenure means that total output is lower and that domestic food require- ments cannot be met satisfactorily because much of the land on large estates is sown to export crops. Moreover, in view of future reforms of the land tenure system, the skill with which the small producers work their often inadequate farms is evidence of their ability to use land efficiently, and it can be assumed that, if the difficulties which now curtail their activities were removed, their contribution to agricultural output would be even larger. (UNECLA 1968: 350–51)

The report underscored the fact that a process of land reform which liberated productive land from a system of under-use and provided small-scale cultivators with sufficient means to cultivate such land as productively as their knowledge and skill permitted would militate against any imminent food scarcity. Throughout the hemisphere – indeed, throughout the world – millions of peasants had already come to that conclusion.

One of the many aims of the Alliance for Progress was to subdue the consequences of such conclusions through the development of commercial, export-oriented agriculture. Behind such objectives lay several imperatives, one of which clearly was the preservation and enhancement of US economic interests. Malthusian thinking played a central role in justifying this. As Dunkerley observes, "Since the Alliance for Progress began ... US planners have provided a remarkably techno- cratic imprimatur to the popular prejudice that the root problem is 'too many people'" (1988: 177). The solution consisted largely of plans for "improvements in the ratio of production to population" (Dunkerley 1988: 176) but in practice such plans emphasised exports at the expense of local consumption. As a result, they were actually a major factor in the eventual deterioration of regional food crop output (Stonich 1991). Most of the countries of Latin America ended up importing basic foods from the United States, which gave the superficial *impression* that popu- lation was outstripping its food supply.

When the Paddocks argued that catastrophic famines would soon sweep through Latin America, they must have known that this was unlikely and that, under any circumstances, food insecurity was not the result of Malthusian pressures. After all, William Paddock had directed the Iowa State College–Guatemala Tropical Research Center in Guatemala in the period after the ouster of Arbenz and then, in 1957, had become the director of La Escuela Agricola Panamerica (EAP) in Honduras. The EAP was established in 1940 by United Fruit (Colby and Dennett 1995: 318).[5] So, it may not be so strange that, reading their book today, it can be seen as an argument against any "disruption of land ownership" (Paddock and Paddock 1967: 89).

For the Paddocks, however, land reform was not only a way of undermining the rights of private property; they also argued that it would reduce food production because, in their view, existing landowners were the repository of all agricultural wisdom (Paddock and Paddock 1967: 89). This was despite the observation by UNECLA that not only were latifundia severely under-producing food, but that they actually tended to be poorly managed (UNECLA 1968: 352). It was, in fact, the resistance of such land-owners and their supporters to what the Paddocks called a "drastic transformation in land use" which seemed more likely to ensure a future food crisis. Not famine perhaps, but it was the reversal of the Arbenz reforms that virtually guarenteed that several generations of Guatemalans would suffer increasing material and nutritional deprivation. By 1981,

> An estimated 83 percent of the rural population lived in poverty … and 41 percent of these people lacked even a minimal diet. As a result, approximately 81 percent of all children less than five years of age suffered from malnutrition at that time, and about 870,000 Guatemalan peasants were suffering from extreme poverty. (Berger 1992: 3)

Deforestation Instead of Land Reform

While the Paddocks were presenting their justification for the landowning patterns of Central America, landlords in many parts of Latin America were engaged in a strategy of land use, with the support and encouragement of international capital, which would eventually transform much forest and farmland to pasture (Williams 1986). It was not merely an echo of the clearances that had swept through rural England and Ireland in Malthus's day; it was the same process, rationalised in much the same way.

---

5. The EAP was founded, among others, by Samuel Zemurray and Thomas Cabot. Zemurray was "Sam the Banana Man", chairman of United Fruit and one of the the most notorious foreign businessmen who dominated the political and economic life of Honduras before the First World War (Langley and Schoonover 1995). The Cabots were major shareholders in the company (Acker 1988: 65; Colby and Dennett 1995: 320, 849).

The lives of the region's peasantry had long been severely circum-scribed by a pattern of development which not only had concentrated prime arable land in the hands of a few families, but had ceded large tracts of territory (and considerable political and economic authority) to foreign companies devoted to production for export. The beef-export boom exacerbated deeply entrenched inequalities and inflamed habitual antagonisms between peasants and large land-owners. Yet, by 1984, the Kissinger Commission report would regard "overpopulation" as "a serious threat to the development and health of the region" and recom-mend "continuation of the population and family programs currently supported by the [US] Agency for International Development" (1984: 388, 381), while it urged further development of the export sector (with especial emphasis on beef). Although such recommendations were con-sistent with the historical role of the United States defining Latin American patterns of resource use with little regard for local needs or consequences, the export policy which Kissinger endorsed was certainly a major factor behind "the transformation of substantial amounts of land from forest or from growing food crops to pasture" (Stonich 1991: 67; cf. Meehan and Whiteford 1985: 183–5).

This policy can only be understood in terms of the influence of the US market – and the USA and international institutions and policies which served the interests of that market and its major players (primarily multinational food companies). Although the USA was a major meat-consuming nation virtually since its inception, pork was the dominant meat until just after the Second World War, when revolutionary new methods of maize cultivation flooded American feed-lots with sufficient cheap grain to fatten unprecedented numbers of cattle (Ross 1980: 207). During this period, beef was actively promoted by major supermarket chains. But in fact most of the rise in beef intake was the result of the mass availability of hamburger manufactured from relatively cheap, low-quality meat, frequently derived from dairy cows. By the late 1970s, at least 40 percent of all beef consumed in the United States was in the form of ground beef (Ross 1980: 213). This reflected a quarter-century of social and economic change, characterised by extensive suburban growth, the expansion of a national highway system and a dramatic rise in working women, all of which factors encouraged the popularity of readily accessible and affordable, mass-produced fast-food to such an extent that, by the 1970s, fast-food was the most rapidly developing part of the US food industry, which was itself a major field for corpo-rate investment.

While pigs and beef cattle were both ultimately dependent on what, by then, under the influence of growing oil prices, was becoming increasingly expensive grain, hamburger was potentially less affected by such constraints. As new technology meant that the lowest grade meat could be processed into an acceptable mass product, it became increasingly worthwhile to import grass-fed cattle from regions such as Central America, once appropriate processing, packing and transport facilities were installed. This was already beginning to occur in the late 1950s (Williams 1986). The dramatic rise in US hamburger consumption therefore coincided not only with the proliferation of fast-food burger franchises (Boas and Chain 1976), but also with the rapid rise in United States beef imports that began in the early 1960s (Edelman 1987). Imports from Costa Rica alone, as a proportion of that country's major exports, rose between 1962 and 1972 from 2.9 to 10 percent (De Witt 1977: 134–5). A similar trend characterised most of Central America, as the size of the region's herd increased to the point where, by 1978, it provided the US market with 15 percent of its annual beef imports (Williams 1986: 77).

From the US viewpoint, these imports were of tremendous value when domestic beef prices, including that of hamburger, began to rise in the 1970s. As Myers has noted,

> Food is the sector of the US economy most susceptible to inflation, and the greatest price increases have been for meat, and especially beef. It is believed that increased imports of cheap Central American beef have done more than any other single governmental initiative. Indeed, the US government calculates that the additional imports save consumers at least $500 million a year. (1981: 5)

From a Malthusian perspective, the trend of increasing food imports in Central America has, as in the case of the Paddocks, been taken as a prima facie indicator of a population crisis. But viewed in terms of the adverse effect of rising cattle production on other forms of land use, the subsistence and environmental crises which have typified the region over the last decades do not fit so conveniently (if at all) into a restrictive Malthusian framework. The proper context – as for understanding the contemporary circumstances of *any* developing country – is that of global political economy, not local reproductive habits.

A major factor has been the role of the major US banks, most of which had an interest in the feed grain and meat industry (Ross 1980: 211–21) and international financial institutions, which began to take an interest in developing Central American beef exports during the 1970s. According to Cheryl Payer, in her analysis of the World Bank, by 1975 "livestock loans constituted nearly one-third of all bank credit projects and in Latin America the figure was extremely high – 70 percent" (1982: 214).

> Of the $3,184.0 million the [World] Bank lent in the Latin American and Caribbean region as of mid-1979 the largest single category was livestock credit, which accounted for $903.0 million, or 28.4 percent of agricultural and rural development lending; in comparison, loans for agricultural (crop) credit amounted to $325.4 million, or only 10.2 percent. (Edelman 1992: 197)

A similar investment strategy was pursued by the Inter-American Development Bank (IDB), which, during the first two decades since its inception in the early 1960s, became one of the most important sources of public external finance for regional development (Arnold 1980: 89). The IDB was created in the wake of the Cuban Revolution, along with the Alliance for Progress, amid growing US fears about regional instability. Some sense of how the USA regarded its ultimate role is suggested by the fact that, in the 1960s, the US Executive Director of the IDB was Robert Cutler, a former president and director of one of the Boston banks for United Fruit. He had also been Special Assistant for National Security Affairs for Kennedy at the time of the invasion of Guatemala (Jonas 1974: 62).

The establishment of the IDB also coincided with the effort to export birth control programmes to the region, in the belief that demographic pressures were one of the major destabilising factors. It was not at all unexpected, therefore, that Antonio Ortiz Mena, the institution's first president, observed in 1971 that

> At this time, one of the most serious challenges we must face is the population explosion. Latin America's annual average population growth is higher than in any other part of the world. (Ortiz Mena 1975: 7)[6]

Such perceptions strongly affected development policy. As Dunkerley notes in his masterly study of the region:

> it has been an enduring characteristic of US government policy prescriptions for Central America's poverty that it be ameliorated through improvements in the ratio of production to population ... prior to those in distribution of income within that population. The most familiar feature of this policy is its attachment to export-led growth as the key to success, but it should be noted that in this zone of the world such a prescription has over the last thirty years been supported by a Malthusian belief that it is not just the inadequacy of production but also an excessive human stock that underlies the problem. (1988: 176)

As we have seen, this can be another way of referring to an excess of troublesome peasants.

---

6. The source of such views may not be too hard to find. Ortiz Mena had been a director of the Mexican Light and Power Company along with William Draper, a major figure in the institutionalisation of birth control in US geo-political policy (see Chapter 4).

The IDB was organised in such a way that each member country had an equal vote – but then had one additional vote for each share of capital stock of the Bank held by that country. As a result, by 1971, the USA alone had 42 percent of all votes (Dell 1972: 38), so that IDB policies tended to reflect the priorities of the US market, with its increasing demands for cheap Central American beef. The availability of low-interest, long-term credit for cattle production readily encouraged the displacement of subsistence crops by ranching and helped to create a situation in which, far from too many people threatening per capita food availability, it was actually the increase in livestock which reduced domestic food supplies. In Costa Rica

> Land converted to cattle farms increased an average of 60,000 hectares per year between 1963 and 1973. By the end of the 1980s, 54 percent of all farmland was in cattle production, and in large part because of this, Costa Rica had the highest deforestation rate in the world. (Honey 1994: 161; Edelman 1992: 248)

And while Central American beef helped to subsidise a level of US protein intake that often far exceeds human metabolic requirements (Ross 1987: 42) – an intake level associated, in fact, with a variety of degenerative diseases – protein consumption in Central America declined. In Costa Rica, which is widely regarded as the most developed country in the region,

> in 1975 the Ministry of Health noted that between 43 percent and 73 percent of the country's preschoolers suffered from nutritional deficits, and the government declared that "childhood malnutrition constitutes the country's most severe social problems [*sic*]". (Whiteford 1991: 128)

The beef boom also had profound environmental consequences. Because of the ease of credit for cattle expansion, there was generally little incentive to intensify production. It was far more lucrative for cattle ranchers to expand their acreage, sometimes ousting peasants and appropriating cropland, at other times moving into forest (Williams 1986). Deforestation is obviously a major global problem, but the evidence from Central America and elsewhere suggests that it can rarely be regarded as exclusively or even primarily a product of population growth, as is often claimed. Yet writers such as Myers, exemplifying today's more sophisticated and subtle Malthusianism, maintain that population – not development policy – is the principal cause of environmental degradation in such regions. Of course, Myers acknowledges other contributing factors, and such apparent fair-mindedness makes his essentially Malthusian message much more acceptable. But in the end he largely lays the blame for global deforestation at the feet (or the axe) of small-scale cultivators. In a recent paper, he writes, for example,

> Driven significantly by population growth and sheer pressure of human numbers on existing farmlands ... slash-and-burn farming by small-holders is the principal factor in deforestation ... Of course one must be careful not to over-simplify the situation. In many areas other factors are at work, notably inequitable land-tenure systems, inefficient agricultural techniques, and faulty development policies overall. *But population growth appears at present to be the predominant pressure on forests* [my italics]. (1991: 242)

The alternative view is that it has, in fact, been the kind of development favoured in recent decades by the World Bank, the IDB and private multinational banks such as Chase Manhattan[7] that has led to the present environmental and nutritional crises in such regions, by failing to challenge the restrictive monopolies over land exercised by regional elites, and, indeed, by tending to enhance their privileges. Where land distribution had been inequitable long before the beginning of the cattle boom, the expansion of cattle ranching only worsened the situation (Carriere 1991: 191). Large numbers of peasants were pushed off their land, reducing the output of staple crops available for local consumption, while ranching – singularly undemanding of labour – failed to absorb the increasing numbers of landless workers. As Carriere observes of Costa Rica, displaced peasants could either choose to drift to urban centres where employment was limited or "move on to fragile marginal lands that can provide temporary livelihoods for a few seasons before becoming degraded beyond redemption" (1991: 192).

While loggers, ranchers and real-estate developers have contributed substantially to the process of deforestation (Carriere 1991: 190), it is almost always the role of peasant cultivators which attracts most attention and blame (cf. Crossette 1996. For that reason, it is worth underscoring that their movement onto vulnerable lands is not simply a survival strategy, but follows from development policies which have often left them no other immediate option. To blame the environmental outcome on their reproductive behaviour is merely to follow in the Malthusian tradition of mystifying the inequities of capitalist development.

The situation in El Salvador was typical. In the second half of the nineteenth century, communal farms, which made up a large proportion of peasant lands, had been dissolved into small private holdings that were eventually consolidated into large coffee plantations. A dual process of increasing landlessness, on the one hand, and land concentration, on

---

7. Chase Manhattan had established a "comprehensive cattle credit program" in Panama in the early 1950s (Freivalds 1985: 241).

the other, was established which became so extreme that, by 1975, less than 1 percent of all landowners possessed 40 percent of the land, while between 40 and 65 percent of households had no land and just under half of those with land had less than one hectare (Mason 1986: 202–3). Social conditions in rural areas were appalling. As North notes:

> Only 15 per cent of the country's school teachers served in the rural areas, where most of the country's 40 per cent-illiterate population lived. With 60 per cent of rural families earning less than the minimum necessary to buy subsistence foods, malnutrition among children stood at shocking levels. Between 1971–1975, among children under five, 48.5 per cent were estimated as suffering from mild malnutrition (in other words, requiring more and better food for recovery), 22.9 per cent from moderate malnutrition (needing medical attention) and 3.1 per cent from severe malnutrition (requiring hospitalization for recovery). Most of these children were rural. But 67 per cent of the country's doctors worked in San Salvador. (North 1981: 65)

By then, coffee was no longer the sole economic imperative for the ruling oligarchy. While it still represented 50 percent of the country's export earnings in 1985 (Dunkerley 1988: 191), cotton had assumed some importance as well. But it was the expansion of cattle grazing which really added to the pressures on rural families in El Salvador, as in most of the countries of the region after 1960. By 1980, more land would be used for grazing cattle in El Salvador than producing food (Mason 1986: 203).

One of the consequences was that El Salvador's rural poor were quite literally squeezed out. Many migrated into neighbouring Honduras where, up to 1950, there were still opportunities for cultivating unclaimed lands or, alternatively, for working on large estates, including the banana plantations of United Fruit (North 1981: 62–3). By the end of the sixties, an estimated one-fifth of Honduran peasants were, in fact, Salvadoreans (Acker 1988: 93). By then, the Honduran landlords were beginning to treat the Salvadorean migrants as a scapegoat for the real problems in the countryside, in particular the increasing monopoly over land.

It is hardly surprising that, as the dramatic expansion of cattle ranching increased the dominance of large estates and further dispossessed the poor (Dunkerley 1988: 193–5), there was increasing popular pressure for agrarian reform. This eventually would culminate in civil war in El Salvador and Nicaragua (North 1981: 61–95), while, in Honduras, peasants organised and invaded land and often had notable success in winning recognition of their rights. But at the same time, ranchers and other major landowners responded with terror and violence in their own bid for more land (Williams 1986: 124–8). As Barry writes:

> Evictions became common during the 1960s and 1970s as the cotton and cattle industries reached out for land occupied by small, powerless campesino families. The land-grabbing resulted in tense and often bloody confrontations between the land-owners and indignant peasants. (1987: 145)

Most of the governments of the region, which represented the power and influence of the landed oligarchies, also became increasingly repressive, which had the effect of transforming popular resistance into revolutionary movements which spread throughout the region during the 1970s (North 1981: 77ff.).

For the Paddocks, who labelled land reform an unrealistic solution to the food crisis anywhere in the developing world, the growing subsistence crisis in El Salvador, Honduras and their neighbours was unrelated to any features of political economy. If, in their view, "the ownership pattern already properly fit ... the limits which local geography has placed on the land" (1967: 87), and if foreign-owned plantations, such as those of United Fruit, somehow represented the natural and inevitable use of Central American land, then Malthusian pressures must be the principal cause of peasant unrest. It hardly seems possible, when so much land is removed from general use, to argue that excess fertility is the primary cause of people's material deprivation. Such an interpretation, by obscuring the economic and social realities of the region, could only intend to undermine the legitimacy of peasant struggles.

6
False Premises, False Promises: Malthusianism and the Green Revolution

One of the legacies of the role of Malthusian thinking in post-war US development policies (including the ongoing commercialisation of Third World agriculture) is that the Green Revolution is still regarded largely as a humanitarian response to population pressures in the Third World. That these pressures were less the result of too many people on the land than of inequalities in access to agricultural resources is far from most people's minds.

The prevailing view of the Green Revolution was enshrined early on by the award of the Nobel peace prize in 1970 to Rockefeller Foundation geneticist Norman Borlaug for his role in developing hybrid wheat in Mexico. A quarter-century later, while much has been learned about its adverse consequences, remarkably little has been done to question the conventional explanation of the origins and aims of the Green Revolution. As a result, prominent Neo-Malthusians such as Paul Ehrlich still describe Borlaug as "a founder of the green revolution" (Ehrlich et al. 1993: 3), as if the latter had never been more than a package of technological innovations, attributable to a handful of scientists, and unrelated to any geo-political agenda.

These are the neutral terms in which the Green Revolution has been persistently represented as the major factor which prevented the famines regularly predicted for much of the Third World (cf. Paddock and Paddock 1967). It is a view which continues to rationalise calls for renewed investment in intensification of agro-technology by organisations such as the International Food Policy Research Institute (IFPRI), the think-tank of the Consultative Group on International Agricultural Research in Washington (which has guided the course of global agricultural development since the early 1970s; see Chapter 7), and the Council on Foreign Relations, which reflects the views of the US policy-making establishment. Both argue that the benefits of the Green Revolution were squandered because developing countries failed to curb their fertility and that Malthusian catastrophe may still be on the horizon (cf. Mathews 1994). They thus share the view expressed by Lester Brown, when he was a Senior Fellow with the Overseas Development Council in Washington, that "Ultimately the only solution to the food problem will be the curbing of world population growth" (1977: 35).

While such a limited view has proven, as we have seen, to be particularly perilous for the fate of peasants, it has proven to be highly serviceable for Western interests. From the 1950s onward, it effectively rationalised the need to develop new high-yielding food crops whose introduction transformed Third World agriculture in a manner which primarily enhanced the interests of Western capital. Whether it also advanced the interests of the land-hungry and nutritionally deprived rural poor is highly problematical. Whether it was even meant to may be more to the point. And in the same way, the current call to revive the Green Revolution may be a response less to a real Malthusian crisis than it is to a crisis in the nature of Western capitalism.

Today, there may still be some time to discuss that point, but in the 1950s there was little debate. A food crisis in the Third World was said to be imminent. The publicly stated starting point was the ostensible threat that rising population presented for the assurance of an adequate diet in developing countries. In policy circles, however, where concern centred more on the implications for political stability of rising pressures for land reform, Malthusian thinking usefully shifted the terms of the argument. The food problem in the Third World could be regarded as

> a direct result of the fact that many of these countries had virtually exhausted the supply of new land that could be readily brought under cultivation but had not yet achieved a takeoff in yield per acre. It was in this context that the green revolution – the combination of new cereal technologies and production-oriented economic incentives – came into being. (Brown 1977: 31)

As recently as 1986, such thinking still led John Mellor, a Cornell agricultural economist who had worked at USAID (Mellor and Adams 1986: 297) and was then located at IFPRI, to advise that "a strategy of development stressing technological change in agriculture represents the most practical means for meeting the ever-increasing food needs of the Third World". Land reform, as we have seen, was not only impractical. In most cases, it was also considered undesirable. On the other hand, the argument that there was no more land to cultivate and that technological change was the best option was a very convenient way to side-step the fact that large farmers were underutilising land which peasants could have brought into production. It was the central justification of the strategy of the Green Revolution, which simultaneously denied the yield-raising potential of land redistribution and represented a commitment to a more entrepreneurial mode of production, oriented to the world market rather than to local subsistence needs.

As US Secretary of Agriculture Orville Freeman would write in *Foreign Affairs* in 1967:

> If we are ever to solve the world food problem, we must now begin concentrating in earnest on increasing food production in the less developed nations. We have a pretty good idea of what is needed. In varying proportion according to particular situations, the hungry countries need: increased quantities of fertilizer and other farm chemicals, improved varieties of seeds, increased availability of water, added credit, productive price policies, improved marketing facilities and expanded research and education. (1967: 592)

There was no mention of access to land, and the ultimate implications for peasant communities were not explicitly addressed. But three decades after the Rockefeller Foundation first established its wheat research centre in Mexico, J. George Harrar, the plant pathologist from the University of Washington who was its first director (Fitzgerald 1986: 463) and who became the president of the Foundation in 1961 (and later its president emeritus), openly observed, in a talk to the Agribusiness Council, that "agriculture is a business and, to be successful, must be managed in a businesslike fashion" (Harrar 1975: xi). Behind the scenes, then, the Green Revolution had never been regarded only, or even primarily, about producing more food, but about creating a global food system in which peasant agriculture, widely regarded as backward and unproductive in terms of a modern market economy (which itself was said to be threatened by demographic pressures in developing countries), was subordinated to or replaced by a more commercial and capital-intensive mode of production, in which the basic units of production resembled Berle's American image of a farm as a food-producing firm. One might go further and suggest that one of the ultimate aims of creating such a system was that local food production in developing countries would actually be *reduced*; that Third World agriculture would be developed in favour of agricultural exports, while the United States profited as a supplier of agricultural inputs and as the principal source of food grains for the Third World.

The Rockefeller Foundation and the Origins of the Green Revolution

This is not surprising. From the onset, the Green Revolution represented an implicit commitment to capitalist relations of production, which, in turn, reflected the fact that the Ford and Rockefeller (and to a lesser degree the Kellogg) Foundations, which played such a significant role in its emergence and expansion, were an intimate and influential part of the US capitalist economy. As such, whatever their philanthropic pretensions, they came to play a prominent part – one whose amplitude and depth still remains to be thoroughly comprehended – in the design and implementation of US development policy after the end of the Second World War. Not unexpectedly, the global agricultural transformation which they promoted became a part of that policy. In that role, it was less about enhancing the food security of the poor in developing countries than about securing the economic security of the United States, through the enhancement of the Western corporate interests with which they were associated.[1]

By the time the Rockefeller Foundation began agricultural research in Mexico in the 1940s, it already had a long history of involvement in agricultural development initiatives at home and abroad. It had been engaged in the development of hybrid grains in the United States and had close associations with the US Department of Agriculture (USDA), especially through its efforts early in the century to eradicate the boll weevil in cotton-growing states in the American South. But many of the ideas about the nature and role of Third World development that characterised later Rockefeller work originated in its agricultural and health programmes in China during the inter-war years when the Foundation was closely associated with American missionary activities in a country which represented, as US Senator Albert Beveridge observed in 1900, "illimitable markets" (in Zinn 1980: 306). More specifically, China was also an important potential market for the source of the Foundation's wealth, Standard Oil, which, eager to sell its kerosene to light the oil-burning lamps of China, supported the US foreign policy toward China commonly known as the "Open Door".[2] One of the

---

1. As recently as 1978, the Rockefeller Foundation had 25.6 percent of its stock (common and preferred) in Exxon and 11.4 percent in Standard Oil of Indiana (United States Senate Committee on Governmental Affairs 1978: 743–4), and, as a US Congressional Report observed, "appeared to place a greater emphasis on receiving maximum return on its investment and tended to support management to a greater degree in its voting of proxies" (United States Senate Committee on Governmental Affairs 1978: 748). It may never be possible – or necessary – to disentangle their common interest in spreading "a package of practices that generally included improved seed and increased cultivation, fertilization and mechanization" (Fitzgerald 1986: 460). In 1974, the Ford Foundation still held 100 percent of Class A (non-voting) stock in the Ford Motor Company (Lundberg 1968: 476) and Benson and Henry Ford II sat on the board of trustees along with Robert McNamara and McGeorge Bundy, two of the leading architects of the Vietnam War. It was, at that time, the richest among the ten leading US foundations, with assets of well over $3 billion and an annual budget of more than $250 million (Hodson 1974: 310).

ways to open that door was through the missionary work with which the Foundation was associated and which conveniently reflected the Baptist upbringing of the elder John D. Rockefeller (Bullock 1980: 31). From the beginning, the varied sides of Rockefeller enterprise – the overtly commercial and the philanthropic – nicely embodied Tuchman's observation that "American infiltration of China ... was a two-pronged affair of business and gospel" (1971: 38).

Rockefeller support of missionary efforts in China was closely associated with the Agricultural College at Cornell University, which, since 1900, had established important connections with American agriculturalists working in China within the framework of Protestant mission activities. Around this time, there had been "a great outpouring of missionaries" to China (Bullock 1980: 31). But by the eve of the First World War, the mission societies had begun to acknowledge how little impact they had had on China after almost a century of efforts. They adopted a more practical approach, which embraced agricultural development as a vehicle for their missionary aims. As Stross observes in his account of their work,

A call for "agricultural missions" sounded in the 1910s and 1920s, providing some missionaries with a hopeful vision: If the church could improve production on Chinese farms China's grateful hinterland would open up and accept the Christian faith. (1986: 92)

One of the most important and well-known of these agricultural missionaries was Cornell-trained John Lossing Buck, who went out to China in 1915 and would later write the much-cited work *Land Utilization in China* (1937),[3] based on a large-scale survey financed by the Milbank Memorial Fund (Caldwell and Caldwell 1986: 11), but which had originated in a conference in 1925 at the Rockefeller-funded Institute of Pacific Relations in Honolulu (Szreter 1993: 697, 699). The way in which the data were presented in this popular form minimised the appearance of inequality in land distribution in pre-revolutionary China, undermining the logic of demands for land reform (Arrigo 1986; Thomson 1969: 211; Thaxton 1983: 28–9). It conformed to Buck's belief that "China's rural problems could be reduced to the simplest matter of matching production

---

2. The so-called "Open Door" policy of the United States sounded relatively benign and even idealistic but, for a country that feared it would lose out in the partitioning of China by other foreign powers, it was obviously designed in the interests of American trade by attempting to ensure that "the door for penetration [of China] should be opened equally to everybody" (Tuchman 1971: 38; cf. Kennan 1951: 23–37; Vevier 1956).

3. Buck's book had a chapter on "Population" by Frank Notestein, who wrote it after the death of his colleague, Edgar Sydenstricker, who was originally going to be the author. Sydenstricker's sister, the writer Pearl Buck, was John's wife (Szreter 1993: 699).

with population by increasing the one and reducing the other" (Stross 1986: 187).

In 1920, Buck had joined the faculty at the University of Nanking as Professor of Agricultural Economy and Farm Management. Nanking (or Nanjing) at that time was the capital of China and the university there had been organised in 1911 by American missionaries. Its Dean – later on, the director of the Agricultural Missions Foundation in New York (Thomson 1969: 73) – was another Cornell graduate, John Reisner, who was instrumental not only in securing Buck to teach agricultural economy, but in obtaining a grant in 1924 from the International Education Board (IEB), which the Rockefeller Foundation had established the previous year. The grant funded a joint project between Nanking and Cornell, which continued to maintain a relationship with China even after funding dried up in 1928 (Stross 1986: 145, 154–6) – scientists from Cornell's Plant Breeding and Agricultural Economics department were working with colleagues at Nanking into the 1930s. By 1931, "the Foundation had spent a total of US$37 million in China ... the highest figure for any foreign recipient" (Thomson 1969: 126). Almost all of this had gone into the medical field, and the support of the Nanking–Cornell project was the major exception (Thomson 1969: 126).

Perhaps the major Rockefeller effort during the 1920s had taken place just about the time that Buck had joined Nanking, and that was the founding of the Peking Union Medical College (PUMC). In 1921, John D. Rockefeller, Jr, and the president of the Rockefeller Foundation, George Vincent, travelled to China for its official opening. According to Bullock, the PUMC

> was a quintessentially American institution being transplanted to China. It was to be sustained financially by funds furnished from the monopolistic growth of the Rockefeller family's Standard Oil Company, nurtured intellectually by the leading medical scientists of the day, and blessed morally by a tacit alliance with evangelical missionary societies. (Bullock 1980: 2)

This was apt. Not only had the senior Rockefeller supported missionary work in China earlier in the century, but these evangelical impulses, along with a desire to circumvent new US tax codes and to polish the otherwise tarnished image of Rockefeller, were present at the very birth of the Rockefeller Foundation in 1913, under the guidance of Frederick Gates, "an erstwhile Baptist fundraiser" (Bullock 1980: 28). Roger Sherman Greene, who was intimately involved with the PUMC, both as vice-president of the Rockefeller Foundation in the Far East and as *de facto* director of the college, was himself the son of missionary parents who had worked in Japan (Bullock 1980: 48).

It is important not to underestimate the relevance for the later work of the Rockefeller Foundation of these formative years during which its interest in developing countries and its view of the role of agriculture in development were conditioned by its missionary associations in China. Thus, without ever abandoning its basic interest in the Westernisation (and Christianisation) of China, in the early 1930s the Foundation increasingly began to shift its strategy from one that had focused almost exclusively on medical education to one that, like its missionising contemporaries, saw rural development as a fundamental factor in creating economic and social stability.

This became an especially crucial concern in the decade after 1927, when the Kuomintang under Chiang Kai-shek purged its ranks of communists and established a national government in Nanking which, until the Japanese invasion of 1937, was regarded in Europe and the United States as the main hope for a China that would be both anti-communist and Westward-looking. Thus, in 1931, Selskar Gunn, a vice-president of the Rockefeller Foundation, first began to envisage a new programme for China. According to Thomson, Gunn's report, written after his second trip there in 1933 and entitled "China and the Rockefeller Foundation", is

> a document of major significance for an understanding of American influence on the development of Kuomintang China. Based on the state of the nation in 1933, it constitutes an evaluation both of China's modernizing process at the mid-point of the Nanking decade and American efforts to assist that process. It also constitutes a prescription for future action. In keeping with the foundation's chief interest, Gunn concentrated his attention on institutions of higher learning. By so doing, however, he was also concentrating on the major channels of Western influence. (Thomson 1969: 130)

An immediate result of Gunn's report was that, in December 1934, the Foundation's trustees approved a grant of US$1 million for a three-year programme in rural reconstruction (Thomson 1969: 139), which easily won the support of the Kuomintang rulers, since rural reconstruction in practice meant the establishment of Kuomintang control over areas reclaimed from the communists (Thomson 1969: 60–70). Thus, in 1937, Mme Chiang Kai-shek wrote to Gunn of how she and her husband intended to "do everything possible to make this program of rural reconstruction an outstanding success" (in Thomson 1969: 147). Within a few months, however, Japan and China were at war. The Foundation's funding continued in various forms until 1942. But the most enduring impact of its work in China would prove to be the lessons it had learned about how to invest its resources strategically in the interests of managed rural change. As Thomson observes:

> If, indeed, there ever was a gradualist alternative to violent revolution in the Chinese countryside, the program of the Rockefeller Foundation came closer to reformers in Kuomintang China. It eschewed social revolution – and most notably was silent on the issue of land reform. But it provided unique support for those who sought to change the conditions of life in village China. (1969: 150)

As long as the advocates of change were not communists and, like Chiang Kai-Shek, were willing to work for the interests of the West.

The Ford Foundation and the Cold War

With the Communist Revolution in China, the Ford Foundation, established in 1936 with resources that dwarfed those of Rockefeller (Mattelart 1979: 156), underwent a dramatic redefinition of its role and aims. Its new role was defined by a report by one of its directors, the lawyer H. Rowan Gaither. The Gaither Report specifically placed the new direction of the foundation within the framework of the emergent Cold War when it noted:

> As the tide of communism mounts in Asia and Europe the position of the United States is crucial. We are striving at great cost to strengthen free peoples everywhere. The needs of such peoples, particularly in underdeveloped areas, are vast and seemingly endless, yet their eventual well-being may prove essential to our security. (in Rosen 1985: 4)

Gaither had already put his words into practice by using Ford resources to help create the RAND corporation. But this was just an early manifestation of what became the Ford Foundation's close involvement in the process of developing and implementing US foreign policy. According to George Rosen, an economist who worked both for the Ford Foundation and RAND,

> when the foundation began to consider its larger role, there was certainly an implicit, if not explicit, agreement between the assumptions and broad policy conclusions of the authors of the Gaither report and the assumptions underlying American foreign policy at the time. (1985: 7)

To implement its newly defined role, the Foundation enlarged its board of trustees, highlighting its increasingly intimate relationship with Washington policy-makers. One of the new board members, for example, was John J. McCloy, who had just left the presidency of the World Bank. The first director (later called president) under the reorganisation was Paul Hoffman, the former president of the Studebaker Corporation and the recent head of the Marshall Plan (Caldwell and Caldwell 1986:

20–21; Rosen 1985: 7–8). Hoffman had also been a member of the Draper–Johnson delegation to Japan in 1947 (Schaller 1985: 127) and later went on to head the UN Development Programme (Raffer and Singer 1996: 61). Another notable figure was Joseph Slater, who had served as secretary-general of the Allied High Commission for Germany in the 1940s and had then been the chief economist for the Creole Petroleum Corporation, a subsidiary of Rockefeller's Standard Oil of New Jersey. Before going to Ford, to run its International Affairs Programme (Caldwell and Caldwell 1986: 49), he had served as the Staff Director of the Draper Committee.

As Rosen notes of the people who came to work for the reorganised Ford Foundation:

> Many of the staff at the next level had been staff members on the Gaither report committee and/or senior government officials. Such a staff insured that there would be easy interchange of ideas between the foundation and higher-level American government. This happened easily and rapidly.
>
> The foundation staff, in particular John Howard, soon established a more or less informal network of relationships with officials of various public agencies, American and international, working in the foreign development field, including the State Department, the Point Four organization, the United Nations, and the Food and Agricultural Organization; with the Rockefeller Foundation, another nonprofit private foundation with lengthy experience in Asia and elsewhere; and with such knowledgeable individuals as Nelson Rockefeller and Howard Tolley. (1985: 8)

Hoffman's writings after he had taken over as head of the Foundation make even clearer the extent to which, at the beginning of the fifties, the thinking of the Ford leadership exemplified the Cold War rhetoric which prevailed in Washington. Like Forrestal and Nitze, Hoffman's vision of the world as the Korean War was beginning was decidedly apocalyptic. Everything about communism was aggressive, deceptive and deceitful. As he wrote in his book *Peace Can Be Won*:

> the Kremlin is looking with ever more naked avidity upon the oil fields of Iran and Saudi Arabia. In Indonesia, Communist agitation, subversion, propaganda and sabotage are increasing in speed and scope. Like a thunderhead over Western Europe is the menace of a Red Army march to the Atlantic. (Hoffman 1951: 14)

One practical manifestation of such views was the Foundation's hiring, in 1951, of Richard Bissell, Jr. Bissell, who had taught economics at Yale and MIT (Jonas 1974: 63), had been in the Office of Strategic Services (OSS) during the war, had been deputy administrator of the ECA under Hoffman and had governed its relationship to the Office of

Policy Coordination (OPC), which, through the activities of the OSS's successor, the CIA, had provided covert political support for the Marshall Plan (Pisani 1991: 6). Bissell stayed at Ford until 1953 or 1954, when he moved officially into the CIA, where he became a deputy director (Pisani 1991: 52, 140; Jonas 1974: 63) and eventually supervised the abortive Bay of Pigs invasion of Cuba in 1961 (Colby and Dennett 1995: 347–8). Before that, however, as Special Assistant to CIA director Allen Dulles, he had sat in on planning sessions for the "liberation" of Guatemala from its popular elected government of Jacobo Arbenz (Jonas 1974: 61–2).

The close ideological and operational association between Ford and the US government was consolidated when McCloy succeeded Hoffman as head of the Foundation, a role he assumed while he was also the chairman of the Rockefeller's Chase Manhattan and of the Council on Foreign Relations, of which he had been a member since 1939 (Bird 1992: 108) and which, by the mid-fifties, was well funded, not only by major US corporations but also by the Ford and Rockefeller Foundations (Bird 1992: 458). McCloy did nothing to discourage relations between Ford and the CIA, and all through the 1950s, while he headed the Foundation, he served informally as President Eisenhower's chief political adviser (Bird 1992: 426–9). By the early 1960s, it had become routine for the CIA to channel funds through the Ford (and Rockefeller and Carnegie) Foundation, to give support and respectability to selected international projects and programmes that served its sense of US strategic interests (Church Committee 1976: 182–3). One of its main concerns was the promotion of Asian studies in a few prominent US universities, including Yale and Cornell (Cumings 1997).

One of the main goals of such centres was to generate plausible academic theories about modernisation which were congenial to Western economic interests. Thus, in the early 1950s, after the Provost of MIT, Julius Stratton, had informed his friend Rowan Gaither about the Institute's plans to establish a new Center for International Studies (CENIS), Ford staff took an early role in the discussions that led to its creation and Bissell strongly endorsed the Foundation's backing of the Institute (Rosen: 1985: 31). That the centre's "ultimate aim ... [was] the production of an alternative to Marxism" (Rosen 1985: 27–9) was hardly surprising in light of the views of its principal staff, which included two of Bissell's former students. These were Walt Rostow, who would play an important role as adviser to Kennedy and Johnson during the Vietnam War, and Max F. Millikan, the Centre's head, who had come in 1952 from his job as director of economic research at the CIA (Rosen 1985: 28). Throughout the fifties, at least, the CIA was a major source of

CENIS funding and the Centre "provided an important go-between or holding area for the CIA, since 'top notch social scientists' and 'area experts' had no patience for extended periods of residence at CIA headquarters'" (Cumings 1997: 19). Among the scholars associated with CENIS, for example, was William Kaufmann, an authority on national security, whose career included work for the CIA, being head of the Social Science Division at RAND, and being on the National Security Council (Brookings Institution 1977).

In a world in which peasants and workers were struggling not just against national elites, but against Western interests in maintaining them, CENIS was a major source of literature on the psychology of development, in works by people such as Daniel Lerner, Lucien Pye and Everett Hagen, who conceptualised the so-called modernisation process as highly dependent on the existence and role of indigenous groups with "a rationalist and positivist spirit" (Lerner 1958: 45). In this sense, modernisation became Westernisation, defined by participation in the capitalist market economy. The conflicts and disruption which often accompanied modernisation were, in the view promoted by the CENIS scholars, less the product of the inequalities which the development process generated than of the way that new Western ideas clashed with the "stabilizing elements in traditional society" (Millikan and Blackmer 1961: 16).

If such views were to be regarded as the product of objective scholars seeking understanding of "the problems of development" in order to enlighten US policy-makers, it was of great importance to camouflage the CIA connection. This was also important so that money was easier to obtain from other sources. One of the most important of these, of course, was the Ford Foundation, which at that time had its own associations with the CIA. In mid-1952, Ford gave CENIS a preliminary grant of $125,000, followed, two years later, by a four-year grant totalling $750,000 (Rosen 1985: 31). Most of these funds were directed toward research on economic development in India, where the portrayal of a rural food crisis – as we shall explore more fully below – was increasingly in terms of over-population.

Meanwhile, some of the individuals who occupied important roles in the centres and institutions being supported by Ford also maintained an intimate association with the power elite and government. One of them was Philip Mosely, who not only directed Columbia University's Russian Research Center, but "was head of the Council on Foreign Relations from 1952 to 1956, a member of various boards and committees at the Ford Foundation, and a prominent leader of the American Political Science Association" (Cumings 1997: 12). In the years leading up to the flowering of McCarthyism, Mosley played a vital role as an adviser to some of Senator McCarthy's predecessors. His testimony on behalf of the Attorney General in 1953 had been instrumental in helping the Subversive Activities Control Board to categorise the Communist Party of the United States as a "communist-action organization" directed by the Soviet Union (United States Supreme Court 1961). Through the 1950s and 1960s, Mosely maintained close contacts with the CIA while he was also "a central figure at the Ford Foundation throughout the formative years of US area studies centers" (Cumings 1997: 12–14).

The Ford Foundation Goes to India

Events in China, as I have suggested, were the principal catalyst for many developments which drew the Ford and Rockefeller Foundations firmly into the field of Cold War policy. In 1949, as Kuomintang forces were being driven from mainland China, the State Department asked Ambassador-at-Large Philip Jessup to conduct a review of US Far Eastern policy. "The task", according to King (1956: 119), "was to seek an understanding of the conditions which led to the impasse in China and to devise ways to prevent these conditions from being repeated in the countries of Southeast Asia." One of Jessup's consultants was Raymond Fosdick, former president of the Rockefeller Foundation (King 1956: 119). The choice reflected the fact that both the Ford and Rockefeller Foundations were turning their attention to the general region of South Asia, where India (and to a lesser extent Pakistan) seemed to them especially vulnerable to communist influence. The Rockefeller Foundation had had a field office in New Delhi since 1935. Between 1942 and 1946, it temporarily replaced the Shanghai office as the Foundation's headquarters for the Far East; after the defeat of Chiang in 1949, it was permanently located in Bangalore (Rockefeller Foundation 1995). The 1950s also saw the Ford Foundation's activities in India expand to the point where they overshadowed all its other programmes outside the United States (Caldwell and Caldwell 1986: 4).

The potential significance of India had been heralded by Notestein after his visit to China for the Rockefeller Foundation, to survey "public health and demography" in that region, on the eve of Chinese communist victory (Ryder 1984: 13). In his report, he had concluded that, if one looked around the developing world and considered the impact of population on social and political stability,

> The subcontinent of India, precariously divided between Hindu and Muslims, comes most forcibly to mind as the next possible location for a serious outbreak of communism. (1984: 676)

Quite apart from the dubious premises of Notestein's Cold War demographic theory, there was good reason to anticipate peasant insurgency in a country where rural conditions were extremely oppressive. Byres and Crow describe the situation at Independence:

> [At] the apex of India's agrarian structure was a landlord class, which leased out land to a subject peasantry from whom it extracted a surplus in the form of rent. Some landlords, in their capacity as moneylenders, drew interest from peasants as well as rent, often keeping peasants in debt bondage. Some landlords used hired labour, frequently in an unfree relationship with the landlord, to work the land that was not leased out...
>
> Among poor peasants, land fragmentation was rife, access to credit was through the village moneylender ... at usurious interest rates, and the level of indebtedness was high...
>
> In 1951, 15 percent of all agricultural families were without land. (1988: 164)

Such conditions cannot be separated from the history of British colonial rule. After an initial period of straightforward plunder (Calder 1981: 691ff.), the East India Company had imposed a regime which was designed to maximise the extraction of revenues. From the end of the eighteenth century onward, as the authority of the Company gradually gave way to increasing rule by representatives of the British state, this brought about the wholesale transformation of Indian society. In particular, the British created new systems of land-ownership to facilitate the payment of rents (Thorner and Thorner 1962: 53–4). To meet these new demands for rent by landlords and by the state, peasants were duly impelled to raise the commercial crops which British industries required (Bhatia 1967: 24–34). This process became more intense as the momentum of British industrialisation grew. That "the importance of India to England in the first half of the nineteenth century lay in the fact that India supplied some of the essential raw materials – hides, oil, dyes, jute and cotton – required for the industrial revolution" (Knowles 1928: 305), helps to explain why the frequency and severity of famines, which had occurred under the rule of the East Indian Company, accelerated under the administration of the British Raj, when food production was increasingly displaced by such commodities.

As the new rulers built the steamships and the railways that linked rural India to the global market, the commercialisation of agriculture accelerated and the pressure on the means of subsistence grew. As the Thorners note:

> Wheat poured out of the Punjab, cotton out of Bombay, and jute out of Bengal. As commercial agriculture and money economy spread, the older practices associated with a self-subsisting economy declined. As industrial

crops (e.g., cotton, groundnuts, sugarcane, tobacco) were more paying than foodgrains, the peasants who could tended to shift over to these. In some districts the peasants shifted over completely to industrial crops and had to buy their foodstuffs from dealers. Villagers sent to market the cereal reserves traditionally kept for poor years. They became less prepared to meet poor harvests. Years of successive drought in the 1870s and 1890s led to great famines and agrarian unrest. (1962: 55)

Yet in India, as in Ireland, such famines came to be regarded as a "natural" measure of population pressure, rather than as a symptom of colonial economic development.

The pressures in the Indian countryside were exacerbated by the decline in the role of local craft production. For a long time, under the rule of the East India Company, India retained a craft and manufacturing sector which actually deluged England with cloth that was cheaper and better made than English material. While the Company itself profited from the export of Indian calicoes and muslins to England, the trade was so harmful to the English woollen industry generally that Parliament eventually introduced measures to protect domestic cloth.

This was not finally achieved until the official ending of the Company's monopoly in India in 1813. With the end of Company rule and the beginning of direct government by the British state, India was subjected to a deluge of English textiles – now cottons – while Indian imports into England were checked by prohibitive duties (Mukherjee 1974: 404). Between 1814 and 1835, English cotton piece-goods exported to India rose from 818,208 yards to 51,777,277 (Bhatia 1967: 17).

This took place at a time of increasing capital penetration of the Indian countryside. One consequence was rising rents which forced many peasants off the land and increased land concentration in the hands of moneylenders and landlords, draining wealth out of rural areas. Yet, at the same time, the agricultural sector was forced to absorb much of the population that had previously earned a living in the craft industries which British colonial policies were now destroying (Dutt 1940: 184–7). Since 1850

a dwindling proportion of the village artisans of the subcontinent have been able to subsist on what they have received for their services from the village. Millions of them have had to find other ways to gain a livelihood or to supplement their scanty earnings from the village. In most cases the only revenue open to them has been agriculture, and they have added steadily to the great pressure on the land which is one of the chief characteristics of contemporary Indian life. (Thorner and Thorner 1962: 57)

But at the same time the potential of Indian agriculture was diminished by a level of administrative neglect that had never been seen during the pre-colonial epoch. As Sir Arthur Cotton, a pioneer in modern irrigation works in India, wrote in 1854: "Public works have been almost entirely neglected throughout India" (in Dutt 1940: 194). As a result, much arable land declined into waste, previously reclaimed areas reverted to swamp where malaria and other diseases spread, and soil productivity generally declined over large areas (Dutt 1940: 204; Mukherjee 1974: 342). Such environmental degradation further increased rural insecurity and forced more people off the land, even as the agricultural sector had to support more people. The result was a decline in small-scale cultivators and a rise in the number of landless rural labourers.

At the heart of the agrarian problem of India was the fact that wealth was drained from the countryside as a result of the landholding and revenue polices created by the British, so that little capital was invested in agricultural development. By the late nineteenth century, the production of industrial crops was rising, but food cultivation, deprived of any incentive or means of innovation, and constrained by such factors as insecurity of tenure, size of landholdings and the role of money-lenders, stagnated. So, as the Thorners note,

> the net effect of British rule was to change drastically the social fabric of Indian agriculture, but to leave virtually unaffected the basic process of production and the level of technique. The upper strata of the new agrarian society benefited handsomely. The position of the cultivators deteriorated. Capital needed for the development of agriculture was siphoned off, and the level of total output tended toward stagnation. (Thorner and Thorner 1962: 111)

Yet through the nineteenth century, partly as a result of public health measures, partly because of the need to deploy more human labour in the absence of capital, Indian population grew. The resultant pressure on the land was not the result of fertility, however, so much as the consequence of the underdevelopment of food production.

The general situation which characterised late British India did not change significantly after Independence, which actually "witnessed the strengthening of the existing structure of land monopoly and the processes of dispossession and marginalisation of the peasantry" (Dewan 1990: 176). The result, as in the century before, was a continuing pattern of popular resistance (Joshi 1969: 447–8), although it was no longer British authority but the government of India which assumed the role of quelling such revolts.

Even as Independence was approaching, two major peasant uprisings had taken place: the Tebhaga movement in Bengal in 1946–47 and

Telangana in former Hyderabad State in South India, which began in 1946 and lasted until 1951 (Banerjee 1984: 17–19; Dhanagare 1991: 154–212). In Bengal, the increasing subordination of the agrarian economy to market demands for cash crops such as jute had led, since the turn of the century, to ever greater misery among smallholders and sharecroppers or *bargadars*. Then, famine had taken one and a half million lives in 1942–43. Although the Bengal famine gave a great impetus to post-war Malthusian thinking in India, it was largely the result of rural commercialisation and rising prices for food grains (Dhanagare 1991: 158–61).

As Dhanagare observes, efforts to organise peasants in Bengal date from the early 1920s (Dhanagare 1991: 162ff.). The Tebhaga movement – the movement for sharecroppers to pay only one-third (instead of one half) of their harvest to *jodedars* (a class of sub-landlords) – grew out of that history, in which the Communist Party of India (CPI) had played a notable role (Dhanagare 1991: 162–7), but it was limited in its aims and impact. The Telangana revolt was more formidable. It was largely the product of the efforts of the CPI and it challenged the economic and political structure of Hyderabad, the largest princely state in pre-Independence India, whose despotic ruler, the Nizam, was one of the wealthiest men in the world. The revolt, which took place in the Telangana districts, where the exploitation of peasants was the most intense in the entire state (Dhanagare 1991: 184–9), represented "an agrarian liberation struggle to get rid of feudal landlordism and the Nizam's dynastic rule" (Banerjee 1984: 19):

> By 1947, a guerrilla army of about 5,000 was operating in Telengana. During the course of the struggle, which continued till 1951, the people could organize and build a powerful militia comprising 10,000 village squad members and about 2,000 regular guerrilla squads. The peasantry in about 3,000 villages, covering roughly a population of three million in an area of about 16,000 square miles, mostly in the three districts of Nalgonda, Warangal and Khammam, succeeded in setting up "gram-raj" or village soviets. The landlords were driven away from the villages, their lands seized, and one million acres of land were redistributed among the peasantry. As many as 4,000 Communists and peasant activists were killed, and more than 10,000 Communists and sympathizers were put behind bars, initially by the Nizam's government, and later by the armed forces of the Indian Government. (Banerjee 1984: 19; cf. Dhanagare 1991: 200)

Regardless of its outcome, the coincidence of the Telangana insurrection with the final victory of the Chinese communists could not fail to signal the revolutionary potential of peasant India. Moreover, even as open armed rebellion waned, the CPI began to emerge as an important electoral force in many regions of the country, especially as the franchise was broadened after independence (Harrison 1960: 178–245). By 1957, it would form the government in the south-western state of Kerala (Nossiter 1982). But such electoral successes did not exclude the possibility of a resurgent militancy in the future, as became evident in 1967 with the short-lived communist-led uprising at Naxalbari in the northern part of West Bengal (Banerjee 1984: i).

It is hardly surprising, therefore, that Paul Hoffman, as the new head of the Ford Foundation, wrote to the US ambassador to India, Chester Bowles, of the need for a rural development programme in India like the one that had been undertaken recently in Taiwan. "If in 1945", he said,

> we had embarked on such a program and carried it on at a cost of not over two hundred million dollars a year, the end result would have been a China completely immunized against the appeal of the Communists. India, in my opinion, is today what China was in 1945. (in Rosen 1985: 11)

And there was a recent programme at hand for Hoffman to draw upon as a model: the Marshall Plan. Well aware of the role it had played in suppressing an effective political role for indigenous communist parties, he could well write, "We have learned in Europe what to do in Asia" (in Raffer and Singer 1996: 61).

Bowles heartily concurred with Hoffman's warning. He published an article in *Foreign Affairs* which underscored his sense of the supreme importance of what would happen now in India. "[T]he success or failure," he wrote,

> of the effort being made in India and other Asian countries to create an alternative to Communism in Asia may mark one of those historic turning points which determine the flow of events for many generations....
> The future of Asia, and eventually the world balance of power, may rest on the competition between democratic India on the one hand and Communist China on the other. If democracy succeeds in India, regardless of what happens in China, millions of Asian doubters will develop new faith in themselves, in their ancient cultures, and in the ideals of the free world. (Bowles 1952: 80)

It was not always clear what those ideals might be, but, if they did not seem to lead to land reform or to popular government, perhaps one had to consider the words of Henry Wallace, one of the most liberal of Roosevelt's New Dealers, when he had criticised Chiang Kai-shek, not for his reactionary and repressive rule, not for an "agrarian policy [which] was one of trying to maintain or restore the *status quo*" (Moore 1966: 192, 193–201), but for "a backward feudal rule which has kept China's 400,000,000 from being the good customers they should be" (in Gardner 1969: 134).

Yet the Kuomintang regime had been subsidised by the United States – it had received up to $2 billion by the time it collapsed (Zinn 1980: 418) – so what was the likelihood of a real alternative to revolutionary change in India, especially if its new leaders were not encouraged more than Chiang had been, to address the material basis of peasant discontent? At the time that Hoffman became head of the Ford Foundation, the problems of rural India were being framed in the Malthusian terms elaborated at Notestein's Office of Population Research at Princeton, where the entire issue of access to land, the basis of recent peasant uprisings, was systematically obscured. The Ford Foundation, like Rockefeller, was helping to develop the logic which would lay the basis for the development of the Green Revolution.

Malthusianism in India

Malthusian thinking already had a long history in Western development thinking about the sub-continent, dating from the middle of the last century. This was in part because Malthus had taught for almost thirty years at the East India College, where, as the Caldwells observe, "he and his successors ensured that generations of British officials and scholars in India saw that country's society in Malthusian terms, as is evidenced by every Indian Census Report until 1951" (1986: 4). The transfer of Malthusian ideas to British India had also been facilitated by the tendency for British policy-makers to see India in terms of their direct or indirect experience with Ireland where British policy had been dominated by a Malthusian perspective (Ross 1996a). The most prominent example is Charles Trevelyan, who, after serving as assistant secretary to the Treasury between 1840 and 1859, during part of which time he had been in charge of famine relief for Ireland, went on to assume the role of Governor of Madras in 1859–60 and Finance Minister for India between 1862 and 1865 (Cook 1993: 28).

Within a few decades, a Malthusian vision had been firmly established among British administrators in India. Lord Lytton, the Governor General of India in the period 1876–80, was one of many who firmly declared that the country's population

> has a tendency to increase more rapidly than the food it raises from the soil … whose consumption, in many places, trenches too closely on the crops already provided by its industry; and which, therefore, runs great risk of having no accumulated produce to depend upon, whenever the earth has failed "to bring forth her fruits in due season" (in Ambirajan 1976: 6)

This, of course, wholly failed to appreciate that one of the reasons the rural population could hardly fail to exceed subsistence capacity was that the colonial regime continually forced the Indian peasant to grow cash crops to meet onerous tax obligations. And Malthusian thinking conveniently helped to justify the high level of taxation. Baden-Powell, in his *Systems of British India*, argued in 1882 that lower land taxes would – like poor relief in England – cause the population to rise, thus wiping out any potential increase in material well-being (Davis 1951: 203).

Through such authoritative interventions, Malthusian ideas flourished in India, preparing the ideological ground for some of the first government-sponsored birth control clinics anywhere in the developing world, in the years between the two world wars (Caldwell and Caldwell 1986: 39). The Final Report of the Bengal Famine Inquiry Commission in 1945 used the famine to further advance the cause of birth control (Caldwell and Caldwell 1986: 39); and the following year the Bhore Committee recommended government provision of free contraception, citing the recent work of the demographer, Kingsley Davis, in particular his article, "Demographic Fact and Policy in India", which had been published in the *Milbank Memorial Fund Quarterly* two years earlier (Caldwell and Caldwell 1986: 69).

A few years later, Davis's *The Population of India and Pakistan* (1951), financed by Milbank and Rockefeller contributions to the Office of Population Research (1951: vi), would further help to obscure the fundamental role of landownership patterns in the problem of Indian agriculture and rural poverty. Davis acknowledged that too little capital was invested in agriculture, but attributed this to the productive and reproductive behaviour of the peasants. "[T]he subcontinent", he wrote,

> includes great tracts of the richest land in the world. The low productivity is due rather to the way the land is handled – to the low proportion of capital invested in it – and hence is correlated with the farmers' poverty and density on the land. The smallness of the capital investment in farming is shown in numerous ways – in the absence or inadequacy of conservation measures, in the primitive techniques of cultivation, in the non-use of both natural and artificial fertilizers, in the failure to improve the breeds of plants and animals. (Davis 1951: 208)

There was no hint at all of how, as Thorner observed, colonial rule had extracted vital resources from the Indian countryside. On the contrary, Davis regarded the lack of capital investment in agricultural development as almost exclusively the result of "population pressure" causing under- and unemployment; he estimated that there was a surplus of 91 million people in the countryside (1951: 211). Even the problem of rural indebtedness was due, in his view, to the fact that there were too many people, which had reduced the size of holdings. So, "the money-lender is a symptom rather than a cause. The true causes lie in the conditions that keep the peasant on the margin of subsistence" (Davis 1951: 211). In this respect, the peasants of Hyderabad had obviously been mistaken to blame their situation on the land tenure system. According to Davis, their plots were so small because of their numbers, and because they were primarily subsistence-oriented, as well, and could not accumulate capital. As a result, they had to borrow, for purposes, moreover, which were typically non-productive – a sure sign of the incapacity of peasants to participate in a modern agricultural economy (Davis 1951: 211).

Davis's interpretation was a symptom of the increasing subordination of demographic thinking to the Cold War. Within a few more years, he would be sitting with William Draper and Margaret Sanger on the Steering Committee of Hugh Moore's World Population Emergency Campaign (Katz 1995) and writing in *The New York Times Magazine*:

> Not only is the glut of people in the poorer areas itself conducive to communism, but in the past communism has made its gains by conquest rather than by population growth. In 1920 it held less than one-tenth of the world's people under its fist: today it holds more than one-third. The lack of unity in the rest of the world against communism suggests that Red expansion may continue. If this happens, and if the conquests are made in the poorer countries, superior population growth will join territorial expansion in increasing communism's share of the world. (in Wilmoth and Ball 1992: 647)

As far as India was concerned, his view of the sources of rural poverty would lend little support to any argument for land redistribution. On the contrary, it reflected a line of reasoning that would increasingly view the West's hold over India in terms of the advancement of commercial agriculture.

In the early 1940s, India had created its Grow More Food (GMF) programme, which had as one of the principal aims to increase the area planted in food grains. At that time, cultivators were encouraged to adopt new seed varieties, but also to use green manures and compost (Brown 1971: 3). After independence, however, the staff of the GMF programme were merged into a new Community Development Programme. "The United States government and the Ford Foundation provided more than $100 million for the Community Development Programme during the First and Second Plans (1951–1952 to 1955–1956 and 1956–1957 to 1960–1961)" (Brown 1971: 4). But during this period, the thrust of agrarian development was changed fundamentally.

By the late 1950s, a general review of what was perceived as a persistent underproductivity in Indian agriculture was undertaken. To do this and to plan immediate appropriate action, the Government of India, through the Ford Foundation, recruited an Agricultural Production Team from the United States to work with a team of Indian agricultural experts. After about fifty or sixty days of work, this committee made public its *Report on India's Food Crisis and Steps to Meet It* in 1959 (Brown 1971: 8). This report became the basis of the new Intensive Agricultural Districts Programme (IADP). A ten–point pilot programme was established as a result of "a Memorandum of Agreement between the Government of India, the respective states, and the Ford Foundation" (Brown 1971: 13).

It is obvious that, in the decades after Independence, the Ford Foundation had acquired enormous influence within the Indian government, in respect to both agricultural development strategy and more general policies. Chester Bowles, the US Ambassador to India in the early 1950s (who would later be a trustee of the Rockefeller Foundation) (Colby and Dennett 1995: 337), wrote in his memoirs of that period:

> Someday someone must give the American people a full report of the work of the Ford Foundation in India. The several million dollars in total Ford expenditures in the country do not tell one-tenth of the story. Under the leadership of Douglas Ensminger, the Ford staff in India became closely associated with the Planning Commission which administers the Five Year Plan. Wherever there was a gap, they filled it, whether it was agricultural, health education or administration. (Bowles 1954: 340)

Bowles himself certainly did not even hint at the full story. On the contrary, he simply described the role of the Ford Foundation as a nongovernmental effort "in the finest traditions" of the United States (Bowles 1954: 340). He offered no hint of how or why the Ford Foundation acquired such a role, of how closely Ford's initiatives were intertwined with US foreign policy, and, especially, of why India was regarded so strategically in the opening decade of the Cold War. Yet, as Rosen has written in his invaluable account of the role of Western economists in South Asia, Bowles, Millikan, Hoffman, Ensminger, all "had a deep personal belief in the importance of the success of the Indian democratic experiment of development, both as a model for the Third World and as important to American security" (1985: 53). But in order to secure India, the Ford analysis of Indian agriculture, as embodied in the 1959 Report, had both to ignore the fact that the country's food problem was largely the product of structural conditions created by British rule and perpetuated by the Congress Party, and to create a sense of immediate crisis resulting from Malthusian pressures.

It is worth quoting the Thorners at length on this point:

> The mode of presentation followed in this *Report* serves to deepen the atmosphere of tension. In a solemn letter of transmittal the members of the team express their "concern" at the "stark threat" of an "ominous crisis" unless action is taken "immediately"....
>
> After all the build-up, the main burden of the *Report* turns out to be a set of proposals focused on attaining by 1966 a Third Five Year Plan target of 110 million tons of foodgrains. The fuss and the furore, the "crisis of overwhelming gravity", one is relieved to learn, are not a matter of 1959, but of 1966. The crucial worry is not how to feed the current population but how to provide for the expected increase....
>
> We may well ask why, if the food-people issue has hung heavy over India for decades, a call went out in the fall of 1958 for a hasty survey by a mission from abroad. One looks in vain through the *Report* for an official statement of the terms of reference of the Team or the specific reasons for which they were invited to India. In the absence of a letter of appointment from the Government of India requesting the Team to make recommendations for dealing with the impending food crisis, one wonders whether the notion of an "ominous crisis" came to India along with the Team. (1962: 113–14)

The Ford team based its prediction of a crisis in the year 1966 on certain assumptions about population growth which would lead to a short-fall of 28 million tons of food grains unless production could triple (Thorner and Thorner 1962: 114). The Thorners do an admirable job of examining the way in which these calculations were made, emphasising the dubious nature of population projections for 1966 based on census data from 1951 and the problematic nature of the estimate of Indian grain requirements by 1966 (Thorner and Thorner 1962: 116–19). In the latter case, the Ford team took a very good crop year as their base, enabling them to calculate a rate of food increase over the next six years which was lower than it would have been if they had selected the previous year as their base. "This", as the Thorners say, "is the sort of jugglery which gives statistics a bad name" (1962: 120).

Nevertheless, it helped to create the air of crisis which permitted the Report to urge the intensive modernisation of Indian agriculture and to justify the simultaneous commitment by the Ford Foundation and the Indian government to family planning – an area in which India would become a model for the developing world. The previous year, the essence of the Second Five-Year Plan had been presented in India's Planning Commission's publication *The New India: Progress through Democracy*, the product of a special study group composed of staff from the Commission and Dr Douglas Ensminger, who had come to the Ford Foundation from the US Department of Agriculture (India Planning Commission 1958: viii) (yet another manifestation of the role that Ford was coming to play as an instrument of US policy). In this work, the position of the Foundation had already been clearly stated when its authors declared:

> that one of India's gravest social and economic problems is an oversupply of agricultural laborers, numbering (with their dependents) about 90 millions throughout India.... A fourth, or possibly as many as a third, of them are believed surplus to the needs of agriculture. (1958: 162)

It soon became commonplace to assert that India would pass its "demographic point of no return" by 1966 (Harrison 1960: 335). And in 1967, in *Famine – 1975!*, the Paddocks cited the 1959 Ford report, endorsing its conclusion that "India's primary problem in achieving human welfare, social justice and democracy" was Malthusian.

The Indian government had already taken its cue. Ten months after the report,

> Nehru opened the Sixth International Conference on Planned Parenthood in Delhi.... During the next week the *New York Times* gave the meeting considerable publicity, pointing out that 587 of the 750 delegates were Indian and that the Indian experts had called for massive aid in the area. On February 21 the delegates unanimously requested the Secretary-General of the United Nations to bring the world organization into the field of family planning assistance. (Caldwell and Caldwell 1986: 43)

The persistent idea that demographic pressure lay behind many of India's social and economic problems had now become a part of the ideological rationale for a particular course of development with which to resolve the problem of a land-hungry peasantry. As Malthusian thinking about Ireland had gained currency during an insurrectionary time in that country, so, in the precarious period after the Second World War, independent India's First Five-Year Plan of 1953 (drafted in 1951) had observed that "The pressure of population in India is already so high that a reduction in the rate of growth must be regarded as a major desideratum" (Myrdal 1968: 1489). As the Caldwells (1986: 4) note, this general view was a significant factor in the Ford and Rockefeller Foundations' interest in that country, in the light of their concerns about the general impact of population pressures on socio-political stability in Asia. It was, therefore, duly elaborated in the country's Second Five-Year Plan (in which the Ford Foundation played a major role), which emphasised the need for rapid industrialisation to cope with rural "underemployment".

However, Myrdal observed,

the discussion of "underemployment" – which is a continuation of the older discussion of "overpopulation" – focused on the idea that huge labor surpluses, especially in agriculture, could be shifted into other sectors to increase labor utilization and aggregate output. (1968: 1153)

It was precisely the Malthusian view of conditions in rural India that prepared the ideological ground for a Green Revolution, which was intended to increase agricultural output through capital- rather than labour-intensive production. Yet there was an alternative. In 1960, Myrdal had argued, the central problem of Asian agriculture – including India – was the underutilisation of rural labour, in conjunction with low productivity. For him, the solution was to devise means for agriculture to become more labour-intensive, to transform it in a way which would enable it to absorb and sustain the seeming surplus of rural labour. But that was precisely what the peasants of Telengana had sought. So what rural India would get instead was the Green Revolution and an increasingly active campaign for birth control.

Byres and Crow (1988: 166–7) date the beginning of the Green Revolution in India from 1964, when, soon after Nehru's death, Chidambara Subramanian, the Minister of Steel and Heavy Industry, became the new Minister of Food and Agriculture. This put the imprimatur on an agricultural development policy which would reflect the interests of the industrial elite, whose principal concern was the availability of cheap food for their largely urban workforce. As Rosen observes, with the ascendancy of Subramanian,

India abandoned institutional change in the form of land reform, extension of cooperatives, and state trading to ensure low prices of food grains in the cities (supplemented by PL 480 grain imports to provide stocks of foodstuffs) as the central policy tools to expand output, for new policies based on the new technology. (1985: 80)

The Ford and Rockefeller Foundations had already helped to ensure that hybrid rice from the Philippines and new varieties of wheat from Mexico were being tested in India and that research on sorghum, millet and maize was also underway. Like Mexicans two decades earlier, Indian scientists reasonably "wanted to generate their own varieties suited to local conditions" (Lele and Goldsmith 1989: 313–25), but, by 1964, the Rockefeller representative in India, Ralph Cummings, took the view that "sufficient testing had been done in India to begin releasing the imported wheat and rice varieties to Indian farmers" (Lele and Goldsmith 1989: 325).

He approached Subramaniam to see if the new agriculture minister would be willing to throw his support to accelerating the process of introducing the

HYVs [high-yielding seed varieties]. Subramanian acknowledges that he decided to follow Cummings's advice quickly.... (Lele and Goldsmith 1989: 325)

It is clear, however, that Cummings was just a mouthpiece for US policy. As Lele and Goldsmith note,

The United States was using its own [food] aid as a source of "leverage" on India in the mid-1960s and was putting pressure on the International Monetary Fund and the World Bank to impose conditionalities for devaluation and give priority to agriculture. (1989: 325)

It is notable that official India's interest in birth control really began to take off at about the same time. Just as the Green Revolution was becoming national policy, John Synder, the Dean of Harvard's School of Public Health, secured Ford Foundation funds to establish a new Center for Population Studies.[4] The Center subsequently managed to establish eight endowed chairs by raising money from wealthy Boston families (Caldwell and Caldwell 1986: 89–90), cashing in on a long-standing concern about population issues on the part of the American upper class. One of the first efforts of the new centre was the so-called Khanna Project, a family-planning programme sponsored by the India government and the Rockefeller Foundation in the Punjab (Mamdani 1972: 25–6), which was one of the key target areas for the introduction of the Green Revolution.

It was also with the assistance of the Rockefeller Foundation that India bought 18,000 tons of Mexican wheat seed in mid-1966 (Lele and Goldsmith 1989: 326). But as Dasgupta noted in a general survey of the initial impact of the Green Revolution, because the success of the new seeds was so dependent on expensive inputs – including chemical fertiliser, pesticides, hired labour and agricultural machinery – they initially were introduced in an extremely selective fashion, in regions with suitable infrastructure and "progressive", that is, large, farmers (1977: 359–60), who, it was commonly believed, would make more efficient use of the new technology (1977: 373). Even when the new technology began to expand to small farmers, larger landowners retained a major advantage. Dasgupta concludes that

The new agricultural strategy ... can be seen as an attempt by the government to solve the food problem of the country without upsetting land relations. It relied heavily on those who had to lose most from a policy of radical land reform. (1977: 373)

---

4. Eventually the Center would be headed by David Bell, after he had left his position as head of USAID during the Vietnam War.

This is hardly new. Recent historical research suggests that pre-famine Ireland

> could have supported a larger rural population by adopting more intensive methods of cultivation. But ... this would have required a major change in the structure of landholding ... [and] a complete overhaul of the political and social structures within which Irish agriculture had developed. (Solar and Goossens 1991: 383)

In the 1840s, that would have constituted a fundamental assault on English colonial rule in Ireland. In the 1950s and 1960s, such an "overhaul" was an equally unwelcome prospect for advocates of capitalist development in the Third World. As one of the principal strategies by which such change could be avoided, the Green Revolution sought to raise productivity through capital-intensive inputs rather than through systematic efforts to harness the great potential of under-utilised rural labour – an alternative which also would have required radical land reform.

7
The Technology of Non-Revolutionary Change and the Demise of Peasant Agriculture

If the Green Revolution ensured the counter-revolutionary modernisation of Third World agriculture, it was in good measure because of the central assumption that the increased output necessary to forestall imminent Malthusian scarcity was only achievable through the introduction of new high-yielding seed varieties (HYVs). From the first, the predicted increased yields from such seeds exaggerated the contrast between traditional and hybrid varieties (proxies for the contrast between peasant and commercial agriculture) and tended to minimise the productive potential of small-holder agricultural practices, while understating the financial, social and environmental costs of the technical innovations on which success of the new seeds would depend. At the heart of the matter lay the question of how land would be apportioned and owned.

The prospective yields of HYVs, as we have noted, depended on substantial use of pesticides, irrigation and fertilisers,. But traditional seeds would also have been responsive to fertilisers. A report from the UN Research Institute for Social Development (UNRISD) pointed out a quarter-century ago that "the potential productivity improvements with older type seeds is very great, even recognizing that the genetic composition of traditional varieties frequently imposes limits on their nutrient intake" (Palmer 1972: 11). Moreover, for fertilisers to make a significant difference, soil moisture was important as well, often to such an extent that, for some hybrids such as rice, "new dwarf seeds perform no better, and frequently worse, than improved traditional varieties in non-irrigated areas". They also needed to avoid water stress at critical times in their growth cycle (Palmer 1972: 1335, 50–53). The new varieties were also less resistant to pests than their predecessors and therefore relied more on pesticide use (Viswanathan 1991: 2039).

While such inputs – irrigation, chemical fertilisers, pesticides – were preconditions for the bountiful harvests promised from the new seeds, they were often beyond the reach of small-holders. As the use of the new seeds spread, they generally remained confined to irrigated areas or they advanced in association with the extension of irrigation. The result was that the Green Revolution accentuated pre-existing differences between regions. In India, for example, "The gains in productivity have remained confined to select areas which have emerged as enclaves of high growth amidst stagnating, backward, and lowyield unproductive agriculture in the rest of the country" (Bhatia 1988: 14).

As we shall see, the latter regions did not lack possibilities for other forms of intensification. But, as long as innovation was confined within the Green Revolution strategy, it not only enhanced such regional disparities; it generally was also the large landowners and more substantial peasants who benefited (Vallianatos 1976: 56). The import of this was often side-stepped, however, by describing such beneficiaries, not in terms of their more favourable material circumstances, but as more "progressive" (Borlaug 1970), a view which conformed to prevailing theories of modernisation.

The Seeds of the Green Revolution

The essence of the Green Revolution, however, was a process of commodisation of agriculture, and this had begun many years earlier. One of its most notable features was the development – long before the emergence of the HYVs – of commercial hybrid seeds which farmers had to purchase every year. As Berlan and Lewontin have written,

> If farmers save seed grown from an initial purchase of a hybrid variety, yields decrease precipitously in the following year. Thus, once farmers turned to planting hybrid corn they had to buy seed from a commercial seed producer every year instead of picking, at harvest time, the healthy and productive ears from their own corn fields for next year's seed, as they had always done. In other words, the adoption of hybrid corn *transformed seed into a commodity* [authors' italics]. (1986: 36)

If anyone knew this, it was Henry A. Wallace. As a new method of plant breeding, hybridisation had developed in the United States around 1910, and he was one of the first people to take commercial advantage of it, founding his own seed-corn business in Des Moines in 1913. By 1920, he had convinced his father, Henry C. Wallace, who had just become Warren Harding's Secretary of Agriculture, to increase federal funding for hybrid-corn research. Such public investment would become one of the essential ingredients of the nascent commercial seed industry, which would include Henry A. Wallace's own company, Pioneer Hi-Bred, which he created in 1926 (Berlan and Lewontin 1986: 44–5; Schapsmeier and Schapsmeier 1968: 27–8) and which is now "the largest seed company in the world" and a major agro-biotechnology company (Hobbelink 1991: 123).

By 1932, Henry A. Wallace had become Franklin Roosevelt's Secretary of Agriculture (and then Vice-President, from 1940 to 1944). While there is no doubt that Wallace had considerable sympathy with the plight of the poor, it was often combined with an innocent faith in the positive benefits of what he called "the modern scheme of things" (Wallace 1964: 41). As a liberal advocate of a modern style of agricultural management, he was also a close associate and friend of Nelson Rockefeller, another vigorous moderniser to whom the term "pragmatic liberal" has been applied (Underwood and Daniels 1982). Both regarded the Rockefeller Foundation as the proper vehicle for transferring an American style of agriculture to Mexico. As Fitzgerald notes:

> The first signs of RF [Rockefeller Foundation] interest in Mexico appeared in early 1933 when John A. Ferrell of the RF's International Health Board (IHB) discussed the prospect with Mexican officials in the public sector. Again, in 1941, the issue was raised with the IHB chief in Mexico, George C. Payne, and later in the year with US Vice-President Henry Wallace. All agreed that the primary need in Mexico was for a programme covering public health, education, and agriculture. (Fitzgerald 1986: 462)

But according to Wallace, while Raymond Fosdick, head of the Rockefeller Foundation, "wanted to set up a public health service in Mexico, I urged him most strongly to put his emphasis on agriculture, so as to make sure that food expanded as fast as people" (Wallace 1964: 38; cf. Fitzgerald 1986: 465). Mexican researchers had already been working on the problem of increasing production, particularly of the staple maize and principally through the development of better criollo seeds, that is, indigenous varieties which had evolved in specific localities through open pollination (Barkin 1987: 112). Moreover, because of their concern for the social consequences of introducing improved seeds, they had

> rejected the route of developing hybrid seeds, contending that they were inappropriate for a country like Mexico, which was not prepared to reproduce and distribute seeds year after year in a quantity commensurate with national needs.... They channeled their energy and resources into improving the system of cultivation, based on better techniques with the use of criollo seeds. (Barkin 1987: 112)

Whereas most of this work was undertaken after 1934, first by the Office of Experimental Fields in Mexico's Ministry of Agriculture and then by the Instituto de Investigaciones Agricolas (IIA), it was to be supplanted just a decade later as a result of an agreement between Mexico and the Rockefeller Foundation which established the Office of Special Studies to preside over research on US-style hybrids (Barkin 1987: 112). All the members of the Foundation's mission to Mexico happened to hold positions in the US Department of Agriculture (Fitzgerald 1986: 462–3). They were led by J. George Harrar, who would later become president of the Foundation. And their main interest was not in maize, the chief food crop of Mexico's rural poor, but wheat, which was primarily a commercial crop.

However, Rockefeller interest in agricultural "modernisation" in Latin America was broader than either Mexico or agriculture. Conveniently for the Rockefellers, in 1940 Franklin Roosevelt had appointed Nelson Rockefeller as the head of the newly organised Office of the Co-ordinator of Inter-American Affairs (CIAA), a section of the US Commerce Department which was chiefly meant to be concerned with securing the loyalty of Latin American countries through the Second World War (Colby and Dennett 1995: 107ff.). This principally involved guaranteeing supplies of raw materials that were vital for the US war effort. In practice, it also meant establishing a fruitful basis for US investment in the post-war period.

The Rockefellers had already proven during the Nazi era that their own loyalties, like those of many prominent industrialists and financiers were somewhat ambivalent. Just as Ford maintained corporate connections with its German subsidiary, which enabled Germany to continue to import crucial supplies of rubber and steel, and as ITT's European communication services provided crucial support for the Nazis throughout the war (Barnet and Muller 1974: 60–61), so the US Attorney General revealed in 1942 that the Rockefellers' Standard Oil company had had long-standing arrangements with I.G. Farben, the great German chemical trust at the very heart of the Nazi war machine (Clairmonte and Cavanagh 1981: 137–8), whose executives would later be tried for war crimes for setting up a factory at Auschwitz employing slave labour, and that these arrangements had critically compromised US efforts to manufacture artificial rubber. Farben also was the second largest shareholder in Jersey Standard (Colby and Dennett 1995: 155; Borkin 1978). So it was not likely that Nelson Rockefeller was too concerned to ensure that the CIAA only expressed the limited national interests of the United States. On the contrary, it clearly was run to secure international post-war opportunities for US business, including those owned or controlled by the Rockefeller family.[1]

With that in mind, in mid-1946, Nelson Rockefeller, his siblings and his father, John D. Rockefeller, Jr, established the American International Association for Economic and Social Development (AIA), a non-profit organisation which operated in conjunction with a profit-making Rockefeller enterprise called IBEC – the International Basic Economy Corporation – which was set up at the beginning of the following year (Colby and Dennett 1995: 212; Lundberg 1968: 750; Lewis 1985: 4). The continuity with Rockefeller's recent activities in Washington was obvious, as IBEC's very name "was inspired by the CIAA's Basic Economy Division, but more than the name was borrowed. Much of the CIAA's top staff also appeared on the boards of AIA and IBEC" (Colby and Dennett 1995: 212).

In fact, AIA was a front for IBEC and one which, by the end of the war, was already showing evidence of Rockefeller interest in the kinds of agricultural developments that foreshadowed the Green Revolution and which would lead to healthy profits for IBEC. As a report by the North American Congress on Latin America (1969) noted:

> AIA, nominally a non-profit organization, conducted a market and product survey of the hybrid seed corn industry in Brazil in 1946. It discovered that only one domestic company produced hybrid seed corn, Agroceres Limitada. AIA persuaded the Agroceres management to form a new company in which Agroceres would provide the technical knowledge; AIA then organized IBEC as a profit-making venture to provide Agroceres with the necessary capital for expansion. IBEC thus came into control of the formerly indigenously-owned Agroceres and since then has cornered over 45 percent of the Brazilian hybrid corn seed market. (BAOBAB Press 1994)[2]

---

1. It is clear that Nelson Rockefeller continuously sought to position his family's interests in Latin America, especially in regard to oil, so that they would have such opportunities *regardless* of who won the war (Colby and Dennett 1995: 91, 95). The Rockefeller-controlled Standard Oil (NJ) had been operating extensively through Latin America since the 1920s (Colby and Dennett 1995: 35 ff.). It is interesting to note that its president at the time, Walter Teagle, played a major role in developing Standard's links with I.G. Farben (Borkin 1978: 47–51). Later, as Higham notes, "Chase Manhattan in Nazi-occupied Paris after Pearl Harbor was doing millions of dollars' worth of business with the enemy with the full knowledge of the head office in Manhattan" (1983: xv). All this reinforces the view that Rockfeller interests and loyalties transcended those of the USA.

2. There are variations on the story of the origins of Agroceres. Jaffé and Rojas write that it "was established in 1945 by scientists of the University of Viscosa, in joint venture with a company owned by the Rockefeller family of the USA" (1993: 16). IBEC eventually became Ibec Inc. in 1980, jointly owned by the Rockefeller family and Booker McConnell, an English agribusiness corporation (Lewis 1985: 1).

Apart from Agroceres, IBEC's activities in Brazil over the next decade showed clear evidence of how Rockefeller interests were expanding into all the facets of what would become Green Revolution technology:

> IBEC set up five key companies designed to provide specialized services to farmers rather than itself engaging in production. They were a hybrid maize seed company (SASA), a hog production company (SAFAP), a grain storage company (CAGSA), a helicopter crop-dusting company (HELICO) and a mechanized agricultural service company (EMA) for clearing virgin land for cultivation. (Lewis 1985: 4)

If the question is asked, in the light of IBEC and the evidence that most Rockefeller activities, including banks, oil companies, the Foundation and investment enterprises, were ultimately interlinked, what circumstances led to the sending of Rockefeller Foundation agricultural researchers to Mexico in the early 1940s, the conventional picture of the motives for the Green Revolution fails. If, some years later, the transfer of the Green Revolution package to countries such as India, the Philippines or Colombia would be rationalised in terms of "over-population", such an argument was scarcely applicable and rarely heard in regard to Mexico in the mid-1940s. Political and economic concerns were more compelling.

In the case of Mexico, foreign investors yearned for a return to the situation which had prevailed in Mexico before the revolution, when the country's economy, under the dictator Porfirio Díaz, was closely linked to foreign and especially North American capital (Platt 1972: 298–300; Cline 1963: 22; cf. Massey et al. 1987: 39–40). A mere 800 haciendas owned about 90 percent of the land, while 97 percent of rural families were landless (DeWalt and Barkin 1991: 13; Massey et al. 1987: 39). By 1910, such oppressive conditions had given rise to a wide-ranging opposition movement of workers, peasants and the national middle class (cf. Friedrich 1970), whose collective efforts converged into what became the Mexican Revolution. But it was an unstable mixture of class interests, and, in the end, its most progressive impulses – embodied in the land reform programme of Zapata (Womack 1968) – were readily curbed by the generals and politicians who eventually established themselves in power.

It was only the global depression of the thirties which briefly created conditions which enabled one of those generals, Lázaro Cárdenas, who became president in 1934, to use the central state to effect a progressive transformation of the rural Mexican economy. There are various interpretations of what Cárdenas – who had already initiated a more limited land reform when he was governor of Michoacán in the late twenties (Monto 1994: 40–41) – had in mind, whether he attempted to fulfil a dream of a kind of agrarian socialism (DeWalt and Barkin 1991: 13) or intended what Thiesenhusen calls "capitalist reformism" (1995: 36). In either case, impelled by pressures rising up from the *campesinos* themselves, he initiated a pervasive programme of land reform (Perelman 1977: 144), primarily through the breaking up of estate lands into communal units called *ejidos*.[3] It was land reform which has been described as "the most far reaching in Latin America before Cuba's and one which really did incorporate the peasants into national life" (Frank 1969: 272).

By 1940, the Cárdenas programme had been so successful that just under half of all cultivable land had been distributed to the *ejidos*. State support for traditional agriculture was such that productivity on *ejido* holdings improved enough to surpass that of private holdings, to the extent that *ejidos* altogether produced just over half of the value of all Mexican farm produce (Hewitt de Alcantara 1976: 6; DeWalt and Barkin 1991: 14). The positive effect on rural conditions generally was so dramatic that, between 1930 and 1940, the number of landless labourers in the country fell from 68 to 36 percent of the rural workforce (Hewitt 1976: 4). As a result, migration out of the countryside "registered its lowest rate in the last 50 years" (Unikel 1975: 534).

The commitments of the Cárdenas years were short-lived, however. Infrastructural support for *ejido* agriculture, including a new National Ejido Credit Bank, was only beginning in 1940, when Cárdenas was succeeded as president by Avila Camacho. By then, the United States had already brought increasing pressure on the Mexican economy:

> In 1938 the oil companies withdrew large sums of money from Mexico; the U.S. government refused to extend its 1933 agreement on silver purchases, and the United States and Britain boycotted Mexican oil, forcing Mexico to work out barter agreements with Germany and Italy that were never fully complied with owing to the start of World War II. As the events in Europe unfolded, Mexico lost important European export markets and its dependence on higher-priced imports from the United States increased; a shortage of foreign exchange forced import limitations, fueling the displeasure of the local and petty bourgeoisie, who demanded an end to cardenismo. (Markiewicz 1993: 107)

But even before the end of his term Cárdenas himself had begun to step back from the central government's commitment to the peasantry and to make concessions to US demands for compensation for lands expropriated from US nationals (Markiewicz 1993: 107–9). More

---

3. *Ejidos* have been defined as "government-sponsored cooperatives whose members enjoy usufruct" (Unikel 1975: 533).

importantly, US pressure was clearly inducing a retreat on agrarian policy: land distribution declined and what land was still distributed was of poorer quality.

> Concessions to private property, the slower rate of land distribution, and the increasingly conservative orientation of government agricultural lending were particularly injurious to the collective ejidos, which depended for their very survival on continued institutional support. (Markiewicz 1993: 109)

The Impact of the Green Revolution in Mexico

Rockefeller family interests had been especially affected by the Cárdenas reforms. Their oil investments in particular had a long history in Mexico. As Baklanoff observes:

> Commercial oil production in Mexico was initiated in 1901 by Edward Doheny, an American entrepreneur, in the Huasteca fields within the Tampico–Tuxpan region. Doheny's Huasteca Petroleum Company was subsequently purchased by the Standard Oil Company of New Jersey. Mexican oil production eventually became concentrated among the "Big Three": Mexican Eagle Company ("El Aguila"), a subsidiary of the Royal-Dutch Shell group, the Huasteca Petroleum Company, now a subsidiary of Standard Oil, and the Sinclair Company.

By 1936, the Mexican Eagle and Huasteca companies controlled over 70 percent of Mexico's crude oil production (Baklanoff 1975: 50). But, under a new Expropriation Law, the Cárdenas administration Mexicanised a large number of foreign-owned industries, including Huasteca, which, as a subsidiary of Standard Oil, was controlled by the Rockefeller family.

Even before he became Roosevelt's Co-ordinator of Inter-American Affairs, Nelson Rockefeller had paid a private visit to Cárdenas in early 1940 to try, unsuccessfully, to reestablish the position of Standard and the other oil companies (Colby and Dennett 1995: 94). Back in Washington, he presented a report to Roosevelt's adviser, Harry Hopkins, which turned out to be "a broad and far-reaching plan for a 'Hemisphere Economic Policy'" (Colby and Dennett 1995: 95) which he hoped to co-ordinate. Meanwhile, the USA had already been exerting pressure to help the more conservative sections of Mexico's ruling party, the PRI, prepare for the post-Cárdenas era. Above all, this meant reversing the redistribution of valuable land to the *ejidos*, and supporting a move toward large commercial farms linked to the global market.

The effectiveness of this shift owed much to the way that Mexican agriculture was transformed by what would be called the Green Revolution. In the early 1940s, the noted US geographer Carl Sauer had pointed out that the agricultural practices of peasants in countries such as Mexico were already good enough to bring about any required in-crease in yields and only needed adequate economic and infrastructural support (DeWalt 1988: 346). However,

> The warnings of Sauer were dismissed by influential people in the Rockefeller Foundation as the concerns of someone who appreciated the quaint customs of the Mexican peasantry and who resented any attempt to change them. (DeWalt 1988: 346)

In fact, the aims of the Rockefeller research programme coincided with efforts to reverse the direction of the Cárdenas reforms:

> there was a tendency ... to concentrate on developing the very highest yielding genetic material, capable of great productivity under optimum conditions available only in the richest agricultural areas of the country, rather than give priority to some less spectacularly productive, but more widely usable, kinds of seeds.... In theory, the new "technological package" was scale neutral, applicable to farms of any size. But given the reality of the Mexican countryside, it was most profitably utilized only by the best-endowed, and most politically powerful, farming groups in the nation. (Hewitt de Alcántara 1976: 308)

This meant that it favoured the minority of Mexican farmers who were chiefly wheat producers, in contrast to the vast majority of Mexican peasants who were subsistence cultivators of maize (Fitzgerald 1986) and who continued to grow it "using rudimentary techniques, few inputs and traditional varieties of seeds" (DeWalt 1988: 347). This, in turn, would mean that it disproportionately enhanced the fortunes of the wheat-raising large farmers of the northern states (Frank 1969: 305), a region that had long been under the influence of US capital (Sanderson 1984).

It became commonplace after the departure of Cárdenas for the collective *ejidos* to be maligned as inefficient, even as the resources that underpinned their success were pillaged by private interests, and to be subdivided into private properties. In the north-western state of Sonora,

> A concentrated official campaign for the division of collective ejidos into individual plots was launched by the government, and the cooperative experi-ments were described as being "communistic." The new local landowning elite, allied to governmental circles, had the greatest interest in "proving" that the ejido farms could not work and in weakening their structures. Internal strife in the ejidos was fomented by the government and its agencies, and the peasants' organizations were divided and torn apart.... Credit, marketing and consumer spending were soon concentrated in the hands of a new, dynamic and enterprising local merchant class which was able to make quick profits at the expense of the ejidatarios. (Stavenhagen 1975: 155)

By 1940, power in the ruling party (the PRI) had shifted to the urban middle and upper classes, whose own priorities recommitted

Mexico to development based on "private initiative", with an economy in which agriculture would subsidise industrial growth (Hewitt de Alcántara 1976: 6; DeWalt and Barkin 1991: 14; Unikel 1975: 536). As Hewitt de Alcántara observes, "The early 1940s thus marked the beginning of an industrial revolution in Mexico patterned fully after the capitalist model" (1976: 8).

Leftists were purged from the Mexican cabinet. Mexico promised to pay the United States $49 million for property expropriated from US citizens during the Cárdenas years and $24 million to settle the oil issue (Markiewicz 1993: 128). There was also a reversal of the Cárdenas programme of land redistribution (Thiesenhusen 1995: 37):

> Avila Camacho and [his successor] Aleman tried to dismantle the peasant-based agrarian structure created by Cárdenas. Collective *ejidos* were broken up and land divided into individual plots. Peasant cooperatives were forced to disband and their financial support was withdrawn. Agricultural investment was concentrated in the construction of roads and massive irrigation works located principally in the North and northwest. Although restricted by law, newly irrigated land was sold to private farmers with no apparent regard for legal amenities. Land distribution came to a virtual halt all over the country. (Sanderson 1984: 138)

Where *ejidos* remained, principally in central Mexico and in the Gulf region, the commitment of state resources after 1940 was relatively meagre. Investment in agricultural infrastructure, especially roads and irrigation, went primarily to the north and north-Pacific areas, which "accounted for two-thirds of private investment in agriculture from 1940 to 1960, with benefits largely accruing to commercial growers" (Thiesenhusen 1995: 37). Just a decade after the Cárdenas reforms had begun to be reversed – and despite the fact that yields on *ejidos*, even on inferior land, were more or less equal to those of private farms of over 12 acres (Perelman 1977: 144) – the polarisation of rural Mexico was dramatically obvious: 87 percent of *ejidatarios* lived at near-subsistence level (Perelman 1977: 6), while a mere 3 percent of all farms accounted for 55 percent of all agricultural output and 80 percent of the increase in the value of production during the 1950s (Barkin 1975: 66; Stavenhagen 1981: 112, 114).

There were several reasons for this. First, from the early 1950s, the Ejido Bank began to encourage the use of new wheat varieties, forcing *ejidatarios* to use costly inputs of fertilisers and insecticides. The rapid process of capital intensification of wheat production served the interests of the private companies which supplied such inputs, but it also imposed terrible debts on the *ejido* sector, which disintegrated under the strain (Stavenhagen 1975: 156). An additional factor was the decisive role of irrigation. Between 1940 and 1979, while *ejido* agriculture either stagnated or collapsed, "irrigation works, particularly in large districts, accounted for from 70 percent to 99.2 percent of government investment in the agricultural sector" (Barkin 1990: 16). But it was always larger farms which benefited. While representing only a very small percentage of all agricultural holdings, they came to possess almost 70 percent of all irrigated land, as well as 75 percent of the value of all agricultural machinery (Barkin 1990: 115).

As Stavenhagen has noted, however, this was only one part of the pervasive injustice which characterised the modernisation of Mexican agriculture after the Second World War. By 1970, at least one half of the agricultural labour force consisted of landless workers who depended on migratory and seasonal work for what was a tenuous existence at best. But because of increasing mechanisation on large farms, the demand for their labour was steadily declining (Stavenhagen 1970: 115–17). Widespread and growing rural unemployment and the fact that government and foreign investment was largely going into industrial infrastructure and manufacturing in a limited number of urban centres produced a scale of migration to Mexican cities which was "without precedent in the demographic development of the country" (Unikel 1975: 493).

At the same time, there was a decline in access to dietary resources, which has proceeded steadily to the point where, now, half of the Mexican population is estimated to be malnourished (Barkin 1990: 28). While it would be easy to assume that this is merely the expected result of excessive population growth, the evidence suggests that it is actually the product of the agricultural policies already described. In the first place, the landless and unemployed are the product, not of large families, but of a modernisation process which has made increasing numbers of the rural population obsolete. There is also less food being produced. This is still blamed on an inefficient agricultural sector and the *ejido* system, rather than on the decline in domestic food production under pressure to export and on an agro-industrial system which compels producers to emphasise profitability and reflects the demands of the international and domestic urban middle-class market far more than the dietary needs of Mexico's rural and urban poor (Pelto 1987). The advance of sorghum acreage is particularly illustrative. According to DeWalt, agronomists within the OSS of the Ministry of Agriculture had begun working in the 1940s with the African food crop sorghum, with the initial idea that its drought resistance might make it useful in dry areas which were unsuited for maize. But, even at that early date, consideration was given to the use of sorghum as an animal feed, as in

the United States (DeWalt 1988: 347). The production of sorghum steadily expanded. Between 1965 and 1980, while the cultivated area in Mexico
grew by 1.5 percent annually, the sorghum area grew by 13 percent. By
1984, there was 50 percent more land in sorghum than in wheat (DeWalt
1988: 348).

In recent years, as a result of government policies that have encouraged
mechanisation, which is particularly suitable for sorghum (Barkin 1990:
23–5), the latter's importance has increased even further. In many areas,
sorghum has also displaced maize and wheat, the staples of the Mexican
working-class diet. But the factor underlying the expansion of sorghum
cultivation is chiefly the demand for it as an animal feed, to fuel an
expanding national and export market for Mexican livestock (Barkin 1990:
27). In terms of the growth of cattle production, the experience of Mexico
over the last few decades parallels trends throughout Latin America and,
indeed, world-wide (Barkin et al. 1990). However, Mexican cattle are less
dependent on pasture than animals in Central America, and are fed on
sorghum, which represents 74 percent of the industrial livestock feed
sold in Mexico (DeWalt 1988: 349), and on feed grains, such as oats and
soybeans, which also have taken over land once used for maize, beans
and wheat (DeWalt 1988: 349). The major consumers of soybeans are
subsidiaries of US multinationals, such as Anderson Clayton and Ralston
Purina, which process them into animal feed (Mexican Soy Buyers 1997).
In this way, meat production is monopolising an increasing share of the
country's agricultural resources, yet not in a way which is nutritionally
advantageous for the majority of Mexicans. As Barkin observes:

> a growing share of rural resources is devoted to fodder production for live-
> stock to provide a high-protein diet for the minority wealthy and middle-class
> Mexicans, whose incomes increased much more rapidly than those of the rest
> of the population during the 1970s.... Enormous quantities of natural re-
> sources are devoted to the production of meat. The proportion of cultivated
> land devoted to animal production has gone from about 5 percent in 1960 to
> over 23 percent in 1980 ... the proportion of grain fed to animals increased
> from 6 percent in 1960 to over 32 percent in 1980. (Barkin 1990: 27)

As a result, Mexico grew increasingly dependent on food imports from
the United States, including staples such as maize and wheat.

In the end, the Green Revolution has done very little for the Mexican poor. Large farms, many of them tied to foreign capital, were the
chief beneficiaries of the new agricultural regime. While investment in
irrigation fed the growth of commercial agriculture, small-scale, rainfall-
based farming became virtually obsolete. The increasing mechanisation
of large farms, moreover, meant that intensive farming had little need

for the labour of the rural poor. Thus, Escobar et al. describe the seventies and eighties as a time of "rural collapse", when increasing numbers of the poor fled the traditional agricultural sector (1987: 42). In broad terms, the poor in the Third World have ended up yet again subsidising North American farmers.

This was compounded by the world debt crisis of the 1980s, which hit Mexico in 1982. Over the rest of the decade, real wages fell by 57 percent, per capita GDP fell by 15 percent, and the number of people living in poverty increased dramatically (Brachet-Marquez and Sherraden 1994: 1298–1300). General food subsidies were cut during this period by 80 percent and, although they regained a role in 1988–89, they never attained pre-1983 levels. Moreover, food subsidies tended to be targeted in favour of urban areas (Brachet-Marquez and Sherraden 1994: 1301). One of the ways in which many families sought to cope with these circumstances was to diversify their means of employment:

> Researchers suggest that poorer households responded to the crisis by send-ing women and children into the labor force (usually in the informal sector) and by relying more on money transfers from migrants and other sources. (Brachet-Marquez and Sherraden 1994: 1299)

The percentage of the labour force in the informal sector seems to have increased from 1.1 percent in 1982, to 9 percent in 1986, to 19.4 percent in 1990 (Brachet-Marquez and Sherraden 1994: 1307). Much of this has occurred in the urban areas, where an increase in the role of child labour undoubtedly has been a factor in the determination of family reproductive strategies.

The Migration of Rural Labour

Another strategy, as it was for Irish peasants, has been to seek work through immigration. While this is often interpreted as a sign of an over-populated countryside, it is primarily a reflection of rural under-development. The Mexican Revolution did little to change this and, as a result, the years just after the First World War saw a great increase in migration as low-paid Mexican workers increasingly became a major asset for the farms of the southwestern United States (Cohen 1987: 46–7; Lowell 1992: 140; Monto 1994: 55). As European immigration was curtailed by restrictive, eugenics-minded legislation in 1921, Mexican labour took on even greater importance, not only in the Southwest, but even in midwestern cities such as Chicago. By 1924, the US Border Patrol had been established to help to maintain a convenient influx of "illegal" migrant labourers from Mexico (Cohen 1987: 47–8) to subserve the fluctuating demands of farmers and industrialists in the United States.

During the Depression years, when unemployed workers in the United States provided a reserve of labour for larger farmers, especially in California, not only was Mexican migration very strictly curtailed, but many Mexicans either returned home voluntarily or were deported (Cohen 1987: 48; Massey et al. 1987: 42; Monto 1994: 55). In the early 1940s, however, the burgeoning war-time US economy, short of cheap labour, once again needed Mexican workers. As large agricultural enterprises in the US began to clamour for open borders and access to Mexicans (Markiewicz 1993: 134), the Bracero Program was inaugurated (it would last until 1965) (Burawoy 1976: 1065), enabling farmers in the United States to secure legally contracted Mexican labourers at low cost (Cohen 1987: 49–51). At the height of the programme in the late 1950s, as many as 400,000 *braceros* (legal workers) entered the US annually (Massey et al. 1987: 43). Meanwhile, as the annual number of *bracero* permits did not satisfy the demand for labour and as many growers preferred Mexican workers to be as cheap as possible, illegal immigration persisted as well (Monto 1994: 57). There is no way to give a precise figure, but it must have exceeded the number of immigrants who actually were caught, which "annually rose steadily from the early 1940s to a peak of over a million in 1954" (Burawoy 1976: 1065).

The reversal of the Cárdenas land reforms certainly facilitated the inception of the *bracero* programme. The dramatic pace of legal and illegal immigration from Mexico during the 1940s reflected a marginalisation of subsistence agriculture which reduced demand for rural labour and transformed rural Mexico into a labour reserve for national and international capital. Where families had rights in *ejido* land, migration was less likely to be permanent or long-term. But unfortunately, by the 1940s, land distribution was at an end and in some regions, especially central Mexico, *ejido* land was even being expropriated (Sanderson 1941: 139–41). Moreover, as Young has shown for some of the small, remote agricultural communities of Oaxaca, in southern Mexico, migration through the 1950s and 1960s had a profound impact on the demographic structure and, therefore, on the subsistence potential, of such regions:

> The bulk of all migrants (80 percent) were ... under 29, and although young men were leaving in increasing numbers, the typical permanent out-migrant was still a young unmarried woman under 20 years of age.... The typical seasonal migrant was a married male with several children. (Young 1982: 161)

The net effect of out-migration was a labour shortage in some households during crucial times in the local agricultural cycle (Young 1982: 162–70).

During the 1960s, as foreign investment in Mexico more than doubled (Barkin 1975: 71), Mexican immigration increased. The connection is made clear in a study by Wilcox Young (1993) of the El Bajio region of Mexico. Located chiefly in the state of Guanajuato on Mexico's central plateau, this region illustrates the effect on one of the country's most fertile regions when it came under the domination of some of the world's largest agro-industrial corporations from the 1960s onward. These firms, which included Campbells, Del Monte, Green Giant, Bird's Eye, Ralston Purina, etc., introduced new commercial crops that were heavily dependent on irrigation and mechanised methods of cultivation and harvesting and required far less human labour than traditional rain-fed agriculture. As a result, the state of Guanajuato became one of Mexico's chief sources of migration (Wilcox Young 1993: 169, 187).

While it became commonplace to explain such migration in terms of population pressure, it was primarily the result of a continuing decline in the demand for rural labour, which worsened dramatically during this period. The landless had no choice except to seek work in Mexico's cities, where unemployment was high, or to try to enter the United States (Cohen 1987: 54). The dramatic growth of Mexico City, which has fired the popular Malthusian imagination, was principally the result of this rural exodus (UN 1991: 3). And such movements increased during the 1970s and 1980s, as Mexico's debt crisis intensified the pressures on the rural poor.

To a large extent, the principal role of what remains of subsistence agriculture in Mexico is to subsidise this migration. While rural food production is now totally inadequate, it none the less enables many rural communities to survive; it underwrites the costs of the reproduction of labour and therefore plays a vital role in the complex dynamic of migration, and will continue to do as long as "the siting of labor force reproduction within rural Mexico remains of enduring significance for US capitalism as well as for Mexican capitalism" (Gledhill 1995: 37). But this situation cannot be sustained indefinitely, as recent events in Mexico suggest. In the early 1990s, the prospect of the commercialisation of the rural areas at the expense of the poor accelerating under the new free trade regime of NAFTA was the principal trigger for an uprising in the southern state of Chiapas – where elaboration of cash crops and cattle grazing has been most intense over the past few decades (Burbach and Rosset 1994) – which has already begun to transform the structure of the entire Mexican political system.

The Political Economy of US Farm Surpluses

While Mexican agriculture was experiencing the first impact of the Green Revolution in the 1950s, grain production in the United States was also expanding, dramatically re-creating the economic and social landscape of the American Midwest. Although living far above the subsistence level of Mexican peasants, hundreds of thousands of small American family farmers were forced off the land as a result of a shift to capital-intensive corporate farming (Ross 1980; Michie 1982: 82–6). Between 1950 and 1969, the number of farms in the United States would fall from 5.4 to 2.7 million, with farms between 1 and 259 acres declining by 58 percent (Ross 1980: 212).

It is one of the seeming paradoxes of this period that, despite such profound social costs, and although surplus grain production had long been one of the chief problems of US agriculture, harvests in the 1950s were encouraged to expand. As surpluses grew, Malthusian thinking provided a major justification for their use abroad, and the preeminent instrument for this was the Public Law 480 (PL 480), the Agricultural Trade Development Assistance Act ("Food for Peace"). But the intentions of PL 480 were exceedingly complex and deceptive. While it made US grain – chiefly wheat – available to selected developing countries at low cost and therefore could claim to have humanitarian intent, the means through which this was achieved were meant, in the words of the act itself, to "promote ... the foreign policy of the United States" (in Hudson 1972: 144).

It was also ostensibly designed to reduce the huge surpluses which filled the storage facilities of the US government. Superficially, this may seem strange, since increased production was apparently being encouraged. But it is important to understand that, over a century ago, large commercial farmers, cognisant that the domestic market could never absorb their harvests of grain, began to exert an unprecedented influence on the Federal government, which led to a policy of creating markets, rather than restraining output.

PL 480 recipients typically were developing countries. The public justification of Food for Peace was humanitarian, with a Malthusian twist. If developing countries were regarded as heading toward a food crisis that had been precipitated by demographic pressures, the USA, as the world's greatest food producer, would provide cheap food to help forestall disaster. The implementation of PL 480 coincided with the first stirrings of the Green Revolution and on the surface appears entirely congruent with its public premises and aims. But there was more to it than that, just as there was to the Green Revolution itself. US concessionary food aid actually played a major role in constraining the agricultural development policies of recipient countries in a way which increased their strategic dependence on economic and political relations with the United States. As Hudson notes, the way that PL 480 food aid has operated does not constitute long-term constructive assistance to the aid-borrowing countries. Neither their farm sectors nor their balance-of-payments position is helped. They are contractually obliged not to implement policies of domestic agricultural self-sufficiency and must enter into agreements assuring the United States a guaranteed future share in their domestic markets. (Hudson 1972: 146)

This did not necessarily clash with the interests of national elites, who saw PL 480 aid as a way of facilitating the process of "modernisation". Through such assistance, they subsidised the transformation of their own systems of agricultural production in a way which effectuated a movement of labour to urban areas, to subsidise industrialisation. In South Korea, for example,

wheat imports ... quadrupled between 1966 and 1977, while rice consumption began a gradual but steady decline. Cheap imported food allowed the government to maintain low grain prices to hold down industrial wages. Low wages subsidized the industrial export strategy, beginning with labor-intensive manufactures of clothing items. Meanwhile, from 1957 to 1982 more than 12 million people migrated from the rural sector to work in industrial cities such as Seoul and Pusan. Thus, rapid industrialization in South Korea, fueled by labor transfers from the countryside, depended on a cheap food policy underwritten by food aid. In this way, the food regime sponsored economic development in one of the "showcase" countries of the Cold War. (McMichael 1996: 62–3)

In sum, PL 480 can be viewed as a multi-purpose policy. Above all, it helped support US farming interests, just as most US foreign aid primarily benefits US business. It enabled the United States to remove surpluses from the domestic market, which bolstered farm prices, while the conditions attached to the receipt of PL 480 food aid conferred additional benefits on US farmers. For example, an agreement with Iran in the 1960s provided 18,000 metric tons of US vegetable oils if Iran also bought a further 55,000 tons on the world market – which would have meant making purchases of US supplies (Hudson 1972: 145). The law also bestowed dramatic benefits on many corporations in the grain sector, not least by helping to create new markets. As a result, Cargill, a multinational grain trader which is perhaps the largest private company in the United States, saw its US grain exports increase 400 percent in the decade 1955–65 (Kneen 1995: 196). PL 480 also created the means for US grain surpluses to be deployed for political ends within the context of the Cold War, as it gave the USA enormous leverage over the diplomatic policy of recipients (Lindenbaum 1987: 430). And, finally, it enhanced the process of agricultural transformation in the Third World, which the USA and international lending agencies were encouraging, precisely because cheap food aid could mitigate the destabilising effects of rapid agricultural change.

Agricultural Modernisation in Colombia

By 1966, the terms of PL 480 had also been restated, so that food aid was explicitly dependent on the recipient country "creating a favorable environment for private enterprise and investment ... [and] development of the agricultural chemical, farm machinery and equipment, transportation and other necessary industries" that were components of the Green Revolution (quoted in McMichael 1996: 70). This is what occurred in Colombia. But it can only be understood as a part of a wider process of agricultural change in a country which came to be regarded by the United States as perhaps the preeminent model for capitalist development in Latin America.

As a result of a pattern of landownership established in the early colonial period, the fertile heartland of Colombia, the broad river valleys of the Andes, has tended to be monopolised by cattle grazers and large commercial agricultural enterprises (Griffin 1981: 134). On the eve of the Second World War, only 10–12 percent of the country's arable land was actually cultivated, while some 43 percent was in pasture (Escorcia 1975: 106–8). Such patterns of land use, which had long excluded peasants from more central and attractive agricultural zones, eventually drove them to migrate into the more remote mountainous regions of the country (Vallianatos 1976: 79) where, despite the hardships, they became the core of subsistence production in Colombia.

But since most of this land was poor, steep and prone to severe erosion, the security of domestic food production was problematic and malnutrition endemic (Reichel-Dolmatoff and Reichel-Dolmatoff 1961). One of the few things that ensured their survival, and actually encouraged the settlement of such regions in the late nineteenth century, was the cultivation of coffee. While the steep slopes of the cordilleras precluded successful long-term cultivation of most subsistence or cash crops, coffee was especially well suited to such gradients where soil was well drained. Its adaptable root systems acted as a deterrent to soil erosion; and it could easily be intercropped with traditional food crops such as plantains, which provided shade for young coffee plants. By 1900, coffee had become a major factor in the establishment of relatively permanent communities southward from Antioquia along the central mountain chains of the Colombian Andes, as peasants came to regard it as a means of making otherwise marginal land commercially productive (Palacios 1980; Parsons 1949; Koffman 1969: 60–61).

Through the 1920s and 1930s, however, the increasing commercialisation of the Colombian economy also stimulated the emergence of large coffee plantations which employed peasants – or *colonos* – to clear frontier land and plant coffee, and then to repeat the process when the coffee trees became productive. They also attempted to deny peasants, tenants and sharecroppers the right to grow coffee on their own subsistence plots. It was only the fall in world coffee prices in the 1930s, which increased the financial risks for large growers, that created a central role in coffee cultivation for small-holders. Production rose during this period as the Federacion Nacional de Cafeteros (National Federation of Coffee Growers), founded in 1927 by large estate owners and exporters with the backing of the state (Mass 1976: 238), extended credit to peasants. But, as Colombia became the world's second major coffee producer after Brazil (Parsons 1949: 140–41) and coffee became the primary basis of capital accumulation in the country, most of the profits flowed out of the peasant regions.

For advocates of modernisation, however, the problem was that "[a]ccumulation of capital in the most important sector of the Colombian economy depended on relations of production and exchange that grossly exploited coffee workers and small and medium producers" (Bergquist 1986: 277). The consequences for population increase in such regions cannot be underestimated. One of the principal costs of coffee production is labour, at least half of which is required for harvesting (De Graff 1986: 79). But while moderate- and especially large-sized estates depended upon seasonal waged labour (Koffman 1969: 67), recruited from among the landless and those whose own holdings were too small to provide an adequate income, small coffee producers, depending largely on extremely labour-intensive techniques to make an adequate living on steep, rugged terrain, relied exclusively on family labour with "an opportunity cost of near zero" (Griffin 1981: 148). As Bergquist observes:

> The cultivation of coffee trees and their harvesting involved huge labor demands and tapped the resources of all family members. Men and older male children did the heavy labor involved in clearing, planting, and weeding the groves. Women and children of both sexes played an important role in the harvest. (1986: 320)

While their standard of living was marginal, characterised by endemic disease and low dietary intake (Koffman 1969: 70; Fluharty 1976: 213; Bergquist 1986: 277–8), it was only the capacity to provide labour for their own holdings, especially for coffee cultivation, and for work on the latifundias, that ensured survival and obviated the need to migrate to the cities, where unemployment was endemic (Griffin 1981: 148). Fertility was therefore directly related to the means of diversifying sources of income. There was nothing Malthusian here. On the contrary,

> The vigorous demographic growth of the coffee zones reflected the domestic social imperatives of family-centered, labor-intensive coffee production. Astronomical birth-rates offset shocking indices of mortality and disease to produce the celebrated population growth of the coffee regions. (Bergquist 1986: 277)

The fact that coffee had simultaneously become the key to the Colombian economy and a cardinal element in the livelihood strategies of many peasant households implied an inevitable tension. It revolved around the fact that

> Colombia's ability to expand coffee production and to capture a larger share of the depressed world market during the crisis of the 1930s – as well as its capacity to mount an impressive record of import-substituting industrialization during the same period – depended on the willingness of small producers and their families to subject themselves to an ever greater degree of exploitation. (Bergquist 1986: 277)

But that willingness had its limits, and the result was a dramatic escalation in rural conflict, as *colonos* began to refuse to surrender lands they had improved, renters stopped paying their quotas and landlords threatened peasants and began to clear them off the land (Galli 1981: 51). By the 1950s, rural violence had reached a level which was virtually without precedent in the developing world. Although violence had long been characteristic of Colombian history, this was exceptional for its intensity: perhaps as many as 200,000 died in what came to be known simply as *la violencia* (Griffin 1981: 125).

A Malthusian perspective on such violence seemed to gain credibility from the fact that in the 1930s Colombia had one of the highest population growth rates in the world (Dix 1967: 38). By 1949, the issue of population had become one of some concern, at the time of a World Bank economic mission to Colombia, the first which the Bank had ever sent to a developing country (Escobar 1995: 24; Knox 1985: vi). Despite the fact that the Bank acknowledged the issue of unequal landownership, it emphasised that "the fundamental problem was not a maldistribution of land but rather a maldistribution of people" (Hayter and Watson 1985: 183). The overriding concern was that there were too many people engaged in agriculture.

Lauchlin Currie, the New Deal economist who led that mission, would observe, years later, in the *Population Bulletin* that the "population bomb" was the greatest threat facing contemporary humanity (Sandilands

1990: 213, 413). But more importantly, in 1961, in his influential work *Operación Colombia*, a book which became a blueprint among the Colombian elite for the country's modernisation, he wrote that

> Colombia's real rural problem was an excess rural population ... This excess should be transferred, forcibly if need be, to the large cities and employed in public works in order to create increased consumer demand, which in turn would be met by increased industrialisation. Colombian agriculture would, meanwhile, be intensively mechanised, and the remaining rural population would be employed by these large, mechanised farming operations. (in Hayter and Watson 1985: 183)

Even before these words were published, much of the rural population had already been driven into the cities by *la violencia* – the decline in the ratio of rural to urban population during the 1940s was one of the highest in the world (Dix 1968: 32) – and the process of agricultural change that Currie advocated was well under way. What the so-called Currie plan signified, however, was that, as in Ireland in the decades after the famine, the clearing of the countryside that already had occurred was not enough to satisfy its beneficiaries. It would continue.

So, it was not fortuitous that, from the mid-1960s onward, Colombia was "the target country for some of the earliest and most extensive pilot programs in the field of population control" (Casselman and Acton 1976: 235). In 1965, PROFAMILIA, the Colombian Association for Family Welfare, was established. Within the next decade, with support from the Ford and Rockefeller Foundations and USAID, it became the main source of contraceptive services in the country. Most importantly, when it began to extend its services into rural areas, it did so in close collaboration with the National Federation of Coffee Growers (Mass 1976: 253), with its class bias against peasant producers. Between 1960–64 and 1972–73, the total fertility rate for Colombia fell dramatically from 7.04 births per woman to 4.6; it continued declining to 3.2 in 1985 (Flórez 1996: 254; Merrick 1990: 147). Although the decline was somewhat earlier in urban areas, it was clearly a rural trend as well (Flórez 1996: 254). However, it is doubtful whether it was principally the result of an increased availability or awareness of contraceptives. In rural areas, at least, where one of the main incentives for high fertility had been the demand for labour on small family coffee-producing farms, the widespread disappearance of such units and the devastating rupture of community life during the period of *la violencia*, played a major role in rural fertility decline.

It is perhaps not surprising, however, that the dramatic rise in rural violence which characterised Colombia in the late 1940s and 1950s, and

which had a strong association with major coffee-producing depart-
ments in the highlands (Koffman 1969: 71), was often attributed to
population pressure. But this overlooks not only the relationship of
fertility to small-holder coffee cultivation, but also the complex interrelationship of coffee production and the national economy. The national
economy was so highly dependent on coffee, which represented about
48 percent of the value of all agricultural production and 10 percent of
GNP (Koffman 1969: 46), that, even when prices fell, production
increased, putting intolerable pressure on peasant cultivators and increasing the likelihood of conflicts over land. Yet the process of capital
accumulation, as a basis for the diversification of exports and development of industry, depended on maintaining coffee production. The
eventual solution could only be to return coffee production to the hands
of large commercial interests and to clear the countryside of peasants.
This is what the violence did. It not only served to curb rising peasant
protest, but enabled large farmers to buy up minifundia at below market
value (Arocha 1975: 230; Williamson 1965: 39), effecting a process of
land consolidation as large areas were depopulated by terror and death
and mass migration to the cities (Fluharty 1976: 210; Galli 1981: 52). In
Tolima, one of the principal coffee regions,

> land from which peasants were systematically uprooted was turned to several
> different purposes. In the south, it was often returned to pasture for extensive
> cattle production; in the north, it was generally put under intensive coffee
> cultivation, while in the southeast, haciendas were sold and/or broken into
> medium-sized commercial plantations of cotton, rice, and sesame. (Galli
> 1981: 55)

But violence was only one part of the modernisation process, and it
is not coincidental that its escalation in the immediate post-war era
paralleled a marked increase in interest in Colombia on the part of
international capital. At a time of mounting struggle for land between
tenant farmers and latifundistas, Laurance Rockefeller obtained a controlling interest in 1.5 million acres of prime agricultural land in
Colombia's Magdalena River Valley – one of the interandine valleys
where valued bottom lands were traditionally monopolised by ranching
interests – not far from the 2,000-square-mile De Mares oil field which
had been a major producer for Rockefeller's Standard Oil of New Jersey
since the early 1920s (Colby and Dennett 1995: 35–6). In 1949, Colombia signed an agreement with the Rockefeller Foundation to develop a
programme of agricultural research, and the following year the Rockefeller Foundation chose Colombia for the site of its first agricultural
research programme outside of Mexico (World Bank 1950: 86; Lele and

Goldsmith 1989: 314). It was to lead to the establishment of the Centro Internacional de Agricultura Tropical (CIAT) at Cali, under Ford and Rockefeller auspices, some twenty years later. Such events reflected the growing Rockefeller attraction to Colombia, where, from the 1950s, IBEC pursued a number of commercial possibilities and eventually spearheaded the creation of the Colombian Finance Corporation (Colby and Dennett 1995: 380). The principal Rockefeller interest was in the expansion of commercial farming, and during the 1950s and 1960s, as this took place and as the use of synthetic fertilisers in Colombia increased on average 6 percent per year (Reinhardt 1988: 143), much of it was supplied by Rockefeller's Esso Chemicals, whose ammonia-urea complex at Barranquilla produced 100,000 tons a year of nitrogen fertiliser.

Rockefeller family interests were echoed by the activities of the World Bank. Colombia was one of the first developing countries to apply for a loan from the Bank, and the first to host a World Bank economic mission (Sandilands 1990: 159; Knox 1985: vi),[4] which arrived in Colombia in 1948. Its report, interestingly, made virtually no reference to the escalating violence or to its impact on the rural population. This gives a certain mordant irony to Currie's view that one of the country's paramount needs was "to plan for and create the conditions that would effect a rapid expansion in Colombia's urban population relative to the rural", one of the principal Western measures of a modern economy (Sandilands 1990: 164; cf. Zamosc 1986: 21). That expansion was already taking place as a result of *la violencia*.

Such outside influences – which continued to regard the goal of Colombian development as the creation of a diversified export economy – also ensured that any movement toward real land reform was minimal (Thiesenhusen 1995: 87). Griffin notes that, while a "successful land reform in Colombia should begin by expropriating the best of the latifundia lands" and "efforts should be focused on the densely populated regions where the problem of underemployment is most intense", the strategy of INCORA, Colombia's land reform agency, was to locate "its projects in sparsely populated areas, in poor zones, on abandoned land", where not only was there no threat to established patterns of land use (Griffin 1981: 140), but its activities could be closely co-ordinated with a general policy of rural pacification (Galli 1978: 76–7). In true Green Revolution fashion, moreover, the agency emphasised improved output and commercial exports, a policy which favoured large holdings and

---

4. It was also the subject of the first World Bank Economic Report in 1952 and of the first country report which the Bank published in book form, in 1972 (Knox 1985: vi).

was supported by its outside sponsors, the World Bank, USAID and the Inter-American Development Bank (Galli 1978: 78).

US shipments of PL 480 wheat also played an important role. Such sales meant that the United States accumulated Colombian currency, a part of which was then loaned back to Colombia on terms that allowed the United States to influence the direction of the country's economy in a particularly tumultuous period of agricultural change. One indication of this is the fact that "the largest P.L. 480 loans, totalling approximately 44 million pesos, were invested in the chemical fertilizer industry" (Hall 1985: 142). While this reduced Colombia's dependence on fertiliser imports, much of the country's own production actually was controlled by foreign (principally North American) companies. The same was true of other chemical inputs:

> EXXON controlled Abonos Colombianos that supplied 35 percent of the fertilizer market. Insecticides and herbicides were mainly manufactured by subsidiaries of foreign companies such as Rohm and Hans, Cyanimid, BASF Chemical, Ciba-Geigy, Dupont, and Shell. Weed killers were the particular reserve of Down Chemical of Colombia, S.A. Moreover, the agricultural input industries had to import large quantities of raw materials. For example, both ammonium sulphate and superphosphates used in making fertilizers were still being imported. (Galli 1981: 44)

By the 1970s, moreover, the Instituto de Mercado Agropecuario (IDEMA), the semi-official marketing agency, was selling PL 480 wheat at a price low enough to discourage domestic production. This conformed to the general development policy of the period, since (unlike in Mexico) wheat farming generally

> was characterized by small farm size and a low degree of commercialization. In Cundinamarca, one of the nation's major wheat-producing states, nearly 40 percent of the wheat was grown on plots of less than ten hectares, with an average of only slightly more than one hectare of wheat per farm. (Hall 1985: 144)

Such wheat production was also regarded as backward technically (Hall 1985: 144) and PL 480 aid provided an instrument through which it could be reduced. As a result, "By 1973, wheat production was less than half its average annual level from 1956 to 1960" (Hall 1985: 144). In contrast, it was large farmers who developed rice production (and the irrigation on which it was based) through public funds which were derived to a large extent from resales of PL 480 wheat and channelled through the Caja de Credito Agrario (Hall 1985: 145). At the same time, "By using P.L. 480 revenues to support rice and restricting rice imports, IDEMA sheltered Colombia's developing rice industry" (Hall

1985: 146) and, in line with government policy generally during that period, enhanced the process of commercial agricultural concentration. Between 1950 and 1982, the area in rice expanded from 133,000 hectares to 474,000 (Goodman and Redclift 1991: 62) and the average size of holdings rose. Where, before 1960, "rice was grown only on very small plots, the great majority less than 5 ha in size", by 1981, "almost half the land cultivated in rice was in holdings of over 100 ha" (Goodman and Redclift 1991: 62). Rice also came to play an increasing role in the diet of urban workers, although the pattern of agrarian development generally meant that an increasing proportion of domestic production was exported, and that Colombia became more dependent on food imports which many people could not afford.

Synthetic Nitrogen in War and Peace

Among the most important of Green Revolution inputs were synthetic fertilisers. But the story of their eventual role in the Green Revolution begins in the early nineteenth century, when a number of imported fertilisers – including Peruvian guano – began to be used in Britain (Bonilla 1974: 142; Pike 1967: 123–5). Guano imports reached their peak in 1858, by which time cheaper nitrates from the Chilean coast, first used around 1840, were emerging as a major source of fertilisers. While much of the trade was handled by British firms, the Germans were the principal importer as the English shifted to superphosphates and nitrates, which were a by-product of the gas industry (Platt 1972: 255).

It was in the 1840s that major advances first began to be made in industrially produced fertilisers, beginning with the suggestion by Justus von Liebig that ammonia could be formed when coal carbonised to produce coal gas and coke. While fertiliser production began to develop into a major European industry during the 1870s, Chilean nitrates still maintained their preeminence until the First World War, when Liebig's suggestion finally emerged as a practical possibility. But how this came about can only be understood in terms of the relationship between technological development and the evolution of industrial capitalism.

It is useful to recall how the suppression of the European uprisings of 1848 had marked the beginning of a period during which the interests of the rising industrial class were effectively consolidated, bringing about a dramatic growth in investment in new enterprises on a global scale. It was a process which coincided with a process of dramatic European imperialist expansion, from the 1870s to the turn of the century (Barratt Brown 1974: 184). More and more capital was invested abroad (Barratt Brown 1974: 133–45; Platt 1972: 98–135), but there was also growing competition for markets and raw materials (Hobson 1902: 17–19). Especially after the great economic crisis of 1873, the costs of this competition gave rise, in both Europe and the United States, to the formation of a new system of great corporations and cartels which sought to rationalise production and markets in specific commodities. Such cartels began to organise themselves globally after 1900, and especially after the First World War (Platt 1972: 173–5; Clairmonte and Cavanagh 1981: 126–7; Williams 1969: 76–7).

One sector in which this occurred and whose very emergence reflected the conflicts that such competition would bring was the European munitions industry. But beyond the conventional production of weapons by companies such as Armstrong in England and Krupp in Germany, there was another aspect of the arms industry that had its origins in a different field entirely. Lacking the great colonial resources of Britain or France, Germany had, however, the great coal reserves of the Ruhr Valley. The coal, which was used to produce steel, much of which went into Krupp guns, left behind a waste product called coal tar which became the basic material of a new industry, which turned it into synthetic dyes. The chief companies engaged in this process by the beginning of the twentieth century were BASF, Bayer, Hoechst and, to a lesser extent, Agfa (Clairmonte and Cavanagh 1981: 136).

These companies were to profit from another line of development as well. As Borkin writes:

> During the latter part of the nineteenth century, a number of prominent scientists expressed the belief, supported by facts and figures, that an exploding world population clearly threatened to outrun the food supply. The ghost of Malthus had returned to haunt the world. The most promising solution was the increased use of fertilizers. (1978: 8)

By the turn of the twentieth century, the Germans, with their great coal reserves, were actively seeking an alternative to Chilean nitrates in the development of organic chemicals. In 1908, Fritz Haber developed a method of using coal and water under high pressure and moderately high temperature to yield ammonia, which was a major constituent of fertilisers. Chemically, there was little difference between fertilisers and explosives. By 1913, BASF had completed a plant which mass-produced synthetic ammonia, based on the so-called "Haber–Bosch" process which won Fritz Haber the Nobel Prize. But its labs had also been oxidising some of the plant's ammonia to produce a synthetic saltpetre, which was an essential ingredient of gunpowder (Borkin 1978: 10). By mid-1914, as it became clear that shortages of saltpetre would force

Germany out of the First World War, efforts began to be made to manufacture synthetic nitrates on a large scale (Borkin 1978: 19).

In the immediate aftermath of the war, BASF, Bayer, Hoechst and four other companies, including Agfa, which had been operating as several cartels since before the war, combined formally to become I.G. Farbenindustries Aktiengesellschaft, commonly known as I.G. Farben (Borkin 1978: 43). According to Borkin, it "was the largest corporation in Europe and the largest chemical company in the world". It began to expand and "One of its first moves was to gain control of Germany's munitions industry" (Borkin 1978: 43). It also entered into negotiations with Rockefeller's Standard Oil, which brought the two companies into close co-operation long after I.G. had entered into an alliance with the Nazis (Borkin 1978: 76–94; Shirer 1960: 144, 190). Its commitment to the Nazi cause, fuelled by the material advantages which the company obtained, led to its ultimate venture: the synthetic coal-oil and rubber factory at Auschwitz, where its operations – and profits – were based on slave labour (Shirer 1960: 664; Clairmonte and Cavanagh 1981: 138; Borkin 1978: 141–56).

Despite the dismemberment of I.G. Farben in 1945, BASF, Hoechst and Bayer all survived, to flourish as individual companies. By the late 1970s, each would be larger than its parent. But now they were all embarked on a new path. As the Green Revolution spread, they became global giants in the field of agro-chemicals, accounting for one-fifth of the world pesticide market by 1988 (Hobbelink 1991: 44). Within four decades, much of the world's food production could be linked to the activities of companies whose idea of corporate responsibility had been demonstrated at I.G. Auschwitz.

The TVA, Munitions and the Post-war Market for Fertilisers

The relationship between munitions and fertilisers may also help to explain one of the less noted advantages to the United States of promoting the process of technological intensification which the Green Revolution represented. In 1916, the National Defence Act had led to the construction of Wilson Dam on the Tennessee River in northwestern Alabama, at a site called Muscle Shoals. It provided the cheap electricity for two plants to manufacture the synthetic nitrogen compounds which could produce either munitions or fertilisers. As Allbaugh notes:

> The close technical bond between fertilizer and munitions lends common sense to the idea of using the same laboratories, plants, and people for work on both. When a munitions plant stands idle, advances in technology soon

make it out of date. Then when it is needed, tax money is spent lavishly in the hurry to rebuild or replace it and to start operation with an inexperienced crew. The country gains from the use of that plant for fertilizer production when its output is not needed for munitions. In this way the plant is kept up to date, and both the plant and the people who run it are kept ready for an orderly shift to munitions production. (1956: 153)

The original plants were idle after the First World War (Allbaugh 1956: 155; Clapp 1955: 137). But, in 1933, the Roosevelt administration created the Tennessee Valley Authority (TVA), which took over Muscle Shoals and eventually constructed and operated a vast complex of thirty-three dams on the Tennessee River. During the Second World War, the government invested more than $250 million to built ten ammonia plants for the manufacture of explosives (Allbaugh 1956: 159). Toward the end of the war, as the need for ammonium nitrate for explosives declined, the plants were converted to production of fertilisers. As Allbaugh explains,

> TVA worked with the Department of Agriculture and with industry … to make the ammonium nitrate more suitable for use as a fertilizer, and diverted its output of this concentrated source of nitrogen almost immediately to agricultural uses. (1956: 159–60)

By 1950, at about the same time that the TVA first entered into distribution contracts with fertiliser companies, six of the plants were sold to private firms (Allbaugh 1956: 160, 167). But the TVA continued to produce fertilisers. It never manufactured more than 3 percent of US output, but it played a major role in developing new production techniques (Clapp 1955: 138–9). With time, it also assumed a leading role in international agricultural development. In 1974, the TVA's National Fertiliser Development Center at Muscle Shoals was separated into two programmes, one national and the other international. The latter was administered by a new organisation, the International Fertilizer Development Center (IFDC), which was funded largely by USAID and which describes a major part of its current role as "increasing and sustaining food and agricultural productivity in the developing countries through the development and transfer of … agribusiness expertise" (IFDC 1997).

It is interesting to see what impact the TVA had on the agriculture of the region, largely through the increased use of fertilisers. Phosphate fertilisers produced by the TVA were especially suitable for grasses and legumes and led to a significant shift in patterns of production:

> In the four states for which data are available (Alabama, Mississippi, North Carolina, and Tennessee), there was an increase from 1935 to 1949 of 314 per cent in fertilizer use in the Valley areas, in contrast to an increase of 114 per

cent in the non-Valley portions. Corn acreage in the Valley has decreased 20
per cent since 1930, cotton acreage 18 per cent. Small grain acreage is up 17
per cent, hay acreage 57 per cent. Sixteen per cent more land is in pasture.
Cattle and calves on the farms are up 38 per cent. (Allbaugh 1956: 172–3)

It does not take much imagination to see the model here for a process
of agricultural transformation that would spread around the world over
the next thirty years. What is especially important is how increasing
fertiliser use enabled agricultural output – much of it eventually directed
to animal feeds, as in the case of Mexico (Barkin et al. 1990) – to rise,
even as family farming and the number of agricultural workers declined.
For an industrialised country with the means to absorb such labour,
that was one thing. The implications for a developing country are entirely
different.

Yet the Green Revolution was, as much as anything, a revolution in
the development of a market for Western fertiliser production and in
the use of the excess productive capacity that existed in the immediate
post-war years. As Borlaug had noted in his Nobel acceptance speech
in 1970, "If the high-yielding dwarf wheat and rice are the catalysts that
have ignited the Green revolution, then chemical fertilizers [are] the
fuel that has powered its forward thrust" (Borlaug 1970). Fifteen years
later, forty years after the initial research in Mexico, it could still be said
that the most revolutionary aspect of the new hybrids was that they
could "yield twice as much additional grain as the traditional ones for
each kilogram of added nitrogen fertilizer up to the first 70 kilograms
of nitrogen per hectare" (Baum 1986: 7–8). Increased yields had depended from the outset on access to substantial chemical fertiliser supplies and, as such, were destined to tie the fate of such agricultural
efforts to their distribution and supply.

Thus, as Brown wrote in 1974,

> The use of the new high-yielding wheat and rice varieties has spurred ferti-
> lizer demand in Asia, since these varieties are far more efficient users of
> chemical nutrients than the traditional ones they are replacing. (1974: 116–17)

This was certainly the view that had been advanced almost a decade
earlier by the governmental and corporate participants at the National
Seminar on Fertilisers in India (Alexander and Giroti 1966). It was the
view which generally had prevailed since the 1950s when most of the
world's nitrogen fertiliser was produced in North America, the USSR,
Japan and Europe. Thus, at least initially, countries to which the Green
Revolution was exported needed to purchase fertilisers in quantities
which increased at a dramatic rate.

The sale of fertilisers provided an excellent solution to the USA's non-agricultural trade deficit (Doyle 1987: 317). That prospect had generated great enthusiasm in the 1960s among Western agribusinesses eager to invest in fertiliser-producing capacity in developing countries such as India. As Frank Parker, Assistant Director for Research and Technology at USAID, observed at the India conference on fertilisers, a recent USAID-commissioned report by the TVA of planned world fertiliser production capacity

> showed that private industry was prepared, almost anxious, to invest in fer-
> tiliser production to meet the growing demand of both the less and more
> developed countries.... "given a favourable climate for investment and rea-
> sonable assurance that a market can be developed". (Parker 1966: 33)

The major oil companies also had a keen interest in agricultural developments that would create an explosive new demand for petroleum-based fertilisers. Most of them were and remain heavily involved in the manufacture of chemicals generally and agro-chemicals in particular (Lundberg 1968: 317). They include Esso Chemical Co., Standard of Indiana's Amoco Chemicals Corp., Mobil Chemical International, Phillips's American Fertilizer and Chemical Co., etc., and chemical companies such as DuPont and Union Carbide, in many of which the Rockefellers have had significant interests.[5] It is not surprising that the Rockefeller Foundation – along with Ford – "played an active part" in the Fertiliser Seminar in India in 1965 (Ranganathan 1966). While the Ford Foundation was intimately involved in India's national planning during this period, the Rockefeller Foundation, according to Lele and Goldsmith of the World Bank, had a "crucially important interaction" with the Indian government and played a significant role in "the technological transformation of Indian agriculture" (1989: 306, 308). Both foundations encouraged the adoption of the Green Revolution strategy to modernise Indian agriculture.

Moreover, as I have suggested, neither operated independently of US foreign policy or of the aims of the World Bank. Although Rockefeller support for hybrid maize research was formally requested by India in 1955 (Lele and Goldsmith 1989: 314), this support only

---

5. Thus, Chase, the Rockefeller bank, was the third largest shareholder in Mobil Corporation, ranked seventeenth among shareholders of Phillips Petroleum Company and ninth for Union Carbide. This, however, barely begins to account for Rockefeller investments in companies involved in agro-chemicals, since Chase and/or the Rockefeller Family Group have significant and influential holdings in other major banks – such as Morgan and Citibank – which themselves are major shareholders in such companies (US Senate Committee on Governmental Affairs 1978: 161, 163, 230).

came a decade later, in the wake of a major drought and dramatic
decline in grain production, when

> President Lyndon Johnson, believing that India was not serious about policy
> reform, put India on a "short tether" regarding food aid to increase pressure
> on its government. Meanwhile, the consortium of India's donors led by the
> World Bank were discussing program support to help India meet critical
> balance-of-payments needs, but wanted it contingent on India's willingness to
> devaluate and to reorient its economic strategy away from import-substituting
> industrialization and toward accelerated agricultural development. (Lele and
> Goldsmith 1989: 325)

As a result, India immediately announced that it would introduce
HYVs onto 32.5 million acres over the next five years. A year later, in
1966, with assistance from the Rockefeller Foundation, it purchased
18,000 tons of Mexican wheat seed (Lele and Goldsmith 1989: 326).
That same year, Frank Parker of USAID announced at the National
Seminar on Fertilisers that the Esso Chemical Company – a subsidiary
of the Rockefeller-controlled Standard Oil of New Jersey (currently
known as Exxon Corporation) – had current and planned investment in
fertiliser plants in India amounting to $200 million (1966: 33). There
clearly was a synchronisation between US foreign policy, the Rockefeller
Foundation and Rockefeller petrochemical interests.

If one of the main objectives of the Green Revolution was to create
a lucrative global market for the industrial products on which "modernised" agriculture depended, it also practically ensured that any country
committed to such a course of agrarian development was unlikely ever
to disengage itself successfully from that market. Quite the contrary. As
rising oil prices in the 1970s were "one of the most important external
causes of mounting LDC debt" (Avery 1990: 507), in many countries
where an increasingly mechanised, commercial agriculture had created
dependence on oil imports, the hold of the international economy
tightened. In the eighties, far from addressing the essential debt question,
which, as Chossudovsky notes, "lies in an unequal structure of trade,
production and credit which defines the role and position of developing
countries in the global economy" (1991: 2527), the World Bank and the
IMF seized upon it to impose programmes of "structural adjustment",
which accelerated the process of internationalisation of Third World
economies. This meant their becoming, in effect, "open economic
territories and 'reserves' of cheap labour and natural resources"
(Chossudovsky 1991: 2527), pushed toward further agricultural "modernisation" under the influence of foreign agribusiness. It was a process
which generated more exports – filling the supermarket shelves of the

developed countries – at the cost of rising domestic food poverty in developing regions. Ignoring this sequence of events, the growing nutritional crisis in the Third World is variously attributed to over-population and/or other environmental stress and has now become the current basis for Neo-Malthusian calls from the Western political and corporate elite for a profitable renewal of the Green Revolution. As US Assistant Secretary of State for Global Affairs Timothy Wirth – for whom the issue of population is "at the top of the agenda" (Stilkind 1995) – has recently declared: "we would be very fortunate if we had another Green Revolution" (Ggedda 1997). But, as ever, who is "we"?

Rationalising the Green Revolution

A large part of the "we" is represented by what is called the Consultative Group on International Agricultural Research (CGIAR). By the mid-1960s, as the Green Revolution had been widely implemented throughout strategic zones in Asia and the Americas, a network of centres for agricultural research and development had been created to further the interests of an emergent global agro-industry. The initial step toward this had been the formation of the International Centre for the Improvement of Maize and Wheat (CIMMYT) in Mexico and IRRI in the Philippines, both under Ford and Rockefeller Foundation auspices (Mason and Asher 1973: 574; Vallianatos 1976: 57–61). By 1971, when there were eight such centres (formally designated as IARCs, or International Agricultural Research Centres) world-wide (Mathieson 1975: 23), it was considered necessary to create a co-ordinating agency. J. George Harrar at the Rockefeller Foundation, and F.F. Hill, an agricultural economist and vice-president of the Ford Foundation, played a major role in the emergence of what became the CGIAR, a system which was explicitly meant to direct the future course of the Green Revolution (Baum 1986).

Although the CGIAR system has been described recently by a spokesperson for the Council on Foreign Relations as "an international, publicly funded effort, located in the developing world" (Mathews 1994), it is far more than that. Its initial funding came through the Ford and Rockefeller Foundations, which remain a major influence within the system. Its headquarters has always been at the World Bank (Mathieson 1975: 23), which provides its secretariat (Mason and Asher 1973: 574). More pointedly, as former Bank president A.W. Clausen has observed, the CGIAR was "designed, sponsored, and promoted" by the World Bank, which continuously "has provided the chairman from among its senior officers" (Clausen 1986: vi).

The CGIAR has been widely regarded as "an historic step in the evolution of a truly global agricultural research strategy", according to a leading Neo-Malthusian, Lester Brown, who began his career at the US Department of Agriculture (Brown 1975: 178). But it was a strategy which, despite all the efforts to portray it as a decentralised, international effort, has embodied and expressed Western corporate interests. Despite the need to portray its aims as ideologically neutral, ostensibly concerned with the purely technical improvement of agricultural production, any consideration of the forces which gave birth to it and which continue to inspire it thoroughly belies this picture.

Much of the initiative for the setting up of the CGIAR came from Robert McNamara, when he was the president of the World Bank, and this raises many interesting questions. When he left government in 1968 after the election of Richard Nixon, the Vietnam War was far from over. For six years, McNamara had been one of the chief architects of that war, and, as I noted in an earlier chapter, there is little reason to think that he moved on to the Bank with any sense that the war had been misguided. As a director of the Ford Foundation (Baum 1986: 36), he found ready support for the establishment of the CGIAR in the person of the Ford Foundation's president, McGeorge Bundy, who, along with his older brother William, had been a Washington colleague of McNamara in the Kennedy administration, helping to shape the course of the war as well. McGeorge Bundy himself had been at the CIA and liased with it from the White House during the Kennedy and Johnson years.

Another contemporary of McNamara and Bundy in Washington during the Kennedy years who was involved in the origins of the CGIAR was David Bell, who had been assistant director of the budget under Truman, served as Kennedy's Budget Director and chaired the top-level committee that wrote the famous Bell Report, which made proposals to reform the Federal government's system of research and development (Nieburg 1970: 334–50). Then, in 1961, the Foreign Assistance Act was passed which became the principal legislative framework for all US economic and military aid, both of which were effectively integrated into one overall structure. Among other things, this act created the US Agency for International Development (USAID) and gave its administrator, who was responsible only to the President and the Secretary of State, the rank of Undersecretary of State (Packenham 1973: 60). In 1963, Bell became the head of USAID (Caldwell and Caldwell 1986: 100).

As such, the man who in 1968 would become the executive vice-president of the Ford Foundation in charge of its international programmes and play a major role in the emergence of CGIAR (Baum 1986) now became the head of an agency which was closely identified operationally with the CIA and which directed the notorious "rural pacification programme" in Vietnam (Halberstam 1972: 346; Sheehan 1988: 310, 495). More recently, he has been the director of the Center for Population Studies at Harvard University and chair of the International Food Policy Research Institute (IFPRI), the major think-tank for the CGIAR system.

Such connections inevitably underline that the Green Revolution, especially in the mature phase co-ordinated by the CGIAR system, represented a new kind of assault on the Third World peasantry, a form of rural pacification that relied no longer on bombs and napalm, but on global financial institutions and development policies which favoured private agribusiness investment. It is not surprising, then, that many of the underlying premises about the Third World that legitimated the efforts of the Bank in the 1970s under McNamara were not really very different from those that had motivated the United States in Vietnam. Central to both was the view that developing countries, especially those of strategic importance for the West, must develop within the orbit of the capitalist market. In both cases, this might require rural populations to be "pacified". But, where in the case of Vietnam, this had been attempted through military means, more sophisticated economic instruments now took over. Nevertheless, the similarities were otherwise striking. As Bello et al. have written, the Bank's involvement in the Philippines

> has been compared to the U.S. military odyssey in Vietnam. The image is apt, for the economic buildup in the Philippines and the military buildup in Vietnam were both massive, capital-intensive "technical fixes" to societies rent by deep-seated social conflicts.... The main elements of [the Bank's efforts in the Philippines] were to be the pacification of the countryside through Rural Development and the transformation of the industrial sector from import-substitution manufacturing to export-oriented industrialization. This strategy was to plug the Philippines more firmly into the international capitalist economic order. (1982: 41)

Whether it was the Philippines, India or Mexico, the result was not favourable to the survival of subsistence cultivators. In many parts of the Third World, while exports – coconuts from the Philippines, cattle feed from Mexico, orange juice from Brazil – have increased, staple food production has declined. As more and more people in such countries depend on inadequate employment to purchase imported foods, nutritional insecurity is on the rise. But Malthusian logic continues to be employed to deny democratic access to cultivable land a significant role in securing rural livelihoods. Instead, it is used to justify an unprecedented escalation in the commitment to bio-technological innovations which will further concentrate power in the hands of multinational agro-industry.

Contemplating an Alternative

Before that happens, it is worth considering the implications of Stewart Odend'hal's work in West Bengal, India, now twenty-five years old, which demonstrated how a system perceived by the West as traditional and inefficient was, in fact, more ecologically rational than the more industrialised system found in the United States, which has been the model for agricultural development in the Third World since the days of Cornell missionaries in China. In India, where cattle were reared on the by-products of crops grown for human use, there was virtually no competition between humans and animals for food or land. Most cattle food – rice straw, rice hulls and chopped banana tree trunks – was locally produced, and cattle converted it into products that humans could use, including calves, work, milk and dung (for fertiliser and fuel). In contrast, in the USA, where agricultural fertiliser is based on petro-chemicals, cattle manure is wasted and ends up, in fact, as a major environmental liability, polluting ground water and causing the eutrophication of rivers and lakes (Odend'hal 1972: 17–19; Pimental and Pimental 1991: 330–31).

Thus, even when it increased output, the Green Revolution actually reduced the overall efficiency of food production because of its waste of potential resources in favour of increasing dependence on costly inputs. In the early nineties, for example, imported pesticide ingredients cost Costa Rica more than $80 million (Wheat 1996). But such costs do not even begin to consider the social, environmental and health consequences of pesticides and herbicides, without which increased yields of new grain varieties were declared to be impossible. India, one of the world's largest users (and manufacturers) of pesticides – many of which are banned or severely restricted in developed countries – "accounts for over one-third of the 500,000 acute pesticide poisonings which the WHO estimates occur every year in the developing world" (Viswanathan 1991: 2039). But pesticides are a major health risk throughout the Third World (Putzel and Cunnington 1989: 53; Canihuante 1997), and not only where new grain varieties have been introduced. Such chemicals are applied as well to many of the cash crops that also tie developing economies into the increasingly intensive global agro-food system. In Costa Rica, for example, the banana plantations, which occupy 5 percent of the country's cultivated land, use 30 kilos of active pesticide ingredients per hectare annually and inflict considerable damage on the health of the workers and their families (Wheat 1996).

This is despite the fact that the long-term efficacy of such chemicals is highly problematical. As Viswanathan observes:

analysis of the environmental and biological effects of pesticides reveals that increasing pesticide use does not boost foodgrain production over the long term but, instead, has led to a resurgence of both target and secondary pests.... Like all wonder drugs, pesticides promised miracles but only delivered addiction. (1991: 2039)

And they may well be counterproductive in the long run. As far as new rice varieties are concerned, despite the

increased use of insecticides there is no proof that losses due to insects in rice have been reduced; rather, at best such losses have remained around 27 per-cent.... One reason for this is that more insect-susceptible varieties of rice have been planted. Further, the use of 2,4–D herbicide has increased the level of attack of insects on rice. (Pimental and Pimental 1991: 329–30)

Such attacks have also been amplified by high fertiliser use, since higher nutrient levels of crops tend to favour insects and disease as well (Pimental and Pimental 1991: 331).

These costs had to be overlooked if industrialised agriculture was to be presented as the key to global human dietary sufficiency – not to mention if it was to foster a profitable market for chemical inputs. But quite apart from the central question of whether more people in developing countries are actually getting fed, the growing evidence that such agriculture is far less efficient than pre-Green Revolution systems has led some writers to the conclusion that high yields alone have been a misconceived measure of success, and that an "analysis of energy costs and energy returns shows that a truly appropriate technology for the poorest regions of the tropical world has yet to be revealed" (Bayliss-Smith 1984: 170).

In fact, even as Rockefeller research efforts were underway in Mexico in the 1940s, an alternative strategy existed. Peasant horticulture, as Sauer had suggested and as many Mexican scientists appreciated, had enormous potential for innovation and productivity. What peasants chiefly lacked was access to cultivable land and the commitment of the state to provide the resources and incentives that small-holder production required – no small thing, since that often mean a radical realignment in basic property relations. We have subsequently learned as well, though perhaps too late, that peasant agriculture may prove far more sustainable than intensive commercial systems of food production – in terms not only of the environment, but of the human communities that are part of them. As Yates noted almost half a century ago:

The long-term objectives of agricultural technique ... should be the development of self-contained systems which do not require excessive supplies of scarce raw materials or external sources of power. (1951: 72)

Instead, they would make more use of human labour, in a
non-exploitative social relations. As Mencher observed of rice
Kerala:

> Kerala agriculture could actually benefit considerably from gre
> intensification, including such activities as improving irrigation channels, and
> in some areas small-scale irrigation works (building storage tanks, etc.) ...
> growing more short-duration green manures which would save on costly
> fertilisers, growing more high-protein lentils, by the much greater develop-
> ment of small fish cultivation, and (as has been noted by a number of people)
> by the better utilisation of small pieces of garden land. (1978: A-104)

Such practices, which would harness rather than discount the potential
of rural labour (and thereby subvert the illusion that "over-population"
was only remediable through fertility control), would require more
general access to land than even the process of land reform under a
left-wing government in Kerala had been able to provide in the face of
opposition from large landowners. Above all, such intensification would
also provide the basis for the relative independence of local production.
But such a development would be antithetical to the kind of market
dependency and technological intensification (in the form of multinational development of agro-bio-techology) which the Green Revolution has deliberately engendered and which the CGIAR continues to
promote, even after the formal end of the Cold War.

Conclusion

Malthusianism after the Cold War: The Struggle Continues

While the Cold War is assumed to have ended with the triumph of the capitalist market, Malthusian thinking, long associated with the struggle against the critics of capitalism, is enjoying renewed vigour. At first, this seems paradoxical, but the recent experience of developing countries suggests why. As policies of free trade, unrestricted and unregulated investment and open capital markets, longtime goals of the United States, are now being implemented with a vengeance, the contradictions of capitalist development have also become more acute. With an unprecedented rise in the international flow of capital (Gomez 1997) has come a dramatic increase in the instability in the world capitalist economy, growing inequalities throughout the Third World (and in many parts of the developed countries), and new forms of resistance to the consequences of capitalist development.

The flourishing of the new rhetoric of sustainable development and globalisation reflects their special appeal to Western policy-makers and capitalists, precisely because they help obscure how the current "free market" regime is exacerbating, rather than resolving, the social and environmental problems that confront most developing countries; and how, far from engendering global harmony, the dynamics of an un-restrained world market are actually accelerating a process of economic and ideological polarisation. But such concepts by themselves cannot entirely defuse the potential consequences of such realities. After the easing of the previous constraints of Cold War ideology, which initially encouraged widespread expectations that attention and resources might be directed to making capitalism more equitable, the increasing fragility and volatility of the global capitalist economy is transforming such expectations into popular struggles for equity and social justice. Whether these take the form of renewed claims for land, concerted opposition to neo-liberal trade policies or assertions of the right to emigrate to seek work in an internationalised economy, they are provoking a defensive reaction in the North, through immigration restriction, enforcement of the right of unimpeded capital investment, and other measures meant to ensure the sustainability of its own privileges. It is also reviving the time-tested myths of legitimation of capitalism. Malthusian thinking, the most consistent feature of which is its resolute defence of inequality, is once again being enlisted to justify, defend or enlarge the rights of private property.

The Globalisation of Garrett Hardin

In this context, the work of Hardin has been revived, by himself and others. Abernethy, for example, suggests that any attempt to promote such an ethic of global redistribution would represent "an attack on the legitimacy of unevenly distributed wealth" and, therefore, on the "legitimacy of ownership" *per se*, and would undermine any likelihood of conserving scarce resources and preventing the so-called "tragedy of the commons" (Abernethy 1991: 323). Extending the logic of Lloyd and Hardin, she maintains that only a system of *inequality* can forestall global resource depletion. An argument which has enormous appeal, not least for transnational corporations who want to represent profits as evidence of profound environmental concerns, it is an expression of an emergent development perspective which can no longer explicitly identify the defence of private interest with resistance to communism, but which remains hostile to the advance of any communitarian or redistributive ethic or to economic democracy of any kind.

While it is clear that there are many environmental problems in the world, Abernethy and others have tried to ensure that any remedial policy focuses primarily on the destructive role of population in developing countries, without any serious effort to consider either the fertility of the poor or the nature of resource use in the historical context of underdevelopment. Their main concern is to legitimise current inequalities in resource control and distribution. Thus, Abernethy's central tenet is that a "one-world redistributive ideology obscures the reality that resources are finite" and only encourages "overpopulated countries to tolerate further growth" (1991: 326). A compelling counter-argument could easily be made that, on evidence, an ideology which favours capitalist monopoly does not exactly seem to discourage the view that resources are infinite. But Abernethy's point is to elaborate the perennial Malthusian view that it is only inequality and the miseries which it entails that can act as sufficient incentive for the irrational and improvident poor to curb their fertility. One of the current corollaries of this view, moreover, is that a tolerant attitude toward immigration is just another way of redistributing resources and that, like any other, it will only offer the poor in developing countries an escape from local "realities". According to Hardin, it only "prolongs the reign of poverty in poor [countries]" (Hardin 1993: 283) by subsidising maladaptive behaviour. Such an argument, which rests on the implicit claim that the profits of capital are global (and should move freely), while poverty is strictly local (and should not freely migrate), cannot be expected to impress the poor as a formula for the improvement of their own lives.

The implications go even further. In a recent article, Abernethy has suggested that "economic expansion ... encourages the belief that formerly recognized limits can be discounted" (1994). From this generalisation, she proceeds to warn against "large transfers of technology and funds to the Third World" which would – like the poor laws a century and a half ago – ameliorate worsening livelihoods and therefore stimulate fertility. As it happens, however, such transfers are not actually occurring. While Hardin and Abernethy vigorously oppose, on classic Malthusian lines, the idea of a "one-world redistributive ideology" which would assist the poor, this is precisely what the neo-liberal order promoted by the developed countries has, in fact, brought to fruition for the rich. Even a quarter of a century ago, according to a Department of Commerce study, the top 298 US-based multinationals received more profits from abroad than at home (Barnet and Muller 1974: 16–17). This is even more the case today, when the newly emergent system of world trade presided over by the World Trade Organisation dramatically favours the flow of resources and wealth from the poor to the richer countries. In other words, the local realities which Abernethy and Hardin would force people in developing countries to face are really only the local consequences of global realities. This is not much different from the situation in India or Ireland a century and a half ago. Now, as then, no matter how much hardship the poor endure, no matter how much they reduce their fertility, their economic fate will still be beyond their control.

Meanwhile, the wealthiest countries are actually cutting back on overseas aid. Aside from the evidence that such aid usually benefits the donor far more than the recipient, much of it now is only in the form of debt relief or rescheduling and actually never amounts to real cash for concrete development (UNICEF 1995). In the end, it is more than likely to be protecting the position of international banks and foreign investors. What is on the rise, in the context of new trade liberalisation policies, is *private* foreign investment in developing countries, but a disproportionate share of this goes to a very few recipients (United Nations

General Assembly 1994), chiefly in Southeast Asia.[1] Although far more in need, Africa received less than 5 percent of direct foreign investment in developing countries in 1994 (UNICEF 1995).

Competing to attract such investment, developing countries are forced to comply with World Bank or IMF recommendations. As the World Bank's chief economist has recently noted, "globalization of world capital markets has raised the rewards for countries that pursue good policies, but may make even more dismal the prospects for those that do not" (Gomez 1997). Unfortunately, "good policies" are those which cut back on state provisions and services. Meanwhile, the profits from corporate investments are increasingly repatriated to the North and do very little to meet the basic educational, medical or social needs of poor countries. It is commonly argued, however, that such investments are one of the most important answers to the problem of international migration, which is often viewed as little more than a response to population pressures in developing countries. As Edward Morse, a former special assistant in the Office of Undersecretary for Economic Affairs in the US State Department and Executive Director of the 1980s Project of the Council on Foreign Relations, has written:

> One means of reducing the scale of legal as well as illegal international migration is the creation of employment opportunities in those developing countries from which the alien workers will tend to come. Capital investments by governments or multinational firms in these developing areas could, by fostering employment, make it more attractive for workers to stay in their native countries. (Morse 1978: 15)

Writers such as Abernethy (1994), however, argue against any development assistance lest it give the poor a sense of "economic optimism" which would simply encourage fertility. But it is not enough only to deny aid or to rule out the hope of migration; she suggests that policies of land redistribution must also be resisted, or they would also favour increases in family size. True to the Malthusian spirit, a single-minded concern with population growth amounts to little more than an endorsement of structural injustice.

Once again, "over-population" is regarded as given, inequality is an historical accident, and the rich owe nothing to the poor. This is Malthus's original vision, but now it is being reinforced by a view of a world of dramatically declining resources in which the future prosperity and well-being of capitalism, especially in the North, are regarded as being under immediate threat from "over-peopled" developing countries, particularly in the form of potential waves of immigration from poorer

---

1. Which, as of mid-1997, are in profound fiscal crisis.

to richer countries. Hardin's own response is the classic Malthusian one, that, in such a world, generosity, however tempting, would be misguided and counterproductive. "Our desire", he writes,

> to help the wretched of the world does our hearts credit, but not our heads: two thousand million people in the world are dreadfully poor by U.S. standards. That is eight times the population of our country. In our softer moments we wish we could share our wealth with all the world's poor. (Hardin 1993: 288)

That it is "our wealth", resourced by nothing more than Western genius – the parallel of the entrepreneur's imagining that workers do not create wealth, but only enjoy the jobs created for them by the wealthy – is one of the oldest myths of capitalism.

Demographers and biologists have not been particularly enlightening in this respect. As I suggested in Chapter 2, Livi-Bacci's overview of the history of world population paid scant regard to the impact of the political economy of English colonialism in Ireland – or anywhere else. Kingsley Davis, who effectively mystified the dynamic of exploitation in rural India, has more recently portrayed the difference in rates of population increase between developed and developing countries primarily as a function of their relative degrees of industrialisation. As a result, he concludes that "there is increasing pressure on industrial countries to accept Third World migrants and to share *their wealth* [my italics] with the less fortunate" (Davis 1986: 23).

In such references to "theirs" and "ours", the nature of contemporary patterns of transfer of resources and wealth is not taken into account, even as multinationals are rapidly gaining new advantages in developing countries. If Abernethy's argument were true – and there is little evidence that it is – that it is material disadvantage, rather than well-being, that will cause people in developing countries to reduce fertility, all that could be said for the activities of such corporations is that they would prove to be the most effective form of birth control. Such activities are actually having an effect on patterns of child-bearing in the Third World – but not for the reason that Abernethy implies. In parts of Chile, Mexico and the Philippines, for example, where increasingly competitive commercial development of cash crops for exports involves the growing use of agro-chemicals, especially pesticides, there is mounting evidence of health risks for rural agricultural labourers (especially women) and their offspring (Instituto de Ecologia Politica 1997; Philippines 1996). In Costa Rica pesticides are reported to be causing sterility among male banana plantation workers (Wheat 1996).

If a major impetus behind economic globalisation is the increasingly necessary effort by giants of international capital to colonise new markets and resources, to forestall the persistent tendency in capitalist economy toward stagnation and declining profits (Magdoff and Sweezy 1977), it is unsurprising that such consequences – and others, including increasing childhood poverty, the use of child labour, a rise in societal violence, and new forms of social and environmental damage – are not regarded by policy-makers and TNCs as the outcome of the global economy of capitalism. On the contrary, by considering only proximate causes and consequences, the development policies of industrial nations reflect quite the opposite view, that such trends are chiefly the result of Malthusian pressures – and demographically induced poverty – in the South. The main response in the North has been to defend itself against the imagined impact of such putative pressures on its own well-being. This leads to the contradiction that as neo-liberalism is dismantling economic forms of protectionism, arguments for new forms of demographic protectionism – in the shape of immigration restriction – are gaining ground.

The Malthusian Ecology of Global Conflicts

What is also increasingly prevalent in development thinking in the North is the view that regional conflicts around the world now arise chiefly from environmental crises in which Malthusian pressures play a paramount role. While this idea may be traced back to the linkage between population and national security concerns in the days of the Draper Committee, it has acquired a new gloss of academic respectability in the work of Homer-Dixon. Writing in the journal of the Population Council, he represents the growing scarcity of natural resources as principally the product of local or regional population growth, and suggests that societies may adapt to them through what he calls "ingenuity" – the social production of new technological or institutional ideas. However, because of their "underdeveloped economic institutions", "social friction", lack of capital investment in research, etc., developing countries are particularly likely to suffer from "a serious and chronic ingenuity gap", which brings about "a downward and self-reinforcing spiral of crisis and decay" (Homer-Dixon 1995: 598ff., 605). The central role of a lack of ingenuity – for whatever reasons – resonates with a sense of a colonialist's disdain for the limited capacity of the colonised, while there is no mention of the historical roots of resource depletion and no reference to current pressures on resource use as a result of structural adjustment and neoliberal trade policies which have forced developing countries to expose themselves to the demands of the international market. The bland phrase "underdeveloped economic institutions" obliquely blames the victim for economic underdevelopment without trying to comprehend, as Frank once wrote, "how their past economic and social history gave rise to their present underdevelopment" (Frank 1969: 3).

In a similar vein, the Environmental and Conflicts Project of the Center for Security Studies and Conflict Research in Switzerland observes that, "by jeopardizing the natural base for economic and social development and causing migration movements, environmental degradation can also lead to internal revolts, violent clashes between ethic groups and insurgency" (ENCOP 1997). When such conflicts are interpreted as a threat to the legitimacy or survival of national governments which are strategically linked to Western economic security, they will be used to justify intervention, and little attention will be paid either to the way that they may have arisen because of foreign interests or to how intervention may serve such interests.

This preoccupation with a future in which environmental conflicts will be "one of the most pressing of mankind's problems" (ENCOP 1997) must also be seen in terms of the role of military production as one of the persistent fixtures of Western capitalist economy. In his classic work, *Imperialism: A Study*, published at the turn of the century, J.A. Hobson argued that imperialistic wars absorbed a significant proportion of public finance in order to secure economic advantages overseas for large domestic capitalist interests. As a result, by 1900,

> The most salient feature of the [government expenditures] is the small and diminishing proportion of the national revenue expended for what may be regarded as directly productive purposes of government. Roughly speaking, over two-thirds of the money goes for naval and military expenditure, and for the payment of military debts, about six shillings in the pound being available for education, civil government, and the dubious policy of grants in aid of local taxation. (Hobson 1902: 95)

The costs of imperialism could never be covered by current taxation and therefore created large national debts. The "floating and dealing" in public loans to finance such debts happened to be particularly lucrative for many American and European capitalists, who acquired considerable influence over government policy in the process. Meanwhile, of course, industry also made profits from the manufacture and sale of the arms which made wars possible. In the end, there was less and less public money for social investment in health, housing and education. Two decades after the end of the Second World War, Melman (1965) was able to document the way that this had depleted the US economy of the resources required to maintain or develop a modern infrastructure or to provide secure and productive employment for the majority of its citizens.

While one may want to regard public expenditure, in a Keynesian sense, as a solution to the chronic problem in capitalist economy of periodic unemployment and stagnation, in practice it has been public investment in the arms industry that has performed this role. Thus, in the United States in 1970, toward the end of the mildest recession of the post-war period, the National Bureau of Economic Research estimated that the unemployment rate was 6.2 percent and manufacturing capacity was characterised by 72.3 percent use (Sweezy 1972: 26). But real unemployment was actually higher, since many people excluded from employment – many black youths – are not counted as unemployed. And it would have much higher still if one considered people employed because of US military production. This would include 2.9 million members of the armed forces, 1.2 million civilian employees of the Defense Department, 3 million workers in defence industries, and over 7 million people employed because of indirect effects of military spending. On that basis, it could be calculated that, had it not been for the defence establishment, US unemployment actually would have been around 25.6 percent, more or less what it had been in the depths of the Great Depression in 1933 (Sweezy 1972: 27).

The problem is that, as advanced industrial capitalism has come to depend on military investment to sustain economic "prosperity", and despite "the conventional wisdom of our time, which views the defence industry as a support for the economy" (Melman 1965: 240–41; cf. Sampson 1977), the concrete benefits of such investment actually have been concentrated within a very small segment of the population. There also has developed a powerful symbiotic relationship between the military sector and monopoly capitalists, who reinforce one another's interests in a way which does little to enhance democratic participation in decision-making about priorities in government spending. As a result, Pentagon budget requests are approved, while domestic social programmes are cut.

So entrenched is the role of military expenditure within the political economy of capitalism that, even without the excuse of a threat from the Soviet Union, it has proven easier to find new rationales for the continuing modernisation of the arms industry than to contemplate the process of conversion to peace-time production. As a consequence, political debate in countries such as Britain and the United States about the aims and responsibilities of domestic government spending has been an artificial one about how to prioritise among varied social programmes, while the question of cutting military programmes is scarcely raised. As the Washington-based Center for Defense Information has reported:

On February 6, 1997, the Clinton Administration released its budget request for Fiscal Year 1998, which included $265 billion for the military. While this represents the thirteenth straight year of reductions in the military budget since the Reagan Administration's spending spree, the Administration's multi-year spending plan calls for military spending to level off this year, and then actually go up....

The President's budget calls for $1.6 trillion for the military between now and the year 2002. During that same period, the Clinton Administration and Congress have agreed that they will achieve a balanced budget. The deficit for 1997 is estimated to be $126 billion. If Congress and the Administration do actually eliminate this annual budget, while at the same time increasing spending for the military, drastic cuts in other federal programs become a virtual certainty. (Center for Defense Information 1997)

The injunction by Neo-Malthusians such as Hardin that "we" must learn to live within limits clearly does not embrace the field of defence expenditure, the linchpin of capitalist political economy. But such spending – and its social costs – can only be justified by fostering the general impression that the world remains a threatening place, even if the public perception of what those threats are has had to change.

One issue which has played a crucial role in this respect is environmental change, whether at the global level, in the sense of atmospheric warming, or on a regional level, where increasing numbers of emigrants from developing countries are now being defined as "environmental refugees". In both cases, ecological change is increasingly portrayed as threatening, economically, socially or politically, to the stability and security of industrial countries, and is in turn ascribed to Malthusian pressures. Despite the fact that predictions about the potential impact of climatic trends on environmental productivity, and especially on the productive capacity of agricultural systems, are highly conjectural, there has nevertheless been a notable tendency to draw far-reaching policy implications – whether to justify military intervention or to promote the merits of further intensification of commercial agriculture – which probably would have been drawn anyway.

Instead of any critical assessment of the unsustainability of a market economy, at least in regard to large-scale environmental problems such as global warming, it is the poor whose lifestyles and habits are meant to change. Even though it is increasingly recognised that present emissions of greenhouse gases are chiefly the result of developed economies, the current Neo-Malthusian argument is that atmospheric pollution increasingly can be regarded as a function of population growth (Ehrlich et al. 1993; Myers 1994). As Myers writes:

the developing countries overall currently produce about 30 per cent of world-wide emissions of carbon dioxide, while possessing 77 per cent of the world population. Medium-level population projections to the year 2025 indicate that developing countries could then be accounting for 64 per cent of all emissions (which would then be much larger in total). (1994: 61)

For this reason the issue of global warming has been addressed by the Population Council, on whose Board of Trustees the president of the World Bank, James Wolfensohn, currently sits (World Bank 1996). The Council concludes that

The industrialized countries are and have been the principal source of greenhouse gases, but rapid population and economic growth in the developing world are expected to raise its emissions above those of the developed countries for most of the twenty-second century... (1994)

But that is over a century from now and is hardly the kind of projection on which responsible present-day development policy ought to be based. Leaving aside the issue of how much of the emissions produced *in* developing countries are actually caused *by* the inhabitants of those countries, as opposed to the activities of foreign companies, it is obvious how the issue is being transformed. Global warming has now become another argument for population control in the developing world.

Several general consequences of global warming are mentioned. First, it is suggested that there may be a decline in surpluses produced by industrial agricultural systems, most notably in the United States (Pimental and Pimental 1991), whose wheat crop is a major source of "food aid" for many developing countries. Secondly, there may be a reduction in the agricultural output of many developing countries (Global Climate Change Information Programme 1997). These two possibilities, taken together, are used to suggest that, if predicted environmental changes occur, many less-developed nations may face increased food shortages which will generate social unrest and lead to population dislocation and the likelihood of increased regional and international emigration. Where once a worsening of the population:resource ratio was envisaged as a major source of social conflict because it was an apparent incitement to "communism", it is now regarded as the potential catalyst for a wide range of equally undesirable and destabilising trends. In this new context – which is only "new" in the sense that the development interests of the West are no longer intimately and explicitly linked to anti-communism – an ecologically driven model of underdevelopment, amplifying what was always an implicit feature of Malthusian thinking, is capable of proving quite as effective as the Cold War as a means of obscuring the actual historical process of development and underdevelopment, and of rationalising policies – such as the further commercialisation of agriculture – designed to counter the alternative of radical structural change in the global economy.

The New Malthusian Fears of Immigration

It is perhaps not surprising that concerns about the impact of environmental change on world agricultural output – and about the anticipated social and political consequences – seem to be reviving European and North American fears of a eugenic, as well as purely Malthusian, nature. In the past, as we have seen, such fears reflected two closely related concerns: about the social and genetic impact of immigration, and about domestic fertility rates, whose decline seemed to exacerbate the potential threat from immigration. In the first decades of this century, these fears not only degenerated into a widespread and rabid preoccupation with the so-called degradation of European (in particular, "Nordic") population and culture (Grant 1918), but eventuated in racist restrictive immigration laws and policies which excluded from the United States alone millions of potential immigrants who were later to die as a result of Nazi persecution (Chase 1977: 289–301).

Not only is concern over immigration being reasserted, but it is taking place within the framework of environmental concerns. In the late 1970s, at the height of the Neo-Malthusian tide which brought the biologists Ehrlich and Hardin to prominence, one of the academics who had raised such fears forty years before, Joseph Spengler, revived his former eugenic apprehensions. Prompted by renewed concerns that European birth-rates were again in decline, Spengler wrote:

> There is need also to guard against the accumulation of unfavorable genes in the human gene pool ... since this pool now is increasingly led by those whose survival into reproductive age has been made possible for the first time by modern medicine. For, in the absence of further development in the field of genetic application, and in the light of the possibility of less rigorous selection in a stationary society, dysgenic selection could increase potential burdens. (1977: 269)

Generally, however, the current anxiety over immigration in Western academic, political and popular thought presents itself in terms of cultural or environmental protectionism. If there is any echo of Spengler, it has been when environmental worries have given rise in countries such as Germany to what has been dubbed "eco-racism" (Foraci and Songur 1993). To long-standing nativist ideologies with their roots in the last century, there has been added the argument that too many immigrants would mean unacceptable pressures on the European environment. While ignoring more fundamental questions about the environmental impact of industrial economy generally, adherents of this viewpoint evoke environmental concerns chiefly as a means of focusing their antipathy to outsiders, raising a cry of "demographic pollution", which echoes not only the spirit of Hardin but, more ominously, that of the Third Reich.

While declining domestic birth-rates have meant that the Western European economies could not only absorb but also benefit from significant numbers of poorly paid and ill-treated immigrants (Wunsch 1978: 234), little effort has made to integrate them into national life (Solomos 1982; Castles 1984), giving rise over time to social and political problems which have generated a varying and volatile mix of xenophobia, discrimination and violence. Not fortuitously, the three countries with the highest levels of immigration in the 1950s and 1960s – Germany, France and Belgium (Wunsch 1978: 234) – subsequently gave rise to extreme right-wing, nativist political movements with evident fascist leanings. Even within the mainstream political parties, however, anxieties about domestic population decline and foreign immigration have been increasingly evident – for example, in the view of Jacques Chirac, former Prime Minister of France, that Europe faces the "terrifying" prospect of being submerged demographically by the peoples of other continents (1985: 163).

It is already ominously apparent that Western Europe generally is taking an increasingly restrictive posture on immigration policy (Information Network on Migration from Third World Countries 1997). Meanwhile, in the United States, where there is mounting preoccupation with immigration (Beck 1994), it is notable that the problem of global warming has been explicitly linked to the need for the USA to develop a population policy. As respected a scientist as David Pimental has recently written:

> Although sound ecological practices in agriculture are needed to help offset projected global warming, of greater importance is the need to control the rapid growth in the U.S. and the world population (1991: 358).

While Pimental notes that the US population is increasing at a modest rate of 0.7 percent per year, he suggests that even this is too high to maintain the current standard of living. Disregarding the fact that the USA suffers from dramatic national disparities in income and opportunity and that it is the high quality of life of a privileged sector to which he implicitly refers, he proceeds to underscore that "One-quarter of this rate of increase is due to immigration" (Pimental 1991: 349). His argument about the need to develop the US economy in a sustainable way therefore pays minimal attention to the consequences of the capitalist mode of production, becoming a defence of its resource base in the face of a demographic threat from outside its borders. As with Hardin and Abernethy, the pressures (which account for the rise in international migration) that the globalisation of capitalism is placing on Third World resources (which sustain the economies of the North) are disregarded.

Others go further. The Federation for American Immigration Reform (FAIR), referring to projected US population growth into the next century, claims that "Nearly all that increase will be attributable to immigration that occurred after 1990" (FAIR 1995). It refers to population growth in the Third World as a major cause of "migration pressures" which are creating "unsustainable strains on our environment and resources". In the view of FAIR and Negative Population Growth (NPG), a Washington-based organisation, virtually all degradation of environmental resources in the United States can be attributed, not to the nature of capitalist economy, but, ultimately, either to reproductive pressures in the Third World, or to the reproductive tendencies of immigrants and their descendants (Nowak 1997). Despite the fact that the litany of environmental damage which the United States has suffered over various periods of time – including such observations as "since the Declaration of Independence was signed, more than five hundred species ... have gone extinct" (Nowak 1997: 7) – can hardly demonstrate that population growth, let alone immigration, was the principal cause, these organisations and academics such as Pimental have called for the USA to devise a policy of immigration restriction in the name of "environmental sustainability". A similar position has been taken by Californians for Population Stabilization (CAPS), which has counted among the members of its advisory board such Neo-Malthusian luminaries as Anne Ehrlich, Kingsley Davis and Garrett Hardin (CAPS 1997), whose recent work has been underwritten by the right-wing Pioneer Fund (Hardin 1993). The fears underlying such developments are remarkably similar to those which possessed many of Malthus's contemporaries and successors in the last century when they grimly contemplated the prospect of a rising working class. The same fears inspire the efforts of writers such as Hardin, Abernethy and others to defend narrow national or class interests in the name of environmental integrity.

The Ehrlichs, at least, have expressed solicitude for the way that Mexicans have benefited the US economy as a "labor pool of last resort" (Ehrlich and Ehrlich 1990: 63). But despite this, they urge that "the flow of immigrants into the United States should be damped, simply because the world can't afford more Americans" (Ehrlich and Ehrlich 1990: 64). This does not mean that they advocate any fundamental transformation in the political economy of the United States. Far from it, what they advocate is essentially what NAFTA seeks – the absorption of Mexico into a North American economic sphere dominated by the United States. As they write:

> it is high time to strengthen the bonds of cooperation among the three large nations of North America. Almost 150 years of peaceful coexistence make the United States, Mexico, and Canada an ideal trio to show how cooperation could help solve transnational environmental and economic problems. We should begin to think in terms of the carrying capacity of North America – not merely of three separate and disparate nations that just happen to occupy the continent. Family sizes, consumption patterns, and technological choices made over the entire continent should be coordinated. (Ehrlich and Ehrlich 1990: 64)

While the ostensible aim is to "improve the standard of living of Mexicans within their own homeland" and to obviate any need for Mexicans to migrate to the United States, the likelihood of such an equalisation of living standards across such a vast landscape under the prevailing economic system is remote, especially when one considers that, even within the United States, an estimated 20 percent of the population lives below the official poverty line. Evidence since the implementation of NAFTA suggests that its actual effect has been to increase US investment in Mexico and that it is primarily from the vantage point of US capital that Mexican immigration will cease to be necessary.

The Contradictions of Sustainable Development

Such developments have been legitimated by the official cessation of the Cold War. But while the globalisation of US capitalist enterprise is promoted as a panacea, it is, in fact, exacerbating many preexisting social and economic problems, including environmental change, food insecurity and international migration. To the extent that these can be attributed to population pressures, however, Malthusian thinking just continues as a rationale for Western policy on fundamental questions about the use and distribution of global resources, justifying social and economic inequality in the name of a greater good. One of the names given to such a good today is "sustainable development".

The contradictions contained in this concept are one of its most interesting features. If we look back at the 1987 Report (*Our Common Future*) of the UN Commission on Environment and Development, chaired by the then Norwegian premier, Gro Harlem Brundtland, which brought the concept to popular attention, it noted that "living standards that go beyond the basic minimum are sustainable only if consumption standards everywhere have regard for long-term sustainability". It takes little imagination to realise that, if consumption patterns in the North are not reduced significantly, then living standards elsewhere cannot be expected to go beyond, let alone reach, such a basic minimum.

And assuredly patterns in the North are unlikely to change when the most fervent advocates of sustainable development are transnational corporations and multi-millionaires such as Maurice Strong. A business-man who made his fortune in mining and oil and had been Canada's governor of the World Bank, Strong had entered "public service" in the 1960s – without giving up his business career – and eventually advised the commission that produced the Brundtland Report (Bruno 1992). He was subsequently chosen to head the Rio "Earth Summit" – the UN Conference on Environment and Development (UNCED) – in 1992. It was an appointment which encouraged the world business community.

At a preparatory UNCED conference in New York, Strong set the limits of the Rio conference when he "called on UNCED to be com-patible with the General Agreement on Tariffs and Trade (GATT), an international trade agreement which emphasises open markets and is strongly supported by internationally oriented companies" (Bruno 1992). Strong was also a member of the Business Council for Sustainable Development, based in Geneva, which, with the World Industry Council for the Environment (WICE) in Paris, co-ordinated the international business community's interest in Rio. Early in the lead-up to the con-ference, Strong appointed as his chief adviser the Swiss industrialist Stephan Schmidheiny, a man with a personal fortune estimated at over $3 billion (Bruno 1992; *Forbes* 1997), who sits on the Board of Directors of Asea Brown Boveri (ABB), the world's largest industrial engineering company. Schmidheiny drew together top executives from companies such as Shell, Ciba-Geigy and Mitsubishi to form the Business Council for Sustainable Development (BCSD) to represent the interests of the international corporate community in environmental issues – or, as it would probably prefer to say, "resource management". Since January 1995, the BCSD and WICE have merged to form the World Business Council for Sustainable Development (WBCSD), with Schmidheiny at its head (Bruno 1992; Greenwire 1995).

As a result, while UNCED underscored the role of population growth in developing countries as a source of environmental degradation, and while it was willing to acknowledge the problems created by economic growth in the North, it predictably addressed very little attention to the role of transnational corporations (TNCs) or the environmental conse-quences of social and economic inequity. A separate NGO document, *Treaty on Transnational Corporations*, had to observe that

The United Nations Conference on Environment and Development (UNCED) has abdicated its responsibility to take measures to control TNC activities, instead promoting TNCs' contribution to "sustainable development" and willingness to regulate themselves. The United Nations (UN) has given up trying to develop a Code for the TNCs and the Centre on Transnational Corporations has been weakened. Proposals on trade-related investment and intellectual property rights in the Uruguay Round of the General Agreement on Tariffs and Trade (GATT) would strengthen the power of TNCs vis-à-vis governments, parliaments and the public. (Global Forum 1992: 1)

The transnational corporations emerged from Rio having defined themselves not as part of the problem, but as charged (by themselves and by governments of the North) with the task of balancing the economic and environmental demands of what ironically is called "Our Common Future". In the neo-liberal environment of the 1990s, they appointed themselves as the "stewards" of the natural world, building on Hardin's logic that only private interests could successfully protect the environment – but only if regulatory constraints on investments were pared away, in the name of "free trade".

One of the best illustrations of how the members of the WBCSD operate is provided by Mitsubishi, one of the world's largest industrial corporations. Publicly, the company boasts of its environmental concerns (Mitsubishi Corporation 1997), and the president of Mitsubishi has written of how the "philosophy of stewardship has served us for more than a century and continues to guide the planning and managing of our business ventures". It was an interesting century. One of the *zaibatsu* that dominated the Japanese economy from the late nineteenth century, and one of the principal beneficiaries of Draper's campaign against their dismantling, Mitsubishi bombers played a central role in terrorising and conquering, first China, and then the rest of Southeast Asia, during the Second World War. Today, in language that has become standard among multinational companies and international institutions such as the World Bank, the president of Mitsubishi merely proclaims that "In this age of global partnerships, in our pursuit of sustainable development, we will continue to collaborate with ... all who share our concern for the environment." Yet in its activities as one of the largest timber companies in the world, Mitsubishi has been described by the Rainforest Action Network as "among the world's worst corporate destroyers of forest" (1997).

The contradictions in the commitment by such corporations to the concept of sustainable development are even more explicit in the "Stockholm Declaration on Growth and Development in the Baltic Sea Region", the product of a meeting organised in April 1996 by the Stockholm Chamber of Commerce and major Swedish industrial corporations (including ABB). The declaration's recommendations, designed to promote "growth and development" in that transnational region, began with the affirmation that "The inviolability of private property must be guaranteed in constitutional law" and ensured by the police and the legal system. All the countries of the region were urged to fulfil the requirements for membership in the World Trade Organisation and to conclude free trade agreements with their neighbours. "Prudent fiscal policies and balanced public finances" were considered equally "essential", as was the need to privatise and to guarantee competition in "all sectors of the economy". And while development must be sustainable, environmental legislation "should be based on cooperation with companies, not confrontation". Finally, labour laws and practices must be modernised, to introduce "the necessary flexibility for new technology and new production methods".

If this meant that modern European corporations might need a smaller labour force, raising questions about the fate of the unemployed, the signatories declared that

> It is not reasonable in a functioning market economy to compel firms to take on social responsibility for employees and their families that goes beyond what is directly connected to their employment. (Stockholm Chamber of Commerce 1996)

Presumably, responsibility for the environment would fare no better.

Privatising the Global Commons

But there is another reason why the issue of population is being highlighted as a key element in dominant thinking about sustainable development. As the Brundtland Report intimated, the long-term sustainability of the capitalist system as presently constituted depends upon the world's poor never achieving more than minimum needs, or curbing their fertility, or both. The alternative prospect of a world capitalist system which is less expansive and less aggressive seems dim. Indeed, we see evidence all around – in the corporate practices of Shell, Mitsubishi or ABB, for example – of just the opposite, of an intensive globalising assault on diverse environments and their inhabitants. It is difficult to imagine how that can be congruent with sustainable development in a global sense except through coercive curbs on the fertility of those communities whose own democratic use of local resources is increasingly incompatible with the demand on those same resources by the dominant agents of the global market.

But it is against the background of threats to the capitalist mode of production, not just from local peoples, but from growing global environmental problems, that the very idea of sustainable development has come to the fore, to attempt to redress some of what the North regards as the more destabilising consequences of its own development strategies. In many, if not most, cases, the ultimate cause of such environmental degradation lies not in local population pressures, but in *exogenous* market demands. Yet it is as an *endogenous* process that environmental degradation is widely regarded; and as such that it is seen as a major worldwide source of population migration. It is in that frame of reference that the North increasingly vocalises concern about the impact *on its own standard of living* of international migration. If such movements are attributed to environmental problems that are ascribed to population pressures in the South, then sustainable development becomes, at one and the same time, an argument for restoring local population–resource balance, for regulating local population numbers, for restricting population movements, and for implementing restrictive demographic policies in Western Europe and the United States. The so-called "eco-racism" of a decade ago has found a counterpart in a more respectable, equally expedient, argument that too many immigrants would mean unacceptable pressures on the US and European environments. It is an argument that defers fundamental questions about the social as well as environmental costs of current trends in Western capitalist development.

But the putative prospects of global warming and population growth together overwhelming the world's agricultural capacity are not merely fuelling Western concerns about immigration. They are also behind calls for a renewal of the Green Revolution. While a Malthusian view of the sources of Third World underdevelopment continues to justify the ongoing industrialisation of agriculture, the argument increasingly is that very few developing countries will be able to provide enough food for their own people – even less so in the event of global warming – and that they are better off importing it from the United States. This ignores the difficulties that are already facing US agricultural production, which is dependent on the same costly inputs that are the essential ingredients of modern industrial agriculture. This has been the case especially since the rise in petroleum prices in the early 1970s. But the costs of US agriculture also include the harmful effects of fertilisers, pesticides and herbicides and the decline of farming communities as mechanisation has replaced human labour (Belden et al. 1986: 78–9).

Above all, US food production in its totality – from the field to the table – consumes prodigious quantities of energy. Processing alone is estimated to use one-third of the total energy absorbed by the system. Yet Neo-Malthusians either ignore the implications of this, just as they dismiss the impact of the industrialisation of Third World agriculture

on peasant food security, or they limit their concern to the future availability of oil resources and growing dependence on foreign reserves, in
order to argue for curbing population growth through immigration
restriction. While it is widely acknowledged that, "If energy-intensive
production technologies were used to feed all the earth's population a
U.S.-style diet, usable world petroleum reserves would be exhausted in
only thirteen years" (Belden et al. 1986: 81), organisations such as
Negative Population Growth choose to emphasise the adverse impact
of immigration on the sustainability of the current US mode of
production (Nowak 1977); while notable academics who have been
enlisted in the Neo-Malthusian cause conclude that, "Although sound
ecological practices in agriculture are needed to help offset projected
global warming, of greater importance is the need to control the rapid
growth in the U.S. and the world population" (Pimental 1991: 358).

Neither view takes account of the global impact of the industrialising
of world agriculture, which has not only pushed millions of small-scale
cultivators onto marginal lands or into tropical forests, or to seek work
in urban centres or in distant countries, but has created an insatiable
demand for synthetic fertilisers and the energy with which to manufacture them. In the United States, for example, "More energy is used
to produce [such] fertilisers than goes into plowing, planting, cultivating
and harvesting all U.S. crops" (Belden et al. 1986: 80). This will not
cease if immigration is halted; and it will certainly not if US agricultural
output is meant to expand still further, as the right-wing Heritage Foundation suggests (Frydenlund 1994), to capture new markets in the developing world, at the inevitable expense of local food production.

Overlooking the fact that this would require the United States to
continue to extract energy resources from the Third World, and that
any country that depended on US food surpluses in such circumstances would necessarily sacrifice any pretence of planning for sustainable development, the more immediate implications are for further
losses in labour-intensive forms of production, through which people
feed themselves with reasonable security in an environmentally friendly
way. It will mean that peasants continue to be transformed into
contract farmers and wage labourers in a domestic agricultural sector
dominated by multinationals, devoted to the production of non-
traditional exports. They will, in effect, constitute local and regional
sectors of an international labour reserve for the developed capitalist
countries.

As ever, Malthusian thinking has blinded us to the idea that there
could be any other realistic scenario. But if the advocates of the capitalist
mode of development genuinely believe this, it is less because they

envisage no effective alternative to guarantee global food security than because they see no alternative to ensure their own prosperity. And because that prosperity seems so uncertain now, the incentive to profit from new investment in the further industrialisation of agriculture is greater than ever before. The arguments in favour of such investment are multifaceted and often contradictory, however. It is suggested that pressure on marginal lands in Third World countries can be alleviated by them relying more on food imports from the United States. But it is also argued that such pressure can be reduced by increasing output per unit of land presently in production. In either case, there is little reference – beyond vague phrases about "poverty alleviation" or food security – to the potential benefits for developing countries of systematic reform of established patterns of landownership.

On the contrary, the dominant theme, within the United States at least, is how further agri-technological innovation will benefit the US economy. As a report by the Working Group on International Trade and Development of the National Center for Food and Agricultural Policy – financed, among others, by USAID, the US Department of Agriculture, and agribusiness giants such as Cargill and Pioneer Hi-Bred – has observed:

> Simply put, it is good business to help developing countries to improve agri-cultural research and thereby speed agricultural development and achieve agricultural transformation. Research by the International Food Policy Research Institute (IFPRI) shows that "each dollar invested in agricultural research [in developing countries] generates $4.39 of additional imports by those countries."
>
> So research-induced change in developing countries can help improve United States trade, and agricultural research constitutes an essential invest-ment for the U.S. which can generate considerable benefits and returns. These benefits are evident in terms of increased export of agricultural commodities. In fact, more than 50 percent of all U.S. agricultural exports are purchased by lower income developing countries. As the agriculture of developing countries is improved through research, the U.S. also exports many production items including fertilizers, chemicals, farm machinery, processing equipment, etc. (Working Group on International Agricultural Research 1997)

Evidence also indicates that the increasing role of capital-intensive bio-technology – for example, Monsanto and DuPont alone have a com-bined annual biotechnology research and development budget of $390 million (Hobbelink 1991: 32) – is rapidly concentrating unprecedented power over global food production in the hands of a relatively small number of agro-industrial corporations (Hobbelink 1991: 40, 44–6), the same ones that, along with the CGIAR and the USDA, are currently hailing genetic engineering as the solution to all of the world's food problems. In such a world, any reference to sustainable development – especially from agribusiness itself – can count for very little.

Monsanto, one of the world's top ten agro-chemical companies (PANNA 1995), exemplifies the way that agro-businesses are exploiting the post-Rio climate to gain new opportunities in the name of sustainability. But for them, sustainability – especially in agriculture – is primarily a question of "technical challenges", not of structural *changes* (Pierle 1995). And, as such, it is a perspective which is amply honoured. In early 1996, Monsanto won the President's Sustainable Development Award (Home Depot 1996). It is an ironic achievement for one of the manufacturers of Agent Orange, the dioxin-containing herbicide which the US used to defoliate Vietnam in the 1960s (*Chemistry and Industry Magazine News* 1996). But perhaps the most threatening aspect of Monsanto's current activities is its work in agricultural biotechnology, a field in which the dominant corporations most frequently refer to the concept of sustainable development, in the face of Malthusian anxieties about world population growth, to justify their technological solutions to food production (Pierle 1995). Among Monsanto's major technical achievements has been the genetic modification of soybeans (creating what it calls "Roundup Ready" soybeans) to resist glyphosate, the active ingredient in their widely sold herbicide Roundup. The result is the fulfilment of the process of seed commoditisation to which Berlan and Lewontin referred, with enormous commercial potential for Monsanto. A recent report notes:

> with every Roundup Ready seed sale, Monsanto sells a season's worth of weed killer as well. The company also keeps close tabs on the crops' progress: Farmers must sign a contract promising not to sell or give away any seeds or save them for next year's planting, and the company inspects its customers' farms for violations. (Arax and Brokaw 1997)

By 1995, the company was certainly optimistic about its own sustained development:

> Monsanto is planning to double the production capacity of its glyphosate manufacturing plant in North Carolina with the expanded facilities coming online in early 1996. Approximately 80% of production at the North Carolina site is intended for export. The company has already doubled the capacity of its facilities in Belgium and Brazil and plans additional expansion of facilities in Australia and Louisiana. Monsanto's plans include construction of a technical manufacturing plant in China to formulate glyphosate for the domestic market and for export to other parts of Asia. (PANNA 1995)

While there is increasing doubt about whether Roundup is as friendly to the environment or people as Monsanto claims (PANNA 1997), an even greater long-term concern may be the adverse impact of transgenic crops on the structure of food production in developing countries. The capital-intensive nature of research and development of such crops, on the one hand, and the incredible profits to be made from them, on the other, have already led to the point where only ten TNCs currently control the world seed market. If they also control access to the inputs on which successful harvests depend, peasants and small farmers will become increasingly dependent on an agricultural economy which not only reduces local biodiversity and increases food insecurity, but which also, in the end, probably will eliminate any viable role for small-holder production.

Beyond Malthus

This is the culmination of the continuing displacement and marginalisation of peasant agriculture by a process of increasing privatisation of communal resources – all in the name of progress, even when it has appealed to Malthusian logic which denies the possibility of progress (or, at least, progress through communitarian or socialist relations of production). It is a process that began at the dawn of European capitalism. It was echoed in the Irish countryside in the eighteenth and nineteenth centuries and is happening all around the world today. If peasants – whether they are Mexicans, Filipinos, Colombians or Indians – are on the move, within their own countries or internationally, it is not because they have had too many children, but because the interests of commercial agricultural development, in the name of Malthusian logic, have made them redundant. In almost every instance, the population movements that are now one of the most dramatic features of contemporary global life are the consequence, not of too many people in developing countries, but of their being denied or deprived of secure access to fundamental productive resources.

As these resources increasingly are developed by transnational corporations for the use and profit of industrial nations, transforming many developing countries into little more than labour reserves, such population movements have accelerated. Meanwhile, the Malthusian argument that such movements must be constrained in the interest of maintaining a lifestyle that prevails chiefly among the most privileged sections of the most affluent industrial nations not only misrepresents the nature of the global economy which induces such migration and which makes such limited affluence possible. It may also prove counterproductive in the long run. To expect the majority of people in developing countries to find sustainable security or hope in such an economy is an illusion.

The only real alternative for them remains real systemic change. Only in a society where resources are more or less equitably apportioned will we be able to move beyond the Malthusian politics of population to a real consideration of human reproductive rights and needs, where the desire for fewer children will be matched by a need for fewer offspring. In the meanwhile, Malthusian ideas will be constantly mobilised to obscure the nature of capitalist exploitation – and, along with it, the role of reproduction within capitalist economy – in order to prevent such change. The idea of a "population problem" – or the idea that it is the "tragedy of the commons" which represents "the central issue underlying contemporary debates on population policy", according to the journal of The Population Council (Lloyd 1980) – will continue to mystify the actual determinants of fertility, in order to maintain the illusion that the economic and reproductive behaviour of the poor is largely irrational, that their own behaviour is the source of most of their misery, and that capitalism and private resource ownership is their only source of hope.

Somehow, it is always the critics of Malthus who are charged with the crime of obscuring reality, for refusing to believe the unwelcome 'truths' which Malthus proclaimed. Over seventy years ago, Talbot Griffith wrote in his book *Population Problems of the Age of Malthus* how

> The Essay was ... a shock and an unpleasant one. It was more than that, it was unanswerable. Under the existing conditions, the truth of the main proposition was so clear and strictly relevant that it was hopeless to argue against the author, much as one might rail against him. (1926: 91–2)

In fact, even in the first decades after the publication of Malthus's first Essay there was an outpouring of important critical work which proved that his arguments were eminently answerable. That Malthusian thinking acquired such prominence in spite of such work had far more to do with the ideological advantages it offered to powerful political and economic interests. As Boner observes, by the end of the Napoleonic Wars,

> Despite all efforts so far made to demonstrate the illusory nature of the Malthusian specter, it had grown into an apparently unshakable obstacle to social change. Malthus had gained powerful support among all groups through which public opinion was activated – churchmen, political economists, Utilitarians, Whigs and Tories; and by their agency in Parliament he had set into action the machinery for bringing his stern prescriptions into practice. (1955: 85)

Boner puts Malthus too much at the centre of things. Parliament was not so much the means of implementing his ideas as his ideas were seen as a way of advancing the class interests which Parliament embodied. But there is no doubt that, through the influence of the groups he mentions – and their control of the principal means of producing opinions – Malthusian ideas became generally accepted. They gradually became less obviously the ideological vantage point of the elite, assuming the status of a generally accepted wisdom that was beyond critical questioning. They remain so today. The Trevelyans and Macaulays of the last century have their modern counterparts in the Drapers, McNamaras and McCloys of this, who, in helping to shape the policies of Western capitalism during the Cold War, have found Malthusianism no less opportune than their predecessors did. No doubt this will be the case for their successors. The fact that Malthusian arguments do not bear up under systematic scrutiny will not really matter if they are tacitly accepted or if the tendency to take them for granted, or to minimise the harm they have done by justifying the consequences of social and economic inequality, means that such scrutiny is too little and too late.

In the end, such arguments will encounter their strongest resistance from the victims of the very development policies which they rationalise. There is a persistent line of such opposition, running from the days when Gerrard Winstanley, a leader of the seventeenth-century English communitarians known as the Diggers, proclaimed on behalf of the dispossessed that "the land ... is their birthright to them and their posterity, and ought not to be converted into particular hands again by the laws of a free commonwealth" (quoted in Beer 1984: 58–9), to the struggles of modern Zapatistas in southern Mexico, who have joined their cause to the wider fight against the predations of neo-liberalism. It suggests that it will not need to be the intellectual critics of Malthus who play the major role in reversing the dehumanising course of capitalist development. It will be the poor themselves. Because no one else has so much to gain and so little to lose.

References

Abernethy, Virginia (1979) *Population Pressure and Culture Adjustment*. New York: Human Sciences Press.

—— (1991) Comment: The "One World" Thesis as an Obstacle to Environmental Preservation, in K. Davis and M. Bernstam (eds.) *Resources, Environment, and Population: Present Knowledge, Future Options*. New York: Oxford University Press, pp. 323-8.

—— (1994) Optimism and Overpopulation. *The Atlantic Monthly* 274(6): 84–91. Internet site: http://www.theatlantic.com/atlantic/atlweb/flashbacks/immigr/populate.html.

Acker, Alison (1988) *Honduras: The Making of a Banana Republic*. Boston: South End Press.

Adams, Richard (1960) Social Change in Guatemala and U.S. Policy, in Council on Foreign Relations, *Social Change in Latin America Today: Its Implications for United States Policy*. New York: Harper and Brothers, pp. 231–84.

Aikin, John (1968) (orig. 1795) *A Description of the Country from 30 to 40 Miles Round Manchester*. Newton Abbott: David and Charles.

Alexander, T.M. and R.S. Giroti (eds.) (1966) *National Seminar on Fertilisers*. New Delhi: Fertiliser Association of India.

Allbaugh, Leland (1956) Fertilizer-Munitions and Agriculture, in Roscoe Martin (ed.) *TVA: The First Twenty Years. A Staff Report*. University, AL: University of Alabama Press, pp. 152–76.

Allen, Kevin and Andrew Stevenson (1974) *An Introduction to the Italian Economy*. Glasgow Social and Economic Research Studies 1. Glasgow: Martin Robertson.

Allen, Robert and Cormac Ó Gráda (1988) On the Road Again with Arthur Young: English, Irish, and French Agriculture during the Industrial Revolution. *The Journal of Economic History* 48(1): 93–116.

Ambirajan, S. (1976) Malthusian Population Theory and Indian Famine Policy in the Nineteenth Century. *Population Studies* 30(1): 5–14.

Anderson, Michael (1971) *Family Structure in Nineteenth Century Lancashire*. Cambridge: Cambridge University Press.

Anderson, Robert, Edwin Levy and Barrie Morrison (1991) *Rice Science and Development Politics: Research Strategies and IRRI's Technologies Confront Asian Diversity*

(1950–1980). Oxford: Clarendon Press.

Anon. (1808) Newenham and Others on the State of Ireland. *Edinburgh Review* July: 336–55.

Anon. (1847) *Thoughts on Ireland*. London: James Ridgway.

Arax, Mark and Jeanne Brokaw (1997) No Way Around Roundup. *Mother Jones – MoJo Wire*. Internet site: http://www.mojones.com/mother_jones/JF97/brokaw.html. Accessed on 25/01/98.

Arnold, Steven (1980) The Inter-American Development Bank Approach to Development Financing, in Jean-Claude Garcia-Zamos and Stewart E. Sutin (eds.) *Financing Development in Latin America*. New York: Praeger, pp. 89–107.

Arocha, Jaime (1975) *"La Violencia" in Monteverde (Colombia): Environmental and Economic Determinants of Homicide in a Coffee-Growing Municipio*. Ph.D. thesis. New York: Columbia University.

Arrigo, Linda (1986) Landownership Concentration in China: The Buck Survey Revisited. *Modern China* 12(3): 259–360.

Associated Press (1996) Some Statistics on Irish and North Irish Beef. 28 March. Internet site: http://www.sddt.com/files/librarywire/96...ines/03_96/DN96_03_28/DN96_03_28_fj.html. Accessed on 04/01/98.

Avery, William (1990) The Origins of Debt Accumulation among LDCs in the World Political Economy. *The Journal of Developing Areas* 24(4): 503–21.

Bandarage, Asoka (1997) *Women, Population and Global Crisis: A Political-Economic Analysis*. London: Zed Books.

Banerjee, Sumanta (1984) *India's Simmering Revolution: The Naxalite Uprising*. London: Zed Books.

Banister, Joseph (1901) *England Under the Jews*. London: J. Banister.

—— (1925) *Our Alien Makers of Revolution*. London: J. Banister.

BAOBAB Press (1994) The Icon of Industrial Greed: Meet the Rockefellers. 4(13). Internet site: http://www.africa2000.com:80/bndx/bao413.htm. Accessed on 16/06/98.

Baran, Paul (1957) *The Political Economy of Growth*. New York: Monthly Review Press.

Barkin, David (1975) Mexico's Albatross: The United States Economy. *Latin American Perspectives* Issue 5, 2(2): 64–80.

—— (1987) SAM and Seeds, in James Austin and Gustavo Esteva (eds.) *Food Policy in Mexico: The Search for Self-Sufficiency*. Ithaca: Cornell University Press, pp. 111–32.

—— (1990) *Distorted Development: Mexico in the World Economy*. Boulder, CO: Westview Press.

—— R. Batt and B. DeWalt (1990) *Food Crops vs. Feed Crops: Global Substitution of Grains in Production*. Boulder, CO: Lynne Rienner Publishers.

Barnes, Allan (1973) United States Private Agencies' Contributions to Population Programs. *International Journal of Health Services* 3(4): 661–5.

Barnet, Richard and Ronald Muller (1974) *Global Reach: The Power of the Multinational Corporations*. New York: Simon and Schuster.

Barratt Brown, Michael (1974) *The Economics of Imperialism*. Harmondsworth: Penguin.

Barry, Tom (1987) *Roots of Rebellion: Land and Hunger in Central America*. Boston, MA: South End Press.

Baum, Warren (1986) *Partners Against Hunger: The Consultative Group on International Agricultural Research.* Washington, DC: World Bank.

Bayliss-Smith, Tim (1984) Energy Flows and Agrarian Change in Karnataka: The Green Revolution at Micro-Scale, in T. Bayliss-Smith and S. Wanmali (eds.) *Understanding Green Revolutions: Agrarian Change and Development Planning in South Asia.* Cambridge: Cambridge University Press, pp. 153–72.

Beames, M. (1983) Rural Conflict in Pre-Famine Ireland: Peasant Assassinations in Tipperary, 1837–1847, in Samuel Clark and James Donnelly, Jr (eds.) *Irish Peasants, Violence and Political Unrest, 1780–1914.* Madison: University of Wisconsin Press, pp. 264–83.

Beck, Roy (1994) The Ordeal of Immigration in Wausau. *Atlantic Monthly* April. Internet site: http://theatlanti...on/immigrat/Beckf.htm. Accessed on 29/10/96.

Becker, Carl (1932) *The Heavenly City of the Eighteenth Century Philosophers.* New Haven, CT: Yale University Press.

Beer, Max (1984) (orig. 1919) *A History of British Socialism.* Nottingham: Spokesman.

Belden, Joseph et al. (1986) *Dirt Rich, Dirt Poor: America's Food and Farm Crisis.* New York: Routledge and Kegan Paul.

Bello, Walden et al. (1982) *Development Debacle: The World Bank in the Philippines.* San Francisco: Institute for Food and Development Policy.

Bence-Jones, Mark (1974) *Clive of India.* London: Constable.

Berger, Susan (1992) *Political and Agrarian Development in Guatemala.* Boulder, CO: Westview Press.

Bergquist, Charles (1986) *Labor in Latin America: Comparative Essays on Chile, Argentina, Venezuela, and Colombia.* Stanford: Stanford University Press.

Berlan, Jean-Pierre and Richard Lewontin (1986) The Political Economy of Hybrid Corn. *Monthly Review* 38: 35–47.

Berle, Adolf (1960) The Cuban Crisis: Failure of American Foreign Policy. *Foreign Affairs* 39(1): 40–55.

———— (1962) *Latin America – Diplomacy and Reality.* New York: Harper and Row.

Bhatia, B.M. (1967) *Famines in India: A Study of Some Aspects of the Economic History of India (1860-1965).* London: Asia Publishing House.

———— (1988) *Indian Agriculture: A Policy Perspective.* New Delhi: Sage Publications.

Bird, Kai (1992) *The Chairman: John J. McCloy – The Making of the American Establishment.* New York: Simon and Schuster.

Black, George (1984) *Garrison Guatemala.* London: Zed Books.

Blight, James and David Welch (1989) *On the Brink: Americans and Soviets Reexamine the Cuban Missile Crisis.* New York: Hill and Wang.

Blum, Jerome (1978) *The End of the Old Order in Rural Europe.* Princeton, NJ: Princeton University Press.

Blum, William (1986) *The CIA: A Forgotten History: US Global Interventions Since World War 2.* London: Zed Books.

Boas, Max and Steve Chain (1976) *Big Mac: The Unauthorized Story of McDonald's.* New York: New American Library/Mentor.

Bodley, John (1976) *Anthropology and Contemporary Human Problems.* Menlo Park, CA: Cummings Publishing.

Boner, H. (1955) *Hungry Generations: The Nineteenth Century Case Against Malthusianism*. New York: King's Crown Press.

Bonilla, Heraclio (1974) *Guano y Burguesía en el Perú*. Lima: Instituto de Estudios Peruanos. Bonner, Raymond (1987) *Waltzing with a Dictator: The Marcoses and the Making of American Policy*. New York: Times Books.

Borkin, Joseph (1978) *The Crime and Punishment of I.G. Farben*. New York: The Free Press.

———— and Charles Welsh (n.d.) *Germany's Master Plan: The Story of Industrial Offensive*. London: John Long.

Borlaug, Norman (1970) *The Green Revolution: Peace and Humanity*. Speech at the Nobel Peace Prize award ceremony, Oslo, Norway, 11 December (1970. Internet site: http://www.theatlantic.com/atlantic/issues/97jan/borlaug/speech. htm. Accessed 08/08/97.

Boserup, Ester (1965) *The Conditions of Agricultural Growth: The Economics of Agricultural Change under Population Pressure*. Chicago: Aldine.

Boulding, Kenneth (1973) Introduction to R. Wilkinson, *Poverty and Progress*. New York: Praeger, pp. xiii–xx.

Boulter, H. (1769–70) *Letters (To Several Ministers of State in England, and Some Others, Containing an Account of the Most Interesting Transactions Which Passed in Ireland from 1724 to 1738)*. Oxford: Clarendon Press. 2 vols.

Bowles, Chester (1952) New India. *Foreign Affairs* 31(1): 79–94.

———— (1954) *Ambassador's Report*. London: Victor Gollancz.

Bowles, Samuel and Herbert Gintis (1976) *Schooling in Capitalist America: Educational Reform and the Contradictions of Economic Life*. New York: Basic Books.

Brachet-Marquez, V. and M. Sherraden (1994) Political Change and the Welfare State: The Case of Health and Food Policies in Mexico (1970–93). *World Development* 22(9): 1295–1312.

Bradley, John (1968) *Allied Intervention in Russia*. London: Weidenfeld and Nicolson.

Brockett, Charles (1988) *Land, Power, and Poverty: Agrarian Transformation and Political Conflict in Central America*. Boston: Unwin Hyman.

Brookings Institution (1977) William W. Kaufmann. Internet site: http://www. brook.edu/PA/SCHOLARS/WKAUFMAN.HTM. Accessed on 10/09/97/

Brown, Dorris (1971) *Agricultural Development in India's Districts*. Cambridge, MA: Harvard University Press.

Brown, Lester (1975) World Population and Food Supplies, in The Agribusiness Council, *Agricultural Initiative in the Third World. A Report on the Conference: Science and Agribusiness in the Seventies*. Lexington, MA: Lexington Books, pp. 161–79.

———— (1977) Population and Affluence: Growing Pressures on World Food Resources, in Robert D. Stevens (ed.) *Tradition and Dynamics in Small-Farm Agriculture: Economic Studies in Asia, Africa, and Latin America*. Ames: Iowa State University Press, pp. 25–53.

Bruno, Kenny (1992) The Corporate Capture of the Earth Summit. *Multinational Monitor* July/August. Internet site: http://essential.org/.../mm0792. html#coporate. Accessed on 30/10/96.

Bullock, M. (1980) *An American Transplant: The Rockefeller Foundation and the Peking Union Medical College*. Berkeley: University of California Press.

Burawoy, Michael (1976) The Functions and Reproduction of Migrant Labor: Comparative Material from Southern Africa and the United States. *American*

Journal of Sociology 81(5): 1050–87.

Byres, Terry and Ben Crow (1988) New Technology and New Masters for the Indian Countryside, in Ben Crow et al. (eds.) *Survival and Change in the Third World.* Cambridge: Polity Press, pp. 163–81.

Cahn, William (1980) (orig. 1954) *Lawrence 1912: The Bread and Roses Strike.* New York: Pilgrim Press.

Calder, Angus (1981) *Revolutionary Empire: The Rise of the English-Speaking Empires from the Fifteenth Century to the 1780s.* New York: Dutton.

Caldwell, John and Pat Caldwell (1986) *Limiting Population Growth and the Ford Foundation Contribution.* London: Frances Pinter.

Canihuante, Gabriel (1997) Chile-Agriculture: Pesticides Take Their Toll. Inter Press Service World News. Internet site: http://www.oneworld.org/textver/ips2/feb/chile.html. Accessed on 16/07/97.

CAPS (1997) CAPS Staff and Board. Internet site: http://www.calweb.com/~caps/staff.html. Accessed on 16/06/98.

Carew, Anthony (1987) *Labour Under the Marshall Plan: The Politics of Productivity and the Marketing of Management Science.* Manchester: Manchester University Press.

Carlyle, Thomas (1882) *Reminiscences of My Irish Journey in 1849.* London: Sampson, Low, Marston, Searle and Carroll.

Carriere, Jean (1991) The Crises in Costa Rica: An Ecological Perspective, in David Goodman and Michael Redclift (eds.) *Environment and Development in Latin America: The Politics of Sustainability.* Manchester: Manchester University Press, pp. 184–204.

Cary, James (1962) *Japan Today: Reluctant Ally.* New York: Frederick A. Praeger.

Casselman, Louise and Janice Acton (1976) Colombia: Anchor of the Caribbean, in Bonnie Mass (ed.) *Population Target: The Political Economy of Population Control in Latin America.* Brampton, Ontario: Charters Publishing, pp. 235–58.

Castles, Stephen, with Heather Booth and Tina Wallace (1984) *Here for Good: Western Europe's New Ethnic Minorities.* London: Pluto Press.

Center for Defense Information (1997) 1998 Military Spending: Behind the Numbers. How the Pentagon is Spending Your Money. *The Defense Monitor* 26(3). Internet site: http:www.cdi.org/dm/1997/issue3/. Accessed on 26/01/98.

Chadwick, Edwin (1862) *On the Social and Educational Statistics of Manchester and Salford.* Manchester: Cave and Sever.

Chamberlain, Neil (1970) *Beyond Malthus: Population and Power.* New York: Basic Books.

Chase, Allan (1977) *The Legacy of Malthus: The Social Costs of the New Scientific Racism.* New York: Alfred A. Knopf.

——— (1982) *Magic Shots.* New York: William Morrow and Company.

Chemistry and Industry Magazine News (1996) Report Reveals Agent Orange Risks. Internet site: http://ci.mond.org/9607/960705.html. Accessed on 29/10/96.

Chirac, Jacques (1985) Jacques Chirac on French Population Issues. *Population and Development Review* 11(1): 163–4.

Chossudovsky, Michel (1991) Global Poverty and New World Economic order. *Economic and Political Weekly* 2 November, 26(44): 2527–37.

Church Committee (1976) *Final Report of the Select Committee to Study Governmental Operations with Respect to Intelligence Activities.* Senate report. Washington, DC:

Government Printing Office.

Claeys, Gregory (1989) *Thomas Paine: Social and Political Thought*. Boston: Unwin Hyman.

Clairmonte, Frederick and John Cavanagh (1981)*The World in Their Web: Dynamics of Textile Multinationals*. London: Zed Books.

Clapp, Gordon (1955) *The TVA: An Approach to the Development of a Region*. Chicago: University of Chicago Press.

Clausen, A.W. (1986) Foreword to Warren Baum, *Partners Against Hunger*. The Consultative Group on International Agricultural Research. Washington, DC: World Bank, pp. v–vi.

Cline, H. (1963) *Mexico. Revolution to Evolution: 1940–1960*. New York: Oxford University Press.

Clive, John (1973) *Thomas Babington Macaulay: The Shaping of the Historian*. London: Secker and Warburg.

Cobbett, William (1984) (orig. 1834) *Cobbett on Ireland: A Warning to England*. D. Knight, ed. London: Lawrence and Wishart.

Cohen, R. (1987) *The New Helots: Migrants in the International Division of Labour*. Aldershot: Avebury.

Cohen, Stephen (1980) (orig. 1973) *Bukharin and the Bolshevik Revolution: A Political Biography, 1888–1938*. Oxford: Oxford University Press.

Colby, Gerard with Charlotte Dennett (1995) *Thy Will Be Done. The Conquest of the Amazon: Nelson Rockefeller and Evangelism in the Age of Oil*. New York: Harper Collins.

Coleman, David (1992) Does Europe Need Immigrants? Population and Work Force Projections. *International Migration Review* 26(2): 413–61.

Coleman, David and Roger Schofield (eds.) (1986) *The State of Population Theory: Forward from Malthus*. Oxford: Basil Blackwell.

Colinvaux, P. (1978) *Why Big Fierce Animals are Rare: An Ecologist's Perspective*. Princeton: Princeton University Press.

Collier, F. (1964) *The Family Economy of the Working Classes in the Cotton Industry, 1784–1833*. Manchester: Manchester University Press.

Collins, E. (1969) Harvest Technology and Labour Supply in Britain, 1790–1870. *Economic History* Review 22: 453–73.

Commissioners (1839) *First Report of the Commissioners Appointed to Inquire as to the Best Means of Establishing an Efficient Constabulary Force in the Countries of England and Wales*. London: Charles Knight & Co.

Connell, K. (1950) *The Population of Ireland, 1750–1845*. Oxford: Oxford University Press.

———— (1965) Land and Population in Ireland, 1780–1845, in D. Glass and D. Eversley (eds.) *Population in History: Essays in Historical Demography*. London: Edward Arnold, pp. 423–33.

Cook, S. (1993) *Imperial Affinities: Nineteenth Century Analogies and Exchanges Between India and Ireland*. New Delhi: Sage Publications.

Coontz, Sydney (1961) (orig. 1957) *Population Theories and the Economic Interpretation*. London: Routledge and Kegan Paul.

Cornell University News Bureau (1962) Press Release. 28 January.

Council on Foreign Relations (1960) *Social Change in Latin America Today: Its Implications for United States Policy*. New York: Harper and Brothers.

Cronin, James (1996) *The World the Cold War Made: Order, Chaos, and the Return of History*. New York: Routledge.

Crossette, Barbara (1996) Report Cites Impact of Poor Farmers on Tropical Forests. *New York Times*, 4 August. Internet site: http://www.mtholyoke.edu/acad/intrel/poortree.htm. Accessed on 14/01/98.

Crotty, Raymond (1983) Modernization and Land Reform: Real or Cosmetic? The Irish Case. *The Journal of Peasant Studies* 11(1): 101–16.

Cullen, L. (1981) *The Emergence of Modern Ireland, 1600–1900*. Dublin: Gill and Macmillan.

Cumings, Bruce (1990) *The Origins of the Korean War, Vol. 2: The Roaring of the Cataract, 1947–1950*. Princeton, NJ: Princeton University Press.

——— (1997) Boundary Displacement: Area Studies and International Studies during and after the Cold War. *Bulletin of Concerned Asian Scholars* 29(1): 6–26.

Daly, Herman (1970) The Population Question in Northeast Brazil: Its Economic and Ideological Dimensions. *Economic Development and Cultural Change* 18(4), Part I: 536–74.

D'Arcy, F. (1977) The Malthusian League and the Resistance to Birth Control Propaganda in Late Victorian Britain. *Population Studies* 31(2): 429–48.

Darlington, C.D. (1969) *Evolution of Man and Society*. London: Allen and Unwin.

Dasgupta, Biplab (1977) *Agrarian Change and the New Technology in India*. Geneva: UN Research Institute for Social Development (UNRISD).

Davies, Margaret Llewelyn (ed.) (1915) *Maternity: Letters from Working Women*. London: Virago.

Davis, Kingsley (1951) *The Population of India and Pakistan*. Princeton, NJ: Princeton University Press.

——— (1986) The History of Birth and Death. *Bulletin of the Atomic Scientists* April: 20–23.

Day, W. (1862) *The Famine in the West*. Dublin: Hodges, Smith and Company.

Deane, Phyllis (1979) *The First Industrial Revolution*. Cambridge: Cambridge University Press.

Declercq, Eugene (1985) The Nature and Style of Practice of Immigrant Midwives in Early Twentieth Century Massachusetts. *Journal of Social History* 19: 113–29.

De Graff, J. (1986) *The Economics of Coffee*. Wageningen: Pudoc.

Dell, Sidney (1972) *The Inter-American Development Bank: A Study in Development Financing*. New York: Praeger.

Department of Caldas (1963) *Programa Quinquenal de Desarrollo y de Diversificación Económica para el Departamento de Caldas*. Colombia. mimeo.

Desmond, Adrian and James Moore (1991) *Darwin*. London: Michael Joseph.

DeWalt, Billie (1988) Halfway There: Social Science in Agricultural Development and the Social Science of Agricultural Development. *Human Organization* 47(4): 343–53.

——— and David Barkin (1991) Mexico's Two Green Revolutions: Feed for Food, in D. McMillan (ed.) *Anthropology and Food Policy: Human Dimensions of Food Policy in Africa and Latin America*. Athens, GA: University of Georgia Press, pp. 12–39.

Dewan, Ritu (1990) *Political Economy of Agrarian Reforms in India – The Nexus with Surplus Extraction*. Bombay: Himalaya Publishing House.

De Witt, R. Peter (1977) *The Inter-American Development Bank and Political Influence with Special Reference to Costa Rica.* New York: Praeger.

Dhanagare, D.N. (1991) *Peasant Movements in India, 1920–1950.* Delhi: Oxford University Press.

Dickson, David (1995) The Other Great Irish Famine, in Cathal Póirtéir (ed.) *The Great Irish Famine.* Dublin: Mercier Press, pp. 50–59.

Digby, A. (1983) Malthus and Reform of the Poor Laws, in J. Dupaquier and A. Vauve-Chamous (eds.) *Malthus Past and Present.* London: Academic Press, pp. 97–109.

Divine, Robert (1981) *Eisenhower and the Cold War.* New York: Oxford University Press.

Dix, Robert (1967) *Colombia: The Political Dimensions of Change.* New Haven, CT: Yale University Press.

Dobb, Maurice (1963) (orig. 1947) *Studies in the Development of Capitalism.* New York: International Publishers.

Dolgoff, Sam (ed.) (1972) *Bakunin on Anarchy: Selected Works by the Activist-Founder of World Anarchism.* New York: Alfred A. Knopf.

Domhoff, G. William (1970) *The Higher Circles: The Governing Class in America.* New York: Vintage.

Donnelly, James (1975) *The Land and the People of Nineteenth Century Cork.* London: Routledge and Kegan Paul.

———— (1995) Mass Eviction and the Great Famine: The Clearances Revisited, in Cathal Póirtéir (ed.) *The Great Irish Famine.* Dublin: Mercier Press, pp. 155–73.

Donnison, Jean (1977) *Midwives and Medical Men: A History of Inter-professional Rivalries and Women's Rights.* London: Heinemann Educational.

Doyle, Jean (1987) U.S. Foreign Agricultural Policy and the Less Developed Countries, in Birol Yesiladaet al. (eds.) *Agrarian Reform in Reverse: The Food Crisis in the Third World.* Boulder, CO: Westview Press, pp. 305–35.

Drake, M. (1969) Population Growth and the Irish Economy, in L. Cullen (ed.) *The Formation of the Irish Economy.* Cork: Mercier Press, pp. 65–76.

Draper, William (1972) Address at Funeral and Memorial Services for Hugh Moore.

Drinnon, Richard (1961) *Rebel in Paradise: A Biography of Emma Goldman.* Chicago: University of Chicago Press.

Dublin Mansion House Relief Committee (1881) *The Irish Crisis of 1879–80.* Dublin: Browne and Nolan.

Dunkerley, James (1988) *Power in the Isthmus: A Political History of Modern Central America.* London: Verso.

Dutt, R. Palme (1940) *India To-Day.* London: Victor Gollancz.

Eakins, David (1969) Business Planners and America's Postwar Expansion, in David Horowitz (ed.) *Corporations and the Cold War.* New York: Monthly Review Press, pp. 143–71.

Edelman, Marc (1987) From Costa Rican Pasture to North American Hamburger, in Marvin Harris and Eric B. Ross (eds.) *Food and Evolution: Toward a Theory of Human Food Habits.* Philadelphia: Temple University Press, pp. 541–61.

———— (1992) *The Logic of the Latifundio: The Large Estates of Northwestern Costa Rica Since the Late Nineteenth Century.* Stanford: Stanford University Press.

Ehrlich, Paul (1968) *The Population Bomb.* New York: Sierra Club/Ballantine.

——— (1971) Foreword, in Lawrence Lader, *Breeding Ourselves to Death.* New York: Ballantine Books, p vii.

——— and Anne Ehrlich (1990) *The Population Explosion.* New York: Simon and Schuster.

——— Anne Ehrlich and Gretchen Daily (1993) Food Security, Population and Environment. *Population and Development Review* 19(1): 1–32.

Eley, Geoff (1983) What Produces Fascism: Preindustrial Traditions or a Crisis of a Capitalist State. *Politics and Society* 12(2): 53–82.

Ellis, P. (1972) *A History of the Irish Working Class.* London: Victor Gollancz.

ENCOP (Environmental and Conflicts Project) (1997) Internet site: http://www.fsk.ethz.ch/encop/. Accessed on 17/01/98.

Engels, Friedrich (1958) (orig. 1845) *The Condition of the Working Class in England.* W. Henderson and W. Chaloner trans. and ed. Stanford: Stanford University Press.

Escobar, Arturo (1995) *Encountering Development: The Making and Unmaking of the Third World.* Princeton, NJ: Princeton University Press.

Escobar, Augustín et al. (1987) Migration, Labour Markets, and the International Economy: Jalisco, Mexico, and the United States, in Jeremy Eades (ed.) *Migrants, Workers, and the Social Order.* ASA Monographs 26. London: Tavistock Publications, pp. 42–64.

Escorcia, Jose (1975) *Colombia: Some Economic and Political Aspects in the Development of the Agrarian and Industrial Sectors.* Ph.D. thesis. San Diego: University of California.

Faber, Daniel (1993) *Environment Under Fire: Imperialism and the Ecological Crisis in Central America.* New York: Monthly Review Press.

FAIR (1995) Immigration and Population Growth – Fair Statement (7 December 1995). Internet site: http://www.rahul.net/iti/kzpg/Archive/Broadcasts/Opinion/US-OpEd/msg00028.html. Accessed on 04/11/97.

Fitzgerald, Deborah (1986) Exporting American Agriculture: The Rockefeller Foundation in Mexico, 1943–53. *Social Studies of Science* 16: 457–83.

Fitzgerald, Frances (1972) *Fire in the Lake: The Vietnamese and the Americans in Vietnam.* New York: Vintage.

Fleming, D.F. (1961) *The Cold War and Its Origins, 1917–1960.* Garden City, NY: Doubleday and Company.

Flew, Antony (1986) Introduction to T.R. Malthus, *An Essay on the Principle of Population and A Summary View of the Principle of Population.* Harmondsworth: Penguin Books, pp. 7–56.

Flórez, Carmen Elisa (1996) Social Change and Transitions in the Life Histories of Colombian Women, in José Miguel Guzman et al. (eds.) *The Fertility Transition in Latin America.* Oxford: Clarendon Press, pp. 252–72.

Fluharty, Vernon (1976) *Dance of the Millions: Military Rule and the Social Revolution in Colombia, 1930–1956.* Westport, CT: Greenwood Press.

Foglesong, David (1995) *America's Secret War Against Bolshevism: U.S. Intervention in the Russian Civil War, 1917–1920.* Chapel Hill: University of North Carolina Press.

Folbre, Nancy (1994) *Who Pays for the Kids? Gender and the Structures of Constraint.* London: Routledge.

Foraci, Franco and Hakan Songur (1993) Dawn of the Eco Racist. *Guardian,* 27 July, Section 2: 14.

Forbes (1997) International Billionaires: The World's Richest People. Internet site: http://www.forbes.com/tool/toolbox/billionaires/billintro.asp. Accessed on 21/07/97.

Foster, John (1974) *Class Struggle and the Industrial Revolution: Early Industrial Capitalism in Three English Towns.* London: Weidenfeld and Nicolson.

—— (1976) British Imperialism and the London Aristocracy, in Jeffrey Skelley (ed.) *The General Strike 1926.* London: Lawrence and Wishart, pp. 3–57.

Foster, T. (1846) *Letters on the Condition of the People of Ireland.* London: Chapman and Hall.

Frank, Andre Gunder (1969) *Latin America: Underdevelopment or Revolution: Essays on the Development of Underdevelopment and the Immediate Enemy.* New York: Monthly Review Press.

Franke, Richard (1987) The Effects of Colonialism and Neocolonialism on the Gastronomic Patterns of the Third World, in Marvin Harris and Eric B. Ross (eds.) *Food and Evolution: Toward a Theory of Human Food Habits.* Philadelphia: Temple University Press, pp. 455–79.

Freedman, Lawrence (1986) *The Price of Peace: Living with the Nuclear Dilemma.* New York: Macmillan.

Freeman, Orville (1967) Malthus, Marx and the North American Breadbasket. *Foreign Affairs* 45(4): 579–93.

Friedl, J. and W. Ellis (1976) Celibacy, Late Marriage and Potential Mates in a Swiss Isolate, in B. Kaplan (ed.) *Anthropological Studies of Human Fertility.* Detroit: Wayne State University Press, pp. 23–35.

Friedrich, Paul (1970) *Agrarian Revolt in a Mexican Village.* Englewood Cliffs, NJ: Prentice-Hall.

Frydenlund, John (1994) Freeing U.S. Agriculture to Take Advantage of the New Global Market. Backgrounder No. 1002. The Heritage Foundation. Internet site: http://www.heritage.org/library/categories/enviro/bg1002.html. Accessed on 17/09/98.

Fryer, Peter (1965) *The Birth Controller.* London: Secker and Warburg.

Galli, Rosemary (1978) Rural Development as Social Control: International Agencies and Class Struggle in the Colombian Countryside. *Latin American Perspectives* 5(4): 71–89.

—— (1981) Colombia: Rural Development as Social and Economic Control, in Rosemary Galli (ed.) *The Political Economy of Rural Development: Peasants, International Capital and the State.* Albany, NY: State University of New York Press, pp. 27–90.

Gardner, Florence (1991) Guatemala's Deadly Harvest. *Multinational Monitor* 12(1 and 2), January–February. Internet site: gopher://gopher.essential.org:70/00/pub/EI/Monitor/text/mon9101. Accessed on 07/20/97.

Gardner, Lloyd (1969) The New Deal, New Frontiers, and the Cold War: A Reexamination of American Expansion, 1933–1945, in David Horowitz (ed.) *Corporations and the Cold War.* New York: Monthly Review Press, pp. 105–41.

Ggedda, George (1997) Official Says 1 Billion Suffer Hunger. *San Diego Source* April 3. Internet site: http://www.sddt.com/files/librarywire/97...es/04_97/DN97_04_03/DN97_04_03_faaa.html. Accessed on 29/01/98.

Gettleman, Marvin et al. (1995) *Vietnam and America: A Documented History*. New York: Grove Press.

Ghosh, R. (1963) Malthus on Emigration and Colonization: Letters to Wilmot-Horton. *Economica* February: 45–62.

Gill, C. (1925) *The Rise of the Irish Linen Industry*. Oxford: Clarendon Press.

Gillin, John (1960) Some Signposts for Policy, in *Social Change in Latin America Today: Its Implications for United States Policy*. Council on Foreign Relations, New York: Harper and Brothers, pp. 14–62.

——— and K.H. Silvert (1956) Ambiguities in Guatemala. *Foreign Affairs* 34(3): 469–82.

Glass, David (1953) Malthus and the Limitation of Population Growth, in David Glass (ed.) *Introduction to Malthus*. London: Watts and Company, pp. 27–54.

——— (1966) Family Planning Programmes and Action in Western Europe. *Population Studies* 19(3): 221–38.

Gledhill, John (1995) *Neoliberalism, Transnationalization and Rural Poverty: A Case Study of Michoacán, Mexico*. Boulder, CO: Westview Press.

Global Climate Change Information Programme (1997) GCCIP: Climate Change and Its Impact on World Agriculture. Internet site: http://www.doc.mmu. ac.uk/aric/agricult.html. Accessed on 16/07/97.

Global Forum (1992) *The NGO Alternative Treaties*. Rio de Janeiro, 1–15 June. Internet site: http//www.infohabitat.org/treaties/tncs.html. Accessed on 1/9/98.

Gomez, Berta (1997) Private Capital Flows To Developing Countries to Remain High. The United States Mission to Italy. Internet site: http://www.usis.it/ wireless/wf970529/97052916.htm. Accessed on 08/01/98.

Gonner, Edward (1966) *Common Land and Enclosure*. London: Frank Cass.

Goodman, David and Michael Redclift (1991) *Refashioning Nature: Food, Ecology and Culture*. London: Routledge.

Gordon, Lincoln (1963) *A New Deal for Latin America: The Alliance for Progress*. Cambridge, MA: Harvard University Press.

Gordon, Linda (1976) *Woman's Body, Woman's Right: A Social History of Birth Control in America*. Harmondsworth: Penguin.

Gould, Stephen (1991) *Bully for Brontosaurus: Further Reflections in Natural History*. Harmondsworth: Penguin Books.

Gouldner, Alvin (1970) *The Coming Crisis of Western Sociology*. New York: Basic Books.

Grant, Madison (1918) *The Passing of the Great Race*. New York: Charles Scribner's Sons.

Green, E. (1956) Agriculture, in R. Dudley Edwards and T. Desmond Williams (eds.) *The Great Famine: Studies in Irish History, 1845–52*. Dublin: Irish Committee of Historical Sciences, pp. 89–128.

Green, Marshall (1993) The Evolution of US International Population Policy, 1965–92: A Chronological Account. *Population and Development Review* 19(2): 303–21.

Greenwire (1995) Business Council for Sustainable Development (Interview with Stephan Schmidheiny, 3 and 4 May). Internet site: http://www.rri.org/Schmid-Int.html. Accessed on 25/10/96.

Griffin, Keith (1981) *Land Concentration and Rural Poverty*. London: Macmillan.

Griffith, Talbot (1926) *Population Problems of the Age of Malthus.* Cambridge: Cambridge University Press.

Groves, Reg (1981) *Sharpen the Sickle: The History of the Farm Workers' Union.* London: Merlin Press.

Halberstam, David (1972) *The Best and the Brightest.* Greenwich, CN: Fawcett Books.

—— (1986) *The Reckoning.* New York: William Morrow.

Hall, Alex (1976) The War of Words: Anti-Socialist Offensives and Counter-Propaganda in Wilhelmine Germany 1890–1914. *Journal of Contemporary History* 11: 11–42.

Hall, Lana (1985) United States Food Aid and the Agricultural Development of Brazil and Colombia, 1954–73, in J. Super and T. Wright (eds.) *Food, Politics, and Society in Latin America.* Lincoln: University of Nebraska Press, pp. 133–49.

Hall, Mr and Mrs S.C. (1984) (orig. 1841) *Hall's Ireland. Mr. and Mrs. Hall's Tour of 1840.* Michael Scott, ed. London: Sphere.

Halliday, Jon (1975) *A Political History of Japanese Capitalism.* New York: Monthly Review Press.

Hammond, J.L. and Barbara Hammond (1987) (orig. 1911) *The Village Labourer 1760–1832: A Study of the Government of England Before the Reform Bill.* Gloucester: Alan Sutton.

Handy, Jim (1994) *Revolution in the Countryside: Rural Conflict and Agrarian Reform in Guatemala, 1944–1954.* Chapel Hill: University of North Carolina Press.

Hardin, Garrett (1951) (orig. 1949) *Biology: Its Human Implications.* San Francisco: W.H. Freeman.

—— (1959) *Nature and Man's Fate.* New York: Mentor Books.

—— (1968) The Tragedy of the Commons. *Science* 162: 1243–8.

—— (1969) *Population, Evolution, and Birth Control: A Collage of Controversial Readings.* San Francisco, CA: W.H. Freeman.

—— (1975) (orig. 1968) The Tragedy of the Commons, in Priscilla Reining and Irene Tinker (eds.) *Population: Dynamics, Ethics and Policy.* Washington, DC: American Association for the Advancement of Science, pp. 11–16.

—— (1985) *Filters Against Folly: How to Survive Despite Economists, Ecologists, and the Merely Eloquent.* New York: Viking.

—— (1993) *Living within Limits: Ecology, Economics, and Population Taboos.* New York: Oxford University Press.

Harrar, George (1975) Foreword, in The Agribusiness Council, *Agricultural Initiative in the Third World. A Report on the Conference: Science and Agribusiness in the Seventies.* Lexington, MA: Lexington Books, pp. ix–xii.

Harris, Marvin (1971) *Culture, Man and Nature: An Introduction to General Anthropology.* New York: Thomas Y. Crowell Company.

—— and Eric Ross (1987) *Death, Sex and Fertility: Population Regulation in Preindustrial and Developing Societies.* New York: Columbia University Press.

Harrison, Lawrence (1985) *Underdevelopment is a State of Mind: The Latin American Case.* Cambridge, MA: Center for International Affairs, Harvard University.

Harrison, Selig (1960) *India: The Most Dangerous Decades.* Princeton, NJ: Princeton University Press.

Hartmann, Betsy (1987) *Reproductive Rights and Wrongs: The Global Politics of Population Control and Contraceptive Choice.* New York: Harper and Row.

Harvey, David (1974) Population, Resources, and the Ideology of Science. *Economic Geography* 50(3): 256–77.

Hayter, Teresa and Catharine Watson (1985) *Aid: Rhetoric and Reality*. London: Pluto Press.

Hechter, M. (1975) *Internal Colonialism: The Celtic Fringe in British National Development, 1536–1966*. Berkeley: University of California Press.

Hersh, Seymour (1983) *The Price of Power: Kissinger in the Nixon White House*. New York: Summit Books.

Hewes, Laurence, Jr (1955) *Japan – Land and Men: An Account of the Japanese Land Reform Program – 1945–51*. Ames: Iowa State College Press.

Hewitt de Alcántara, Cynthia (1976) *Modernizing Mexican Agriculture: Socioeconomic Implications of Technological Change 1940–1970*. Geneva: UN Research Institute for Social Development.

Hewitt, Margaret (1958) *Wives and Mothers in Victorian Industry*. Rockliff: London.

Hewlett, Sylvia Ann (1975) The Dynamics of Economic Imperialism: The Role of Foreign Direct Investment in Brazil. *Latin American Perspectives* 2(1): 136–49.

Higham, Charles (1983) *Trading with the Enemy: An Exposé of the Nazi–American Money Plot, 1933–1949*. London: Robert Hale.

Hitchens, Christopher (1990) *Blood, Class and Nostalgia: Anglo-American Ironies*. New York: Vintage.

Hobbelink, Henk (1991) *Biotechnology and the Future of World Agriculture*. The Fourth Resource. London: Zed Books.

Hobsbawm, Eric (1964) *Labouring Men: Studies in the History of Labour*. London: Weidenfeld and Nicolson.

——— (1979) *The Age of Capital, 1848–1875*. New York: New American Library.

——— (1994) *Age of Extremes: The Short Twentieth Century, 1914–1991*. London: Michael Joseph.

——— and George Rudé (1968) *Captain Swing*. New York: W.W. Norton.

Hobson, John (1902) *Imperialism: A Study*. London: George Allen and Unwin.

Hodgkin, Thomas (1981) *Vietnam: The Revolutionary Path*. London: Macmillan.

Hodgson, Dennis (1983) Demography as Social Science and Policy Science. *Population and Development Review* 9(1): 1–34.

Hodson, H.V. (ed.) (1974) *The International Foundation Directory*. London: Europa Publications.

Hoffman, Paul (1951) *Peace Can Be Won*. Garden City, NY: Doubleday.

Hofstadter, Richard (1955) *The Age of Reform*. New York: Vintage Books.

——— (1965) *The Paranoid Style in American Politics and Other Essays*. New York: Alfred A. Knopf.

Home Depot (1996) President's Council on Sustainable Development. Internet site: http://www.homedepot.com/FI/pcsd.htm. Accessed on 29/10/96.

Homer-Dixon, Thomas (1995) The Ingenuity Gap: Can Poor Countries Adapt to Resource Scarcity? *Population and Development Review* 21(3): 587–612.

Honey, Martha (1994) *Hostile Acts: U.S. Policy in Costa Rica in the 1980s*. Gainesville: University Press of Florida.

Horner, J. (1920) *The Linen Trade of Europe During the Spinning-Wheel Period*. Belfast: M'Caw, Stevenson and Orr.

Horowitz, David (1971) Politics and Knowledge: An Unorthodox History of

Modern China Studies. *Bulletin of Concerned Asian Scholars* 3(3–4): 139–68.

House of Commons (1836) *Second Report From the Select Committee Appointed to Inquire into the State of Agriculture. Reports from Committees*, Vol. 8 (Part 1), pp. 225–516. London.

House of Commons (1838) *Accounts and Papers. Estimates; Army; Navy; Ordnance; etc.* Westminster.

House of Commons (1880a) *Accounts and Papers.* Vol. 76. London: HMSO.

House of Commons (1880b) *Accounts and Papers. Law and Crime.* Vol. 60. London: HMSO.

House of Commons (1969) (orig. 1835) Proceedings. *Select Committee Report on the Origin, Nature, and Extent of Orange Institutions in Great Britain and the Colonies with Minutes of Evidence.* Shannon: Irish University Press.

Hudson, Michael (1972) *Super Imperialism: The Economic Strategy of American Empire.* New York: Holt, Rinehart and Winston.

Hughes, J. (1847) *A Lecture on the Antecedent Causes of the Irish Famine in 1847.* New York: Edward Dunigan.

Hughes, Robert (1987) *The Fatal Shore: The Epic of Australia's Founding.* New York: Alfred A. Knopf.

Hutchins, B. and A. Harrison (1966) *A History of Factory Legislation.* London: Frank Cass.

Huzel, J. (1969) Malthus, the Poor Law, and Population in Early Nineteenth Century England. *Economic History Review* 22: 430–52.

IFDC (1997) IFDC: International Fertilizer Development Center. Internet site: http://www.ifdc.org/ Accessed on 16/11/97.

Independent, The (1995) Shell "Is Biggest Global Warmer". December 10: 1.

India Planning Commission (1958) *The New India: Progress through Democracy.* New York: Macmillan.

Information Network on Migration from Third Countries (1997) *The Member States of the EU and Immigration in 1994: Less Tolerance and Tighter Control Policies.* Luxembourg: Office for Official Publications of the European Communities.

Instituto de Ecologia Politica (1997) Pesticide Use and Women Workers in Chile. Internet site: http://www.ecs.earlham.edu/www/faculty/f...iticsAndEnv Action/Conferences/chile.html. Accessed on 16/07/97.

Jackson, T.A. (1970) (orig. 1947) *Ireland Her Own: An Outline History of the Irish Struggle.* London: Lawrence and Wishart.

Jacoby, Erich (1949) *Agrarian Unrest in Southeast Asia.* New York: Columbia University Press.

James, Patricia and John Pullen (1988) Review of E. Wrigley and D. Souden (eds.) The Works of Thomas Robert Malthus. *The Economic History Review* 41(2): 320–21.

Japanese Ministry of Agriculture, Forestry and Fisheries (1995) A Weekly Update of News No. 134, July 21. Internet site: http://www.maff.go.jp/mud/134.html. Accessed on 18/08/98.

Johnson, J. (1970) The Two "Irelands" at the Beginning of the Nineteenth Century, in N. Stephens and R. Glasscock (eds.) *Irish Geographical Studies.* Belfast: Queen's University Press, pp. 224–43.

Johnson, Stanley (1987) *World Population and the United Nations: Challenge and Response.* Cambridge: Cambridge University Press.

Jonas, Susanne (1974) Anatomy of an Intervention: The U.S. "Liberation" of Guatemala, in Susanne Jonas and David Tobis (eds.) *Guatemala.* New York: NACLA, pp. 57–73.

────── and David Tobis (eds.) (1974) *Guatemala.* New York: NACLA.

Jones, David (1983) The Cleavage Between Graziers and Peasants in the Land Struggle, 1890–1910, in Samuel Clark and James Donnelly, Jr (eds.) *Irish Peasants, Violence and Political Unrest, 1780–1914.* Madison: University of Wisconsin Press, pp. 264–83.

Jones, Howard Mumford (1964) *O Strange New World. American Culture: The Formative Years.* New York: Viking Press.

Jordan, D. Merchants (1987) "Strong Farmers" and Fenians: The Post-Famine Political Elite and the Irish Land War, in C. Philpin (ed.) *Nationalism and Popular Protest in Ireland.* Cambridge: Cambridge University Press, pp. 320–48.

Jordan, W.K. (1959) *Philanthropy in England 1480–1660: A Study of the Changing Pattern of English Social Aspirations.* London: George Allen and Unwin.

Joshi, P.C. (1969) Land Reforms in India, in A. Desai (ed.) *Rural Sociology in India.* Bombay: Popular Prakashan, pp. 444–75.

Kamarck, Andrew (1972) *Climate and Economic Development.* Washington, DC: Economic Development Institute, International Bank for Reconstruction and Development.

────── (1976) *The Tropics and Economic Development: A Provocative Inquiry into the Poverty of Nations.* Baltimore: Johns Hopkins University Press for the World Bank.

Kater, Michael (1989) *Doctors under Hitler.* Chapel Hill: University of North Carolina Press.

Kay, James (1969) (orig. 1832) *The Moral and Physical Condition of the Working Classes Employed in the Cotton Manufacture in Manchester.* Manchester: E.J. Morten.

Kegel, Charles (1958) William Cobbett and Malthusianism. *Journal of the History of Ideas* 19: 348–62.

Kennan, George (1951) *American Diplomacy, 1900–1950.* New York: Mentor Books.

────── (1978) Moscow Embassy Telegram #511: "The Long Telegram", in Thomas Etzold and John Gaddis (eds.) *Containment: Documents on American Policy and Strategy, 1945–1950.* New York: Columbia University Press, pp. 50–63.

Kennedy, R. (1973) *The Irish: Emigration, Marriage and Fertility.* Berkeley: University of California Press.

Kerr, B. (1943) Irish Seasonal Migration to Great Britain, 1800–38. *Irish Historical Studies* 4: 365–80.

Keynes, John Maynard (1956) *Essays and Sketches in Biography.* New York: Meridian Books.

────── (1971) (orig. 1919) *The Economic Consequences of the Peace.* The Collected Writings of John Maynard Keynes, Vol. II. London: Macmillan for The Royal Economic Society.

King, John Kerry (1956) *Southeast Asia in Perspective.* New York: Macmillan.

Kirk, Russell (1954) *The Conservative Mind.* London: Faber and Faber.

Kissinger Commission on Population and Development in Central America (1984) *Population and Development Review* 10(2): 381–9.

Kneen, Brewster (1995) The Invisible Giant: Cargill and Its Transnational Strategies. *Ecologist* 25(5): 195–9.

Knox, A. David (1985) Foreword, in Vinod Thomas et al., *Linking Macoeconomic and Agricultural Policies for Adjustment with Growth: The Colombian Experience.* Baltimore: Johns Hopkins University Press for the World Bank, pp. iv–vi.

Knowles, Lilian (1928) *The Economic Development of the British Overseas Empire.* London: Routledge.

Knowles, Michael (1975) Thomas Babington Macaulay, in *The New Encyclopaedia Britannica.* Volume 11, pp. 223–4.

Koffman, Bennett (1969) *The National Federation of Coffee-Growers of Colombia.* Ph.D. thesis, University of Virginia.

Kolko, Gabriel (1968) *The Politics of War: The World and United States Foreign Policy, 1943–1945.* New York: Random House.

—— (1969) *The Roots of American Foreign Policy: An Analysis of Power and Purpose.* Boston, MA: Beacon Press.

Kolko, Joyce and Gabriel Kolko (1972) *The Limits of Power: The World and United States Foreign Policy, 1945–1954.* New York: Harper and Row.

Lader, Lawrence (1971) *Breeding Ourselves to Death.* New York: Ballantine Books.

Lafeber, Walter (1980) (orig. 1967) *America, Russia, and the Cold War 1945–1980.* New York: John Wiley and Sons.

Lamb, H. (1982) *Climate, History and the Modern World.* London: Methuen.

Landau, Saul (1988) *The Dangerous Doctrine: National Security and U.S. Foreign Policy.* Boulder, CO: Westview Press.

Landman, J. (1931) Current Status of Human Sterilization in the United States. *Eugenical News* 16(7): 111.

Langer, W. (1975) The Origins of the Birth Control Movement in England in the Early Nineteenth Century. *Journal of Interdisciplinary History* 5(4): 669–86.

Langguth, A. J. (1978) *Hidden Terrors.* New York: Pantheon Books.

Langley, Lester and Thomas Schoonover (1995) *The Banana Men: American Mercenaries and Entrepreneurs in Central America, 1880–1930.* Lexington: University of Kentucky Press.

Ledbetter, Rosanna (1972) *The Organization that Delayed Birth Control: A History of the Malthusian League, 1877–1927.* Ph.D. thesis. Ann Arbor: Northern Illinois University.

Leitch, Alexander (1978) *A Princeton Companion.* Princeton: Princeton University Press. Internet site: http://mondrian.princeton.edu/CampusWWW/Companion/woodrow_wilson_school.html. Accessed 08/02/97.

Leffler, Melvyn (1992) *A Preponderance of Power: National Security, the Truman Administration, and the Cold War.* Stanford: Stanford University Press.

Lele, Uma and Arthur Goldsmith (1989) The Development of National Agricultural Research Capacity: India's Experience with the Rockefeller Foundation and Its Significance for Africa. *Economic Development and Cultural Change* 37(2): 305–43.

Lerner, Daniel (1958) *The Passing of Traditional Society: Modernizing the Middle East.* Glencoe, IL: Free Press.

Lewis, Robert (1985) The Rise and Fall – and Rise Again – of IBEC, in J. Freivalds (ed.) *Successful Agribusiness Management.* London: Gower, pp. 1–11.

Lindenbaum, Shirley (1987) Loaves and Fishes in Bangladesh, in M. Harris and E. Ross (eds.) *Food and Evolution: Toward a Theory of Human Food Habits.* Philadelphia: Temple University Press, pp. 427–43.

Litoff, Judy (1978) *American Midwives, 1860 to the Present.* Westport, CT: Greenwood Press.

Livi-Bacci, Massimo (1992) *A Concise History of World Population.* Carl Ipsen, trans. Oxford: Blackwell.

Lloyd, William (1980) W.F. Lloyd on the Checks to Population. *Population and Development Review* 6(3): 473–96.

Lodge, George (1966) Revolution in Latin America. *Foreign Affairs* 44(2): 173–97.

Longfield, A. (1929) *Anglo-Irish Trade in the Sixteenth Century.* London: G. Routledge and Sons.

Lorimer, Frank (1931) Trends in the Natural Increase of Population Groups in the United States. *Eugenical News* 16(7): 99–100.

Lowell, B.L. (1992) Circular Mobility, Migrant Communities, and Policy Restrictions: Unauthorized Flows from Mexico, in C. Goldscheider (ed.) *Migration, Population Structure and Redistribution Policies.* Boulder, CO: Westview Press, pp. 137–57.

Lucas, A. (1960) Irish Food before the Potato. *Gwerin* 3(2): 8–43.

Lundberg, Ferdinand (1968) *The Rich and the Super-Rich: A Study in the Power of Money Today.* New York: Bantam Books.

McCay, Bonnie and James Acheson (1987) *The Question of the Commons: The Culture and Ecology of Communal Resources.* Tucson: University of Arizona Press.

MacConnell, Sean (1996) Volume of Beef Exports Constant But Value Falls. *The Irish Times* 3 December. Internet site: http://www.irish-times.com/irish-times/paper/1996/1203/hom13.html. Accessed on 04/01/98.

McCracken, E. (1971) *The Irish Woods Since Tudor Times.* Newton Abbot: David and Charles.

McCreery, David (1994) *Rural Guatemala, 1760–1940.* Stanford: Stanford University Press.

MacHale, John (1888) (orig. 1847) *The Letters of J. MacHale.* Dublin: M.H. Gill & Son.

McLaren, Angus (1984) *Reproductive Rituals: The Perception of Fertility in England from the Sixteenth Century to the Nineteenth Century.* London: Methuen.

McMichael, Philip (1996) *Development and Social Change: A Global Perspective.* Thousand Oaks, CA: Pine Forge Press.

McMillan, Robert (1955) Land Tenure in the Philippines. *Rural Sociology* 20(1): 25–33.

McNamara, Robert (1968) *The Essence of Security: Reflections in Office.* New York: Harper and Row.

MacNeil, J. (1886) *English Interference with Irish Industries.* London: Cassell and Co.

Magdoff, Harry and Paul Sweezy (1977) *The End of Prosperity: The American Economy in the 1970s.* New York: Monthly Review Press.

Malthus, Thomas 1798) *An Essay on the Principle of Population.* London.

——— (1830) *A Summary View of the Principle of Population.* London: John Murray.

Mamdani, Mahmood (1972) *The Myth of Population Control: Family, Caste, and Class in an Indian Village.* New York: Monthly Review Press.

Manchester, William (1968) *The Arms of Krupp, 1587–1968.* New York: Bantam Books.

Mantoux, Paul (1961) *The Industrial Revolution in the Eighteenth Century.* New York: Macmillan.

Marchetti, Victor and John Marks (1974) *The CIA and the Cult of Intelligence*. New York: Dell.

Markiewicz, Dana (1993) *The Mexican Revolution and the Limits of Agrarian Reform, 1915–1946*. Boulder, CO: Lynne Rienner Publishers.

Marlow, J. (1973) *Captain Boycott and the Irish*. London: André Deutsch.

Marr, David (1995) The Rise and Fall of "Counterinsurgency": 1961–1964, in Marvin Gettleman et al. (eds.) *Vietnam and America*. New York: Grove Press, pp. 205–15.

Marx, Karl and Frederick Engels (1972) *Ireland and the Irish Question: A Collection of Writings*. New York: International Publishers.

Mason, E. and R. Asher (1973) *The World Bank Since Bretton Woods: The Origins, Policies, Operations, and Impact of the International Bank for Reconstruction and Development and Other Members of the World Bank Group*. Washington, DC: Brookings Institution.

Mason, T. David (1986) Population Growth and the Struggle for the Hearts and Minds of Rural Populations in Central America, in Jon Saunders (ed.) *Population Growth in Latin America and U.S. National Security*. Boston, MA: Allen and Unwin, pp. 183–222.

Mass, Bonnie (1976) *Population Target: The Political Economy of Population Control in Latin America*. Brampton, Ontario: Charters Publishing.

Massey, D. et al. (1987) *Return to Aztlan: The Social Process of International Migration from Western Mexico*. Berkeley: University of California Press.

Mathews, Jessica (1994) A Small Price to Pay for Proving Malthus Wrong. Opinion. *International Herald Tribune*, 9 June.

Mathias, Peter (1969) *The First Industrial Nation: An Economic History of Britain, 1700–1914*. London: Methuen.

Mathieson, William (1975) The Emerging Structure for Worldwide Support of Agricultural Research, in The Agribusiness Council, *Agricultural Initiative in the Third World. A Report on the Conference: Science and Agribusiness in the Seventies*. Lexington, MA: Lexington Books, pp. 21–6.

Mattelart, Armand (1979) *Multinational Corporations and the Control of Culture: The Ideological Apparatuses of Imperialism*, Michael Chanan, trans. Brighton: Harvester Press.

May, Brian (1981) *The Third World Calamity*. London: Routledge and Kegan Paul.

Meehan, Mary (1996) A Secret War Against the Poor. *Our Sunday Visitor* 21 January. Internet site: http://www.catholic.net/rcc.Periodicals/OSV/96jan21. html. Accessed on 26/08/97.

Meehan, P. and M. Whiteford (1985) Staple Theory and the Rise of Commercial Cattle Production in a Rural Costa Rican Community, in W. Derman and S. Whiteford (eds.) *Impact Analysis and Development Planning in the Third World*. Boulder, CO: Westview Press, pp. 178–95.

Meek, Ronald (ed.) (1971) *Marx and Engels on the Population Bomb*. Berkeley: Ramparts Press.

Mehler, Barry (1988) Brief History of European and American Eugenics Movements. Excerpts from *A History of the American Eugenics Movement*. Ph.D. thesis. University of Illinois. Internet site: http://www.ferris.edu/ISAR/news/eugenics/movement.htm. Accessed on 13/01/98.

—— (1994) The Roots of the I.Q. Debate. Excerpt from In Genes We Trust:

When Science Bows to Racism. *Reform Judaism.* Winter. Internet site: http://www.ferris.edu/ISAR/IQ.htm. Accessed on 13/01/98.

Mellor, John and Richard H. Adams, Jr. (1986) The New Political Economy of Food and Agricultural Development. *Food Policy* November: 289–97.

Melman, Seymour (1965) *Our Depleted Society.* New York: Holt, Rinehart and Winston.

Melograni, Piero (1976) The Cult of the Duce in Mussolini's Italy. *Journal of Contemporary History* 1: 221–37.

Mencher, Joan (1978) Why Grow More Food? An Analysis of Some Contradictions in the "Green Revolution" in Kerala. *Economic and Political Weekly. Review of Agriculture,* December: A-98-A-104.

Merrick, Thomas (1990) The Evolution and Impact of Policies on Fertility and Family Planning: Brazil, Colombia, and Mexico, in Godfrey Roberts (ed.) *Population Policy: Contemporary Issues.* New York: Praeger, pp. 147–65.

Metz, Steven (1995) *Counterinsurgency: Strategy and the Phoenix of American Capability.* Carlisle Barracks, PA: Strategic Studies Institute, U.S. Army War College. Internet site: http://carlisle-www.army. mil/usassi/ssipubs/pubs95/cntrinsr/cntrinsr.txt. Accessed on 06/01/1998.

Mexican Soy Buyers (1997) Directory. Principal Purchasers of Soybeans and Soybean Products in Mexico. Internet site: http:///www.aces.uiuc.edu/~mexsoy/buyers.html#ANDERSON. Accessed on 18/06/97.

Michie, A. (1982) Agricultural Modernization and Rural Inequality in the United States and India, in R. Anderson et al. (eds.) *Science, Politics, and the Agricultural Revolution in Asia.* Boulder, CO: Westview Press, pp. 77–102.

Millikan, Max and Donald Blackmer (eds.) (1961) *The Emerging Nations: Their Growth and United States Policy.* Boston, MA: Little, Brown and Company.

Mills, Lennox et al. (1949) *The New World of Southeast Asia.* Minneapolis: University of Minnesota Press.

MIT Libraries (1995) *Francis Amasa Walker, 1840–1897.* Institute Archives. Internet site: http://nimrod.mit.edu/depts/archives/homepage/biographies/walker.html.

Mitsubishi Corporation (1997) Environmental Report. Internet site: http://www.mitsubishi.co.jp/environment/envir_rep. Accessed on 26/06/98.

Mokyr, J. (1985) *Why Ireland Starved: A Quantitative and Analytical History of the Irish Economy, 1800–1850.* London: George Allen and Unwin.

Monto, Alexander (1994) *The Roots of Mexican Labor Migration.* Westport, CT: Praeger.

Moody, T. (1981) *Davitt and Irish Revolution, 1846–82.* Oxford: Clarendon Press.

Moore, Barrington, Jr (1966) *Social Origins of Dictatorship and Democracy: Lord and Peasant in the Making of the Modern World.* Boston, MA: Beacon Press.

Morgan, Lynn (1993) *Community Participation in Health: The Politics of Primary Care in Costa Rica.* Cambridge: Cambridge University Press.

Morineau, M. (1979) The Potato in the Eighteenth Century, in R. Forster and O. Ranum (eds.) *Food and Drink in History.* Baltimore: Johns Hopkins University Press, pp. 17–36.

Morris, Charles (1988) *Iron Destinies, Lost Opportunities: The Arms Race Between the U.S.A. and the U.S.S.R., 1945–1987.* New York: Harper and Row.

Morris, Margaret (1976) *The General Strike.* Harmondsworth: Penguin.

Morris, R. J. (1976) *Cholera 1832: The Social Response to an Epidemic.* London: Croom Helm.

Morris, William (1984) *Political Writings of William Morris.* A.L. Morton, ed. London: Lawrence and Wishart.

Morse, Edward (1978) Introduction, in Georges Tapinos and Phyllis Piotrow, *Six Billion People: Demographic Dilemmas and World Politics.* New York: McGraw-Hill Book Company, pp. 1–18.

Morton, A.L. (1979) (orig. 1938) *A People's History of England.* London: Lawrence and Wishart.

Moss, David and Ernesta Rogers (1980) Poverty and Inequality in Italy, in Vic George and Roger Lawson (eds.) *Poverty and Inequality in Common Market Countries.* London: Routledge and Kegan Paul, pp. 161–94.

Mukherjee, Ramkrishna (1974) *The Rise and Fall of the East India Company: A Sociological Appraisal.* New York: Monthly Review Press.

Müller, Klaus-Jürgen (1976) French Fascism and Modernization. *Journal of Contemporary History* 11: 75–107.

Myers, Norman (1981) The Hamburger Connection: How Central America's Forests Become North America's Hamburgers. *Ambio* 10(1): 3–8.

———— (1991) The World's Forests and Human Populations: The Environmental Interconnections, in Kingsley Davis and Mikhail Bernstam (eds.) *Resources, Environment, and Population: Present Knowledge, Future Options.* New York: Oxford University Press, pp. 237–51.

———— (1994) Population and Environment: The Vital Linkages, in Department for Economic and Social Information and Policy Analysis, *Population, Environment and Development: Proceedings of the United Nations Expert Group Meeting on Population, Environment and Development, 1992.* New York: United Nations, pp. 55–63.

Myrdal, Gunnar (1968) *Asian Drama: An Inquiry into the Poverty of Nations.* New York: Pantheon.

Newby, Eric (1987) *Round Ireland in Low Gear.* Glasgow: Collins.

Newenham, Thomas (1805) *Statistical and Historical Inquiry into the Progress and Magnitude of the Population of Ireland.* London: C. and R. Baldwin.

Nieburg, H. (1970) *In the Name of Science.* Chicago: Quadrangle Books.

Nitze, Paul (1995) *George C. Marshall Lecture.* Delivered 3 November 1995. Internet site: http://www.ci.vancouver.wa.us/vancable//marshall/1995lec.htm. Accessed 16/04/97.

Niven, N. (1846) *The Potato Epidemic, and Its Probable Consequences.* Dublin: James McGlashan.

North, Liisa (1981) *Bitter Grounds: Roots of Revolt in El Salvador.* Toronto: Between the Lines.

Nossiter, T. J. (1982) *Communism in Kerala: A Study in Political Adaptation.* London: C. Hurst and Company (for the Royal Institute of International Affairs).

Notestein, Frank (1975) William H. Draper, Jr., 1894–1974. *Population Index* 41(1): 28–9.

———— and Edgar Sydenstricker (1930) Differential Fertility According to Social Class. A Study of 69,620 Native White Married Women under 45 Years of Age Based Upon United States Census Returns of 1910. *Journal of the American Statistical Association* 25(169): 9–32.

Nowak, Mark (1997) *Immigration and U.S. Population Growth: An Environmental Perspective.* Washington: Negative Population Growth.

Odend'hal, Stewart (1972) Energetics of Indian Cattle in Their Environment. *Human Ecology* 1(1): 3–22.

O'Donovan, J. (1940) *The Economic History of Livestock in Ireland.* Dublin: Cork University Press.

Ó Gráda, Cormac (1972) Irish Agricultural Output Before and After the Famine. *Journal of European Economic History,* pp. 149–65.

O'Reilly, K. (1986) Contraception, Ideology, and Policy Formation: Cohort Change in Dublin, Ireland, in W.P. Handwerker (ed.) *Culture and Reproduction: An Anthropological Critique of Demographic Transition Theory.* Boulder, CO: Westview Press, pp. 221–36.

O'Rourke, J. (1902) *The History of the Great Irish Famine of 1847, with Notices of Earlier Famines.* Dublin: James Duffy and Co.

Ortiz Mena, Antonio (1975) *Development in Latin America, A View from the IDB: Addresses and Documents, 1971–75.* Washington, DC: Inter-American Development Bank.

Osborn, Frederick (1974) History of the American Eugenics Society. *Social Biology* 21(2): 115–26.

Owen, Robert (1823) *Statements Showing the Power that Ireland Possesses to Create Wealth Beyond the Most Ample Supply of the Wants of its Inhabitants.* London: A. Applegath.

Pacciardi, Randolfo (1954) Democracy Lives in Italy. *Foreign Affairs* 32(3): 440–45.

Packenham, Robert (1973) *Liberal America and the Third World: Political Development Ideas in Foreign Aid and Social Science.* Princeton, NJ: Princeton University Press.

Paddock, William and Paul Paddock (1967) *Famine 1975!* London: Weidenfeld and Nicolson.

Page, Joseph (1972) *The Revolution that Never Was: Northeast Brazil, 1955–1964.* New York: Grossman Publishers.

Paine, Thomas (1969) (orig. 1791) *Rights of Man.* London: Dent.

Palacios, Marco (1980) *Coffee in Colombia, 1850–1970: An Economic, Social, and Political History.* Cambridge: Cambridge University Press.

Palmer, Ingrid (1972) *Science and Agricultural Production.* Geneva: United Nations Research Institute for Social Development.

PANNA (Pesticide Action Network of North America) (1995) Monsanto and Biotech Company Join Forces. PANUPS. Internet site: http://ekolserv.vo.sl...5_07–09/PANUPS950801b. Accessed on 31/10/96.

PANNA (Pesticide Action Network of North America) (1997) Monsanto: Roundup Not Environmentally Friendly! Internet site: http://users.patra.hol.gr/~cgian/epafine.htm. Accessed on 16/07/97.

Parker, Frank (1966) Fertilisers in Indian Economic Development, in T.M. Alexander and R.S. Giroti (eds.) *National Seminar on Fertilisers.* New Delhi: Fertiliser Association of India, pp. 30–37.

Parker, Phyllis (1979) *Brazil and the Quiet Intervention, 1964.* Austin: University of Texas Press.

Parkinson, F. (1974) *Latin America, The Cold War, and The World Powers 1945–1973: A Study in Diplomatic History.* Beverley Hills: Sage Publications.

Parsons, James (1949) *Antioqueño Colonization in Western Colombia.* Berkeley: University of California Press.

Payer, Cheryl (1982) *The World Bank: A Critical Analysis.* New York: Monthly Review Press.

Pelto, Gretel (1987) Social Class and Diet in Contemporary Mexico, in M. Harris and E. Ross (eds.) *Food and Evolution: Toward a Theory of Human Food Habits.* Philadelphia: Temple University Press, pp. 517–40.

Perelman, Michael (1977) *Farming for Profit in a Hungry World: Capital and the Crisis in Agriculture.* Montclair, NJ: Allanheld, Osmun.

Pfister, C. (1990) Food Supply in the Swiss Canton of Bern, 1850, in L. Newman et al. (eds.) *Hunger in History: Food Shortage, Poverty, and Deprivation.* Oxford: Blackwell, pp. 281–303.

Philippine Reporter, The/Philippine News (1995) 6.21 Million Pinoy Work Overseas. Internet site: http://www.mabuhay.com/phil_reporter/news/X0002_621MILL. html. Accessed on 23/08/97.

Philippines (1996) Philippine Case Study: A Developing Country's Perspective on POPs. Prepared for the IFCS Meeting on POPs, 17–19, June, Manila. Internet site: http://irptc.unep.ch/pops/indxhtms/manexp7.html. Accessed on 23/08/98.

Philips, C. (1961) (orig. 1940) *The East India Company, 1784–1834.* Manchester: Manchester University Press.

Phillips, Joseph (1948) Too Many People. *Newsweek,* 27 September: 37.

Pierle, Michael (1995) The Ethic of Sustainability: Not "Either/Or" But "Both/ And". Remarks at World Resources Institute Conference. Monsanto Crossroads. Internet site: http://www.monsanto.c...16Pierle_Michael.html.

Pike, Frederick (1967) *The Modern History of Peru.* London: Weidenfeld & Nicolson.

Pimental, David (1991) Global Warming, Population Growth, and Natural Resources for Food Production. *Society and Natural Resources* 4: 347–63.

———— and Marcia Pimental (1991) Comment: Adverse Environmental Consequences of the Green Revolution, in Kingsley Davis and Mikhail Bernstam (eds.) *Resources, Environment, and Population: Present Knowledge, Future Options. Population and Development Review* Supplement to Vol. 16. New York: Oxford University Press, pp. 329–32.

Pinchbeck, Ivy (1969) (orig. 1930) *Women Workers and the Industrial Revolution, 1750–1850.* London: Virago.

Piotrow, Phyllis (1973) *World Population Crisis: The United States Response.* New York: Praeger.

Pisani, Sallie (1991) *The CIA and the Marshall Plan.* Edinburgh: Edinburgh University Press.

Platt, D. (1972) *Latin America and British Trade, 1806–1914.* London: Adam and Charles Black.

Polanyi, Karl (1944) *The Great Transformation: The Political and Economic Origins of Our Time.* Boston, MA: Beacon Press.

Pomeroy, William (1974) *An American-Made Tragedy: Neo-Colonialism and Dictatorship in the Philippines.* New York: International Publishers.

Population (1991) Bangladesh Cyclone a Malthusian Nightmare. *Population* 17(6): 1.

Post, Ken (1989) *Revolution, Socialism and Nationalism in Viet Nam,* Vol. 3. Dartmouth: Aldershot.

Probert, Belinda (1978) *Beyond Orange and Green: The Political Economy of the Northern Ireland Crisis.* London: Zed Books.

Prest, J. (1972) *Lord John Russell.* London: Macmillan.

Prosterman, Roy and Jeffrey Riedinger (1987) *Land Reform and Democratic Development.* Baltimore: Johns Hopkins University Press.

Putzel, James (1992) *A Captive Land: The Politics of Agrarian Reform in the Philippines.* Manila: Ateneo de Manila University Press.

—— and John Cunnington (1989) *Gaining Ground: Agrarian Reform in the Philippines.* London: War on Want.

Raffer, Kunibert and Hans Singer (1996) *The Foreign Aid Business: Economic Assistance and Development Co-operation.* Cheltenham: Edward Elgar.

Rainforest Action Network (1997) Mitsubishi Boycott in Full Force, Say Environmental Human Rights Groups. Internet site: http://www.ran.org/ran/info_center/press-release/mit_boy.html. Accessed on 18/8/98.

RAND (1997) Major Sponsors of RAND Research. Internet site: http://www.rand.org/organization/LISTS/Majorspons.html. Accessed on 04/08/97.

Ranganathan, C.R. (1966) Foreword, in T.M. Alexander and R.S. Giroti (eds.) *National Seminar on Fertilisers.* New Delhi: Fertiliser Association of India.

Reichel-Dolmatoff, Gerardo and Alicia Reichel-Dolmatoff (1961) *People of Aritama: The Cultural Personality of a Colombian Mestizo Village.* Chicago: University of Chicago Press.

Reinhardt, Nola (1988) *Our Daily Bread: The Peasant Question and Family Farming in the Colombian Andes.* Berkeley: University of California Press.

Ricardo, David (1988) Ricardo on Population. *Population and Development Review* 14(2): 339–46.

Ridley, J. (1970) *Lord Palmerston.* London: Book Club Associates.

Robinson, Caroline (1933) Collegians' Race Suicide. *Birth Control Review* 17(2): 48–50.

Rockefeller Foundation (1995) Record group 6.7, New Delhi, Field Office Records. Administrative History. Internet site: http://www.rockefeller.edu/archive.ctr/admin.delhi.html. Accessed on 27/5/96.

Romero Medina, Amanda (1992) Forced Displacement in Colombia: Causes and Effects. Presented at the CIIR conference, "Forced Migration and National Sovereignty: Refugees, Displaced People and Involuntary Migrants. London, 19–20 June.

Rosen, George (1958) *A History of Public Health.* New York: MD Publications.

Ross, Eric B. (1980) Patterns of Diet and Forces of Production: An Economic and Ecological History of the Ascendancy of Beef in the United States Diet, in Eric Ross (ed.) *Beyond the Myths of Culture: Essays in Cultural Materialism.* New York: Academic Press, pp. 181–225.

—— (1983) The Riddle of the Scottish Pig. *BioScience* 33(2): 99–106.

—— (1985) The "Deceptively Simple" Racism of Clark Wissler. *American Anthropologist* 87: 390–93.

—— (1986) Potatoes, Population and the Irish Famine: The Political Economy of Demographic Change, in W. Penn Handwerker (ed.) *Culture and Reproduction: An Anthropological Critique of Demographic Transition Theory.* Boulder, CO: Westview Press, pp. 196–220.

—— (1987) Patterns of Diet and Forces of Production: An Economic and

Ecological History of the Ascendancy of Beef in the United States Diet, in Eric B. Ross (ed.) *Beyond the Myths of Culture: Essays in Cultural Materialism*. New York: Academic Press, pp. 181–225.

—— (1991) The Origins of Public Health: Concepts and Contradictions, in Peter Draper (ed.) *Health Through Public Policy: The Greening of Public Health*. London: Green Print, pp. 26–40.

—— (1994) A Malthusian Premise Empties the Countryside. Opinions. *International Herald Tribune* 5 July: 6.

—— (1996) The Case for the Vietnam War. *Parameter* Winter: 39–50.

—— (1996a) Ireland: "Promised Land" of Malthusian Theory? *Working Paper Series* No. 230. The Hague: Institute of Social Studies.

Rostow, Walt (1952) *The Strategies of Economic Growth: A Non-Communist Manifesto*. Cambridge: Cambridge University Press.

Rothschild, Emma (1996) The Debate on Economic and Social Security in the Late Eighteenth Century: Lessons of a Road Not Taken. *Development and Change* 27(2): 331–51.

Royal Commissioners on Agriculture (1881) *Preliminary Report, with Minutes of Evidence (Part I)*. British Parliamentary Papers. Vol. 5. Shannon: Irish University Press.

Ryder, Norman (1984) Frank Wallace Notestein (1902–83). *Population Studies* 38(1): 5–20.

Sadler, M. (1829) *Ireland; Its Evils, and Their Remedies: Being a Refutation of the Errors of the Emigration Committee and Others, Touching That Country*. London: John Murray.

—— (1842) *Memoirs of Michael Thomas Sadler*. London: R.B. Seeley and W. Burnside.

Salaman, R. (1943) *The Influence of the Potato on the Course of Irish History*. Dublin: The Richview Press.

—— (1985) (orig. 1949) *The History and Social Influence of the Potato*. Cambridge, MA: Cambridge University Press.

Salomon, Rafael (1997) Disney's World of Labor Exploitation. Consumer Action Center. Internet site: http://www.coopamerica.org/imssclcv.htm. Accessed on 19/01/98.

Sampson, Anthony (1977) *The Arms Bazaar*. London: Hodder and Stoughton.

Sanderson, S. (1984) *Land Reform in Mexico: 1910–1980*. Orlando: Academic Press.

Sandilands, Roger (1990) *The Life and Political Economy of Lauchlin Currie: New Dealer, Presidential Adviser, and Development Economist*. Durham, NC: Duke University Press.

Sanger, Margaret (1926) The Function of Sterilization. *Birth Control Review* 10(10).

Santow, Gigi (1993) *Coitus Interruptus* in the Twentieth Century. *Population and Development Review* 19(4): 767–92.

Sauer, R. (1978) Infanticide and Abortion in Nineteenth-Century Britain. *Population Studies* 32(1): 81–93.

Saunders, John (1986) *Population Growth in Latin America and U.S. National Security*. Boston, MA: Allen and Unwin.

Scally, Robert (1975) *The Origins of the Lloyd George Coalition: The Politics of Social-Imperialism, 1900–1918*. Princeton, NJ: Princeton University Press.

Schaller, Michael (1985) *The American Occupation of Japan: The Origins of the Cold War in Asia*. New York: Oxford University Press.

Schapsmeier, Edward and Frederick Schapsmeier (1968) *Henry A. Wallace of Iowa: The Agrarian Years, 1910–1940*. Ames: Iowa State University Press.

Scheer, Robert (1974) *America After Nixon: The Age of the Multinationals*. New York: McGraw-Hill.

——— (1995) Behind the Miracle of South Vietnam, in Marvin Gettleman et al. (eds.) *Vietnam and America*. New York: Grove Press, pp. 135–55.

Scheper-Hughes, Nancy (1979) *Saints, Scholars and Schizophrenics: Mental Illness in Rural Ireland*. Berkeley: University of California Press.

——— (1992) *Death Without Weeping: The Violence of Everyday Life in Brazil*. Berkeley: University of California Press.

Schneider, Jane and Peter Schneider (1976) *Culture and Political Economy in Western Sicily*. New York: Academic Press.

——— (1992) Going Forward in Reverse Gear: Culture, Economy and Political Economy in the Demographic Transitions of a Rural Sicilian Town, in John Gillis et al. (eds.) *The European Experience of Declining Fertility, 1850–1970: The Quiet Revolution*. Oxford: Blackwell, pp. 146–74.

Schuster, M. Lincoln (1940) *A Treasury of the World's Great Letters*. New York: Simon and Schuster.

Searle, G.R. (1976) *Eugenics and Politics in Britain, 1900–1914*. Leyden: Noordhoff International Publishing.

Seccombe, Wally (1986) Marxism and Demography: Household Forms and Fertility Regimes in the Western European Transition, in James Dickinson and Bob Russell (eds.) *Family, Economy and State*. Toronto: Garamond Press, pp. 23–55.

Select Committee on Emigration from the United Kingdom (1827) *Minutes*. London.

Semmel, B. (ed.) (1963) *Occasional Papers of T.R. Malthus on Ireland, Population, and Political Economy from Contemporary Journals, Written Anonymously and Hitherto Uncollected*. New York: Burt Franklin.

Shafer, D. Michael (1988) *Deadly Paradigms: The Failure of U.S. Counterinsurgency Policy*. Princeton, NJ: Princeton University Press.

Sheehan, Neal (1988) *A Bright Shining Lie: John Paul Vann and America in Vietnam*. New York: Random House.

Shirer, William (1960) *The Rise and Fall of the Third Reich: A History of Nazi Germany*. New York: Simon and Schuster.

Sierra Club (1997) Sierra Club's Conservation Policies on Population. Internet site: http//www.sierraclub.org/population/PPOLICY.HTML. Accessed on 06/10/97.

Simmons, Harvey (1978) Explaining Social Policy: The English Mental Deficiency Act of 1913. *Journal of Social History*. 11(3): 387–403.

Simon, Julian (1981) *The Ultimate Resource*. Princeton, NJ: Princeton University Press.

Sligo Independent, The (1879) The Weather – Harvest Prospects. 30 August: 2.

Smart, W. (1964) (orig. 1910) *Economic Annals of the Nineteenth Century, 1801–1820*, Vol. 1. New York: Augustus Kelley.

Smith, Adam (1947) (orig. 1778) *The Wealth of Nations*, Vol. 1. London: J.M. Dent and Sons.

Smith, Bruce (1966) *The RAND Corporation: Case Study of a Nonprofit Advisory Corporation.* Cambridge, MA: Harvard University Press.

Smith, Dusky Lee (1970) Sociology and the Rise of Corporate Capitalism, in Larry Reynolds and Janice Reynolds (eds.) *The Sociology of Sociology: Analysis and Criticism of the Thought, Research, and Ethical Folkways of Sociology and Its Practitioners.* New York: David McKay Company, pp. 68–84.

Snell, K.D.M. (1985) *Annals of the Labouring Poor: Social Change and Agrarian England, 1660–1900.* Cambridge: Cambridge University Press.

Solar, Peter and Martine Goossens (1991) Agricultural Productivity in Belgium and Ireland in the Early Nineteenth Century, in Bruce Campbell and Mark Overton (eds.) *Land, Labour and Livestock: Historical Studies in European Agricultural Productivity.* Manchester: Manchester University Press, pp. 364–84.

Solomos, John (1982) *Migrant Workers in Metropolitan Cities.* Strasbourg: European Science Foundation.

Solow, B. (1971) *The Land Question and the Irish Economy, 1870–1903.* Cambridge: Harvard University Press.

Spengler, Joseph (1977) (orig. 1971) Economic Growth in a Stationary Population, in J. Overbeek (ed.) *The Evolution of Population Theory.* Westport, CT: Greenwood Press.

Staley, Eugene (1954) *The Future of Underdeveloped Countries: Political Implications of Economic Development.* New York: Council on Foreign Relations.

Stavenhagen, Rodolfo (1975) Collective Agriculture and Capitalism in Mexico: A Way Out or a Dead End? *Latin American Perspectives* Issue 5, 11(2): 146–63.

Steele, E.D. (1974) *Irish Land and British Politics: Tenant-Right and Nationality, 1865–1870.* London: Cambridge University Press.

Stein, George (1987) The Biological Bases of Ethnocentrism, Racism and Nationalism in National Socialism, in Vernon Reynolds et al. (eds.) *The Sociobiology of Ethnocentrism.* London: Croom Helm, pp. 251–67.

Stephanson, Anders (1989) *Kennan and the Art of Foreign Policy.* Cambridge, MA: Harvard University Press.

Stephen, L. and Sidney Lee (eds.) (1921–22) *The Dictionary of National Biography.* London: Oxford University Press.

Stilkind, Jerry (1995) U.S. Official Gives Population Stability Highest Priority. The United States Mission to Italy. Internet site: http://www.usis.it/wireless/wf951218/95121813.htm. Accessed on 28/01/98.

Stockholm Chamber of Commerce (1996) The Stockholm Declaration on Growth and Development in the Baltic Region. Baltic Sea Business Summit, 24–25 April 1996. Internet site: http://www.chamber.se/bsbstext.html. Accessed on 26/10/96.

Stoddard, Lothrop (1920) *The Rising Tide of Color Against White World Supremacy.* New York: Charles Scribner's Sons.

—— (1925) *The Revolt Against Civilisation; The Menace of the Under Man.* London: Chapman and Hall.

Stone, Lawrence (1977) *The Family, Sex and Marriage in England, 1500–1800.* London: Weidenfeld and Nicolson.

Stonich, Susan (1991) The Promotion of Non-Traditional Agricultural Exports in Honduras: Issues of Equity, Environment and Natural Resource Management. *Development and Change* 22(4): 725–55.

Strachey, John (1936) *The Theory and Practice of Socialism*. New York: Random House.

Strangeland, C. (1966) (orig. 1904) *Pre-Malthusian Doctrine of Population: A Study in the History of Economic Theory*. New York: Augustus M. Kelley.

Stross, Randall (1986) *The Stubborn Earth: American Agriculturalists on Chinese Soil, 1898–1937*. Berkeley: University of California.

Sweezy, Paul (1972) *Modern Capitalism and Other Essays*. New York: Monthly Review Press.

Szreter, Simon (1993) The Idea of Demographic Transition and the Study of Fertility Change: A Critical Intellectual History. *Population and Development Review* 19(4): 659–701.

Taatgen, H. (1992) The Boycott in the Irish Civilizing Process. *Anthropological Quarterly* 65(4): 163–76.

Thaxton, Ralph (1983) *China Turned Rightside UP: Revolutionary Legitimacy in the Peasant World*. New Haven, CT: Yale University Press.

Thiesenhusen, William (1995) *Broken Promises: Agrarian Reform and the Latin American Campesino*. Boulder, CO: Westview Press.

Thompson, E.P. (1963) *The Making of the English Working Class*. New York: Vintage.

Thompson, Kenneth (1981) *Cold War Theories, Vol. 1: World Polarization, 1943–1953*. Baton Rouge: Louisiana State University Press.

Thomson, D. (1966) *Europe Since Napoleon*. Harmondsworth: Penguin.

Thomson, James, Jr (1969) *While China Faced West: American Reformers in Nationalist China, 1928–1937*. Cambridge, MA: Harvard University Press.

Thorner, Daniel and Alice Thorner (1962) *Land and Labour in India*. London: Asia Publishing House.

Times, The (1880) *The Great Irish Famine of 1845–46*. London: *The Times*.

Tomaselli, Sylvana (1989) Moral Philosophy and Population Questions in Eighteenth Century Europe, in Michael Teitelbaum and Jay Winter (eds.) *Population and Resources in Western Intellectual Traditions*. Population and Development Review Supplement to Volume 14. Cambridge, MA: Harvard University Press, pp. 7–29.

Treble, James (1979) *Urban Poverty in Britain 1830–1914*. London: Batsford Academic.

Trevelyan, C. (1848) *The Irish Crisis*. London: Longman, Brown, Green and Longmans.

Trevelyan, G. (1978) (orig. 1932) *The Life and Letters of Lord Macaulay*. Oxford: Oxford University Press.

Treverton, Gregory (1987) *Covert Action: The CIA and the Limits of American Intervention in the Postwar World*. London: I.B. Tauris.

Tuchman, Barbara (1971) *Stilwell and the American Experience in China, 1911–1945*. New York: Bantam Books.

Underwood, James and William Daniels (1982) *Governor Rockefeller in New York: The Apex of Pragmatic Liberalism in the United States*. Westport: Greenwood Press.

UNECLA (UN Economic Commission for Latin America) (1968) *Economic Survey of latin America 1966*. New York: United Nations.

UNFPA (1991) *Population, Resources and the Environment: The Critical Challenges*. New York: United Nations Population Fund.

UNICEF (1995) Aid Programmes Cut, Only Reach 0.7% Target. Internet site:

http://www.unicef.org/pon95/aid-0004.html. Accessed on 17/06/98.

Unikel, Luis (1975) Urbanization in Mexico: Process, Implications, Policies, and Prospects, in S. Goldstein and D. Sly (eds.) *Patterns of Urbanization: Comparative Country Studies*. Dolhain (Belgium): Ordina Editions, pp. 465–568.

United Nations (1991) *Population Growth and Policies in Mega-Cities: Mexico City*. Department of International Economic and Social Affairs. New York: United Nations.

United Nations General Assembly (1994) Net Flows and Transfer of Resources Between Developing Countries and Developed Countries, G.A. res. 49/93, 49 U.N. GAOR Supp. (No. 49) at 122, U.N. Doc. A/49/49 (1994). University of Minnesota Human Rights Library. Internet site: http://heiwww,unige.ch/humanrts/resolutions/49/93GA1994.html. Accessed on 13/07/97.

United States Defense Department (1971) *The Pentagon Papers: The Defense Deapartment History of United States Decisionmaking on Vietnam, Vol. II*. The Senator Gravel Edition. Boston, MA: Beacon Press.

United States Information Service (1997) *Transcript: Briefing by Gordon, Walters on European Trip*. Internet site: http://www.usis.it/wireless/wf970522/97052212.htm. Accessed on 08/01/1998.

United States Senate Committee on Governmental Affairs, Subcommittee on Reports, Accounting and Management (1978) *Voting Rights in Major Corporations*. Washington, DC: US Governmental Printing Office.

United States Supreme Court (1961) Communist Party of the United States v. Subversive Activities Control Board 367 U.S. 1. Internet site: http://www.vcilp.org/Fed-Ct/Supreme/Flite/opinions/367US1.htm. Accessed on 05/01/1998.

Vallianatos, E.G. (1976) *Fear in the Countryside: The Control of Agricultural Resources in the Poor Countries by Nonpeasant Elites*. Cambridge, MA: Ballinger Publishing Company.

Vevier, Charles (1956) The Open Door: An Idea in Action, 1906–1913, in William A. Williams (ed.) *The Shaping of American Diplomacy*, Vol. 2. Chicago: Rand McNally, pp. 444–52.

Viswanathan, Aparna (1991) Pesticides: From Silent Spring to Indian Summer. *Economic and Political Weekly* 26(44): 2039–40.

Wakefield, E. (1881) *The Disaffection of Ireland; Its Cause and Its Cure. A Plea for the Tenant Farmers of Ireland and English Workmen*. London: Edward Stanford.

Walinsky, Louis (ed.) (1977) *The Selected Papers of Wolf Ladejinsky: Agrarian Reform as Unfinished Business*. Washington, DC: World Bank.

Walker, Francis (1896) Restriction of Immigration. *The Atlantic Monthly* 77(464): 822–829. Internet site: http://www.theatlantic.com/atlantic/atlweb/flashbks/immigr/walke.htm. Accessed on 26/08/97.

Wallace, Henry (1964) The Most Important Investment, in Gove Hambidge (ed.) *Dynamics of Development: An International Development Reader*. New York: Frederick A. Praeger, pp. 37–41.

Ward, J. and R. Wilson (eds.) (1971) *Land and Industry: The Landed Estate and the Industrial Revolution. A Symposium*. Newton Abbot: David and Charles.

Waterman, A.M.C. (1992) Analysis and Ideology in Malthus's *Essay on Population*. *Australia Economic Papers* 31(58): 203–13.

Watson, Roger (1969) *Edwin Chadwick, Poor Law and Public Health*. Harlow: Longman.

Weindling, Paul (1989) *Health, Race and German Politics Between National Unification and Nazism, 1870–1945.* Cambridge: Cambridge University Press.

Wells, Roger (1983) *Insurrection: The British Experience, 1795–1803.* Gloucester: Alan Sutton.

———— (1988) *Wretched Faces: Famine in Wartime England, 1763–1803.* New York: St. Martin's Press.

Wheat, Andrew (1996) Toxic Bananas. *Multinational Monitor* 17(9). Internet site: http:www.essential.org/monitor/hyper/mm0996.04.html. Accessed on 21/01/98.

White, Theodore (1953) *Fire in the Ashes: Europe in Mid-Century.* New York: William Sloane.

Whiteford, Michael (1991) From *Gallo Pinto* to "Jack's Snacks": Observations on Dietary Change in a Rural Costa Rican Village, in Scott Whiteford and Anne Ferguson (eds.) *Harvest of Want: Hunger and Food Security in Central America and Mexico.* Boulder, CO: Westview Press, pp. 127–40.

Wilcox Young, Linda (1993) Labour Demand and Agroindustrial Development: The Evidence from Mexico. *The Journal of Development Studies* 30(1): 168–89.

Wilkins, Mira (1974) Multinational Oil Companies in South America in the 1920s: Argentina, Bolivia, Brazil, Chile, Colombia, Ecuador, and Peru. *Business History Review* 48(3): 414–46.

Wilkinson, Richard (1973) *Poverty and Progress: An Ecological Perspective on Economic Development.* New York: Praeger.

Williams, Eric (1944) *Capitalism and Slavery.* London: Andre Deutsch.

Williams, Raymond (1983) *Cobbett.* Oxford: Oxford University Press.

Williams, R.G. (1986) Coffee, Cotton, Cattle and the Crisis in Central America. Chapel Hill: University of North Carolina Press.

Williams, T. Harry (1969) *Huey Long.* New York: Bantam.

Williams, William A. (1962) (orig. 1959) *The Tragedy of American Diplomacy.* New York: Dell.

Williamson, Robert (1965) Toward a Theory of Political Violence: The Case of Rural Colombia. *Western Political Quarterly.* March: 35–44.

Wilmoth, John and Patrick Ball (1992) The Population Debate in American Popular Magazines, 1946–90. *Population and Development Review* 18(4): 631–68.

Wilson, Charles and B. Lenman (1977) The British Isles, in Charles Wilson and G. Parker (eds.) *An Introduction to the Sources of European Economic History, 1500–1800. Vol 1: Western Europe.* London: Weidenfeld and Nicolson, pp. 115–54.

Winter, Jay (1977) Britain's "Lost Generation" of the First World War. *Population Studies* 31(3): 449–66.

———— (1989) Socialism, Social Democracy, and Population Questions in Western Europe: 1870–1950, in Michael Teitelbaum and Jay Winter (eds.) *Population and Resources in Western Intellectual Traditions.* Cambridge: Cambridge University Press, pp. 122–46.

Wirth, Alexander (1964) *Russia at War, 1941–1945.* New York: Avon Books.

Wohl, Anthony (1983) *Endangered Lives: Public Health in Victorian Britain.* Cambridge, MA: Harvard University Press.

Wolf, Eric (1969) *Peasant Wars of the Twentieth Century.* New York: Harper and Row.

Wollstonecraft, Mary (1975) (orig. 1792) *A Vindication of the Rights of Woman.*

Harmondsworth: Penguin.

——— (1994) (orig. 1790) *Vindication of the Rights of Men*. New York: Woodstock Books.

Womack, John, Jr (1968) *Zapata and the Mexican Revolution*. New York: Vintage Books.

Woodham-Smith, Cecil (1962) *The Great Hunger: Ireland 1845–1849*. New York: E.P. Dutton.

Working Group on International Agricultural Research (1997) *The Crucial Role of International Agricultural Research: Improving Global Food Production, Benefitting U.S. Agriculture, Enhancing the Economies of Developing Countries and Stimulating U.S. Trade*. Washington, DC: National Center for Food and Agricultural Policy. Internet site: http://www. winrock.org/citdc/iar.htm. Accessed on 18/01/98.

World Bank (1950) *The Basis of a Development Program for Colombia. Report of a Mission Headed by Lauchlin Currie*. Baltimore: Johns Hopkins University Press.

——— (1996) James D. Wolfensohn: World Bank Group President. Internet site: http://www.worldbank.org/html/extar/wolfbio.html. Accessed on 23/8/98.

Wrigley, Eric (1989) The Limits to Growth: Malthus and the Classical Economists, in Michael Teitelbaum and Jay Winter (eds.) *Population and Resources in Western Intellectual Traditions*. Cambridge: Cambridge University Press, pp. 30–48.

——— and R. Schofield (1981) *The Population History of England, 1541–1871: A Reconstruction*. Cambridge, MA: Harvard University Press.

Wunsch, G. (1978) A Review of the Prospects, in Council of Europe, *Population Decline in Europe: Implications of a Declining or Stationary Population*. London: Edward Arnold, pp. 233–41.

Yanaga, Chitoshi (1968) *Big Business in Japanese Politics*. New Haven, CT: Yale University Press.

Yates, F. (1951) Manuring for Higher Yields, in F. Le Gros Clark and N.W. Pirie (eds.) *Four Thousand Million Mouths: Scientific Humanism and the Shadow of World Hunger*. London: Oxford University Press, pp. 44–73.

Yergin, Daniel (1978) *Shattered Peace: The Origins of the Cold War and the National Security State*. Boston, MA: Houghton Mifflin.

Young, Arthur (1967) *A Six Months Tour Through the North of England*. New York: A.M. Kelley.

Young, Kate (1982) The Creation of a Relative Surplus Population: A Case Study from Mexico, in Lourdes Benería (ed.) *Women and Development: The Sexual Division of Labor in Rural Societies*. New York: Praeger, pp. 150–77.

Zamora Chavarría, Eugenia María (1994) The Precarious Situation of Latin America's Children. *NACLA Report on the Americas*. Internet site: http://pangaea.org/kids/latin/poverty.htm. Accessed on 13/10/97.

Zamosc, Leâon (1986) *The Agrarian Question and the Peasant Movement in Colombia: Struggles of the National Peasant Association, 1967–1981*. Cambridge: Cambridge University Press.

Zinn, Howard (1980) *A People's History of the United States*. London: Longman.

Zlotnick, Jack (1962) Population Pressure and Political Indecision. *Foreign Affairs* 39(4): 684–94.

Index

Printed in the United States
119959LV00001B/25-96/A

9 781856 495646